THE GUYS WHO WROTE 'EM

Sean Egan was born in London. His first professional writing work was a brief stint providing scripts for the television soap opera *EastEnders*. He is currently a journalist specialising in popular music and tennis. He has written for, amongst other outlets, *Billboard, Billboard.com, Classic Rock, Discoveries, Goldmine, Mojo4Music.com, Record Collector, Record Mart & Buyer, RollingStone.com, Serve And Volley, Sky Sports, Tennis World, Uncut* and *Vox*. He also writes CD liner notes.

He is the author of four previous non-fiction books, one of which – *Jimi Hendrix And The Making Of Are You Experienced* – was nominated for an Award for Excellence in Historical Recorded Sound Research by the Association for Recorded Sound Collections. He also wrote the critically acclaimed novel *Sick Of Being Me*.

Also by this author:
Star Sail: The Verve (Omnibus)
Animal Tracks: The Story of The Animals - Newcastle's Rising Sons (Helter Skelter)
Not Necessarily Stoned But Beautiful: The Making of Are You Experienced [US title: *Jimi Hendrix and the Making Of Are You Experienced*] (Unanimous/A Capella)
Our Music Is Red With Purple Flashes: The Story Of The Creation (Cherry Red)
Sick Of Being Me (Askill)

THE GUYS WHO WROTE 'EM

Songwriting Geniuses of Rock and Pop

Sean Egan

British Library cataloguing in publication data available

Textual design and cover: Bernie Ross

ISBN 0-9545750-1-6

Askill Publishing
PO Box 46818
LONDON
SW11 6WE

TABLE OF CONTENTS

INTRODUCTION

Non-performing songwriters live in a strange twilight world.

Their songs are known to, and loved by, millions. Yet, while their names can often ring a bell in the minds of those who idly inspect the contents of the parentheses on record labels (or, these days, CD booklets), their faces are generally unknown. This may have its upside: the press hounded Elvis Presley but were utterly uninterested in the daily lives of his composers Jerry Leiber and Mike Stoller and left them in peace. However, there is more than one type of recognition. The vast majority of purchasers of records by Presley are usually aware of the fact that the artist has not written the song that moves or excites them but at the same time invest their gratitude for the pleasure they obtain from the song 100% in the artist. This idolatry of - to use a phrase by the Rolling Stones - the singer not the song reaches almost absurd heights when it comes to the field of biographies. Endless numbers of books have been written about Presley but none about Leiber & Stoller and the various other brilliant songsmiths without whom he would not have had a career. The idea that a singer - even one with a talent as exquisite as Presley's - would have had a perspective on the act of musical creation anything like as interesting as those who actually crafted the words and melodies on his records is patently absurd.

The Guys Who Wrote 'Em seeks to put right the lack of proper recognition and appreciation for those pop geniuses who for most of their careers have chosen to use their musical skills to help others achieve stardom. It focuses on some of the most important and/or interesting composers in rock and pop music since the late-'Fifties, each chapter looking at the career and songwriting techniques of a particular writer or writing team. Due to the range of subjects and the timeframe chosen, the chapters contribute incrementally to a recounting of the story of post-Elvis popular music, from original rock and roll, through Brill Building hit-making, through the beat group boom, through Motown, through bubblegum, through glam rock, through the mellow, pre-punk Seventies and culminating in the modern sequencer-assisted pop production-line. The recounting, though, is from an unusual, lateral angle.

My grateful thanks go to the composers who granted me lengthy interviews for this book: Matt Aitken, Jeff Barry, Nicky Chinn, Lamont Dozier, Graham Gouldman, Ellie Greenwich, Bobby Hart, Brian Holland, Eddie Holland, Joey Levine, Jerry Leiber, Tony Macaulay, Barry Mann, Mike Stock, Mike Stoller, Chip Taylor and Cynthia Weil. The interviews were conducted over a period of around three years, from 2000 to 2002, and none have been published before.

Before you delve in, a brief health warning about chart positions in this book. The sources for chart positions, unless specified, are *Billboard* magazine for the US and *The Guinness Book Of Hit Singles* for the UK. Both are only reliable up to a point. In the UK during the 1960s, there were four competing pop charts, the most authoritative of which was considered to be that compiled and published by the *New Musical Express*. However, because the authors of *The Guinness Book Of Hit Singles* chose to rely on the charts compiled by *Record Retailer* (now called *Music Week*) and because *The Guinness Book Of Hit Singles* is the most readily available source for chart statistics for that period, the *Record Retailer* charts have become the definitive 'Sixties chart by default, thus occasionally leading to 'official' chart positions which jar with most people's memories (e.g., 'Please Please Me' was the first Beatles number one on just about every chart except *Record Retailer*'s). Meanwhile the *Billboard* chart tended to underestimate the sales of the songs at the pop end of the musical spectrum. As Cynthia Weil points out, "Back in those days, there was both *Cash Box* and *Billboard* and actually *Cash Box* was the bigger of the two. For some reason, our kind of songs were always lower on *Billboard* than they were on *Cash Box*. It was really *the* magazine in those days. We didn't even get *Billboard*." Sadly, *Cash Box* no longer exists and, for music journalists, looking up placings on its charts rather than *Billboard*'s would be prohibitively time-consuming. Nonetheless, no song was ever a hit in one chart but a no-show in the other, so the positions contained herein always give at least a fair indication of a record's popularity.

Oh, the book's title? It comes from a billing for a Monkees tour which featured Boyce & Hart, composers of many of their hits. Their songs for The Monkees weren't on the same level as the greatest Leiber & Stoller songs but this book clebrates high quality lightweight pop as much as it does heavyweight, classic rock.

1
LEIBER & STOLLER

Jerry Leiber and Mike Stoller are the first word in rock songwriting. It would be inconceivable to write a book of this kind without including a chapter recounting the achievements of the men who were rock and roll's first non-performing composers to become famous, who wrote some of the greatest records by the original and - to some - greatest rock icon Elvis Presley, who gave rock and roll a respectability with the witty and sophisticated records they wrote for The Coasters, who secured hits for artists as diverse as The Drifters, The Monkees and Elkie Brooks spanning several decades and who, as if their composing achievements weren't enough, had a parallel career as producers in which they were every bit as inventive and prone to strokes of genius.

Jerry Leiber was born on April 25th 1933 in Baltimore, Maryland, where he spent his life until the age of twelve. Unusually for the time, his mother was the breadwinner, the result of Leiber's father dying when he was five. In addition to young Jerome, there were two daughters to support, both older than Jerry. Leiber's mother managed this through what he describes as "a very modest little combination dry goods and grocery shop." The store was located on the periphery of a black neighbourhood. "I wasn't what you call actively interested but I was very much exposed to the blues and language and attitude and these things kind of surfaced later on when I was in my late teens," he says. Leiber's mother ran this concern for six-and-a-half years until deciding in 1945 to relocate to Los Angeles, partly because Jerry's eldest sister was living there and partly because his other sister was due to attend the University of California.

Music was to some extent in Leiber's blood. His brother-in-law Frank Tableporter was a successful songwriter. Tableporter was the brother of another songwriter, Teepee Mitchell, and their father before them was a songwriter. Leiber: "The whole family were songwriters and I was exposed to this general influence that seemed to me a lot of fun." Leiber had studied piano for around two and a half years in Baltimore and drums for the same amount of time. Lack of opportunities for practise once he moved to LA meant the end of his days of playing instruments but he also says, "I was getting more and more interested in the lyrical end of songs." Leiber states, "fifteen going on sixteen" as the age when he decided that he wanted to be a professional songwriter. However, the lyrics he began writing were not the Tin Pan Alley kind favoured by his relatives but ones designed to accompany twelve-bar blues, which was now emerging as one of his greatest loves. It was, of course, a highly unusual love for a white boy at the time. Did his family not find it strange? "My family didn't even know what I was doing," he says. "I could have been hijacking trucks. They didn't really know what I was about. Later on, when I started to have a modicum of success, I'd tell my mother and she'd be pleased at the success, or I'd show her a royalty cheque, but her attitude was always, 'That's very nice Jerry but I really think you should get a job'. Nobody was making any judgment about anything. Nobody was that interested either."

Leiber had one musical foil before meeting Mike Stoller, a boy called Jerry Horowitz who, like him, attended Fairfax High School. "I was in my middle year and I hooked up with him to write songs," he recalls. "But he couldn't make the constant schedule that it demanded to enable us to finish the song, get enough work done, whatever. So we had to separate. I put it to him in a very business-like way. 'I tell you what,' he said. 'I have the number of someone that I played a dance with last week who I think might be just the right guy for you' and he gave me Mike Stoller's phone number."

Before his first meeting with Stoller, though, came a significant occurrence in Leiber's life when he informed a record industry figure called Lester Sill of his songwriting ambitions. Lester Sill was the national sales and promotion man for Modern Records, a family-owned, Los Angeles-based rhythm and blues record company. Says Leiber, "After school, I would work at Norty's Record Shop, which was two blocks down the street from the school. Lester came into Norty's Record Shop to more or less test out the viability of the new records that he had coming out. I was a clerk there at the time and Lester came in and struck up a conversation with me. At some point, he said, 'So what do you want to do when you grow up?' And I said, 'I want to be a songwriter'. He said, 'Really? Have you written any songs?' I said, 'Yes but I don't have any proper music put to them yet'. 'Well could you sing me a song or two?' I said, 'In here? Norty'll fire me'. He was in the back doing inventory. Lester said, 'Don't worry about Norty. He's a friend of mine. Sing me a song'. So I sang him part of a song. He said, 'You're going to be a good songwriter. Now you get yourself a partner who can write these lyrics and music down on a lead sheet'. I said, 'What's a lead sheet?' and he explained to me what a lead sheet was. And then it all started to come together because I think I had Stoller's number in my pocket then and I knew there was an urgency in calling him because I needed someone to write the music down."

Mike Stoller (rhymes with "stroller") was, like Leiber, 17 when he met his future lifetime writing partner. Also like Leiber, he had relocated to Los Angeles, having been born on March 13th 1933 in Belle Harbor, Long Island (New York). From the age of four, he grew up in Sunnyside, a part of Long Island City, just across the river from Manhattan. "I would say lower middle class, economically," he says of his background. "My dad was an engineer but without a degree. He did a variety of things. He was an architectural draughtsman. A little later on he was involved in stage equipment." Stoller was something of a musical prodigy, despite an inauspicious beginning to his musical education. "I guess when I was five I had a few lessons from my aunt, who was a brilliant pianist, organist, harpsichordist, but a recluse so she wouldn't perform publicly," he says. "After a few lessons I couldn't really deal with it because she would slap my hands if my fingers weren't curved properly, so I stopped taking lessons." However, Stoller resumed his piano playing after a stay in an inter-racial summer camp when he was seven. "I heard a black teenager playing for his own amusement on an old upright piano that was in a barn (which served as our recreation hall) during the daytime when no one else was around. He played great boogie woogie and that turned me on and I just wanted to do what he was doing. I wanted to make that beautiful music. When he left I tried to imitate what his fingers were doing. By the time I was eight or nine I was playing pretty good boogie woogie. Probably better than I do today." Remarkably, Stoller's proficiency at boogie woogie and blues is pretty much self-taught, something partly attributable to the fact that despite the modesty of his family's means, a piano was readily accessible: "We always had one. Just part of the furniture." Stoller did eventually resume formal lessons: "My mother wanted me to learn classical music and I did take some lessons from the neighbourhood piano teacher who went door to door teaching kids in the community." Those formal lessons, which began when he was nine and ended when he was ten or eleven, were sporadic and he frequently neglected to practise. "Then a neighbour heard me playing boogie woogie and he arranged an introduction to James P. Johnson, who he knew." Johnson, known as the King Of The Stride Piano, is recognized as one of the greatest jazz pianists in history and numbered amongst his former students no less than Fats Waller. "I took about five lessons with James P. Johnson," says Stoller. "I was ten years old, maybe eleven. Although he lived in Queens, in a community called Jamaica, it involved taking a couple of subways and a bus to get there and after the first visit when my mother went with me, I would go on my own. It was a long trip. Of course, had I been older, I could have learned so many things from a brilliant musician like that. But all I wanted to know was boogie woogie." When Stoller was sixteen, he began receiving piano lessons from his reclusive aunt once more: "I figured I could deal with her at that point in my life and I was doing very well, but at that point we moved to Los Angeles and that was the end of my piano studies. They were never intensive." The next formal musical education for Stoller - who also learned tuba in New York - took place in Los Angeles. "I began to study composition just about the time I met Jerry with a composer named Arthur Lang," he recalls. "I studied for a year or two with him. But of course by that time Jerry and I were very busy writing rhythm and blues."

Stoller, who later studied with atonal composer Stefan Wolpe in New York, can read music but thinks notation ability is irrelevant: "I still don't read that well. I can write faster than I can read, I suppose because piano music is rather complex to read. I did study the tuba in school - they drafted me; they needed a tuba player in the orchestra and the marching band - and that's where I first learned to read really well, but that was one note at a time. I don't think it aids you in writing, in creating melodies. But I think it certainly helps me at this stage to remember what I wrote!"

In contrast to the indifference of Leiber's family, Stoller says he always felt encouraged by his parents: "Especially by my mom. My mom had been a model and a showgirl. She'd been in one of George Gershwin's shows, was a friend of George and Ira and a school chum of their younger sister, Frances. She was always very encouraging to anything that my sister or I wanted to do."

Stoller's family's relocation to Los Angeles was due to a business opportunity that arose for his father. He says, "When I got to LA I went to high school for one semester, graduated and went on to Los Angeles City College. I made a few friends who were musicians and music fans. One fellow who was a good pianist had a job on a Sunday afternoon that paid three dollars. He got another one that paid five so he gave me the three dollar job with a pick-up band. A bunch of guys got together and played standards. The drummer on that Sunday afternoon dance took my phone number and I thought he was gonna call me for some more gigs, but as it turned out, he was in high school with Jerry and Jerry had been writing songs with him. He couldn't devote enough time to it anymore, so he gave Jerry my phone number."

Leiber recalls that first telephone contact: "I said, 'Are you Mike Stoller?' He said, 'Yes'. I said, 'Do you play piano?' He said, 'Yes'. I said, 'Do you read music?' He said, 'Yes'. I said, 'Can you write notes on paper?' He said, 'Yes'. And I said, 'Well, I was told that you might be interested in writing songs, and that's why I'm calling you. Would you like to write songs with me?' He said, 'No'. I was shocked! I had to bug him for another forty-five minutes on the phone to convince him to let me come over and talk to him."

Stoller explains, "I was not particularly eager to write songs because I didn't know what he was talking about. I assumed he meant something that I just didn't care for. By this time I was a big modern jazz or be-bop fan. I assumed he meant some kind of corny romantic song that I wouldn't like. But he was very persistent so I said, 'Hey, you wanna come over, come over'." When Leiber arrived at Stoller's house, things got off to a shaky start. Stoller: "I guess the first thing I noticed about him when he got to my house - in fact I forgot to ask him to come in after I opened the door - was the fact that he had one blue eye and one brown eye, so I just kind of stared at him for a while until I finally regained my composure and asked him to come in." However, things improved when Stoller realized he and Leiber had something in common: "He showed me his notebook of lyrics and I saw immediately they were in the form of twelve-bar blues. They had a line of lyric and a line of ditto marks and a rhyming line. I said, 'Oh, I didn't know you were talking the blues when you said song writing'. I obviously was familiar with the blues because I'd been buying records with boogie woogie instrumentals and listening to the vocals on the other side. Of course, I bought them for the side that was the piano instrumental, but I was quite familiar with blues poetry and blues lines. So I went to the piano and started playing and we started writing."

Though that first songwriting session didn't produce any classics, it did engender a relationship, both professional and personal, which has lasted over half a century. The loquacious Leiber and the studious Stoller had, says Leiber, "a sort of instant rapport, especially writing. We just fell in together."

The pair's writing processes in the early days were somewhat different to today but Leiber points out, "In the early days, it was always spontaneous." One method was for Stoller to set music to words Leiber had already devised. Explains Leiber, "Those lyrics that I had in my notebook, they were written and I would present them to Mike and he would go to the piano and he'd fiddle around with some riffs, some licks and some rhythm patterns and chords 'til we found something that we both liked. Not all these songs that are twelve- or eight-bar blues have what you would call conventional melodies." Writing music to pre-written words - which the pair still sometimes do, despite writing in far more sophisticated idioms than the blues these days - is traditionally supposed to be much harder than the other way round, but Stoller says, "That's easy for me. I love to have Jerry bring me a finished lyrics I can play with." Stoller describes the other main method of composing in those early days: "I would be jamming at something at the piano - a rhythm, a riff - and Jerry would pace around and shout out fragments of lines, phrases, and if something happened at the same time and it felt good, then we would stop and examine it and work on it until it became a song - which sometimes was very, very quickly. We wrote rapidly in those days. It took us only about ten minutes to write 'Hound Dog'."

Could that rapid work rate have something to do with the fact that 12-bar blues, which they were writing exclusively in the beginning, are easy to write? "Easy for me, maybe not for you," says Stoller. "Some of them, in the beginning, we would write in a kind of spontaneous combustion and a lot of the melodies as such were based on blues inflections. 'Kansas City' [1952] was probably the first one of the 12-bar blues that had a more specific melody."

Over the course of fifty-plus years, naturally, techniques have altered. "It's changed a lot," says Stoller. "Sometimes elements of that process happen but more often Jerry will write a part of a lyric or a chorus of eight bars and I'll set that to music and then we'll take it from there. Or I'll write a tune and bring it to Jerry. So it's changed but nevertheless as a song is being worked on, some of the old process comes into play."

When the pair started out, there was a tradition in popular music, now almost dead, for one person to solely write the lyrics and the other to concentrate exclusively on the melodies and it is to this tradition that they have adhered. But have the pair ever swapped roles? "We really edit each other," says Stoller. "Sometimes more, sometimes not at all. We ask each other, 'Should that note go up or down?' or 'Should this word be this or that?' Because we're a team." Has Stoller ever written an entire verse of lyric? Stoller: "I don't recall if I have but if I did it wouldn't be as good as a verse that Jerry wrote." Leiber: "Once in a while I may come up with a note or two and once in a while he may come up with a word. But certainly I'm not a composer and Mike is not a lyric writer."

Within weeks of meeting, Leiber and Stoller were going places, courtesy of Lester Sill. Leiber: "I think I got Mike to write a couple of lead sheets. I had Lester's card and I contacted him." Stoller says of Sill, "He was extremely encouraging to us. He was a wonderful man. He had a sense of talent. He set up an appointment for us with Modern Records." However, on the day of the meeting, Mike Stoller, with the intemperateness of youth, became affronted at being kept waiting for twenty minutes in Modern Records' outer office and suggested to Leiber that they leave. Leiber: "I said, 'We're gonna blow the appointment and it's not so easy to get these appointments'. He said, 'I don't care. I've waited too long. I wanna get out of here'."

"So we walked out of the office," says Stoller, "and it was on

Canon Drive in Beverly Hills. We took a walk up the street and we saw a sign on a little building across the street that said 'Aladdin Records'. We walked in and I guess they were amused at these two white kids coming in to play songs because they were a rhythm and blues record company and almost all the performers were black. Maxwell Davis, who was their musical director (what we'd call producer and arranger now) listened to a couple of our songs and we left jubilantly with our first songwriting contracts." Being presented with a contract within hours of arriving at record company offices without an appointment would be unthinkable today. For more than one reason. Stoller: "Probably couldn't have been legal since we were under age."

Lester Sill, meanwhile, didn't hold the pair's storming out against them and another appointment was arranged with Modern. Through Sill they made some valuable contacts, including Gene Norman, who Leiber describes as "a very powerful disc jockey." Norman promoted an annual blues jamboree at the Shrine Auditorium in Los Angeles and it was at one of these concerts that a Leiber & Stoller song was performed in public for the first time. The song in question was 'Real Ugly Woman' and was sung by bluesman Jimmy Witherspoon in December 1950. The performance was recorded and released as a single (though was actually the second Leiber and Stoller song to be commercially issued). 'Real Ugly Woman' was actually written with Witherspoon in mind and the pair were not a little impressed at the fact that Witherspoon was willing to perform it. "He happened to be my favourite singer," says Leiber. "In fact, Jimmy Witherspoon was one of the reasons that I decided finally to write songs. I used to get jobs after school hours and in the summer. I was working in a cafeteria in downtown LA as a busboy and there was a short order cook there who always had his little radio going on all the time on the blues station. I remember going by one night and I heard 'Ain't Nobody's Business' by Jimmy Witherspoon and I thought, 'That's it - that's what I'm gonna do'." Stoller was equally thrilled at Witherspoon's decision to record that and others of their songs.

The first Leiber & Stoller composition to be released on record was 'That's What The Good Book Says', issued in early February 1951. They had sung the number for a vocal group called The Robins after being invited into the Modern offices to present songs. The Robins liked it enough to record it in mid- or late-December 1950. When released, it was credited to "Bobby Nunn & The Robbins" (sic). Stoller: "We were not present at that recording session but it was recorded and that was a thrill to have our names on a record." This thrill was not even nullified by the fact that both names were spelt wrong: the label rendered them as "Leiber" and "Stroller." Did the young composers assume that they would now become millionaires? Stoller: "Hardly. We were just thrilled at something that legitimised our feeling that we could write songs." Did they like what was done with the song? "Not particularly," says Leiber, "but we also realized the song wasn't too good." Stoller says of the song, "It had all kinds of comical references to biblical characters." Leiber is caustic about its qualities: "That might be one of the worst songs we've ever written."

So started Leiber and Stoller's career as freelance songsmiths. In those early days, Stoller explains, "All we had in terms of a contract was on a song-by-song basis because [the record companies] each had their own publishing companies. We weren't signed to them because we weren't performing." Nevertheless, they placed a steady string of songs over the following couple of years. Amongst the artists who recorded their work were Little Willie Littlefield, Johnny Otis, Little Esther, Little Mickey Champion, Charles Brown, Amos Milburn and Big Mama Thornton. Jimmy Witherspoon also recorded several more of their songs.

All of these artists of course, were black, which begs the question of whether the pair ever experienced scepticism from black performers about two whites - and furthermore kids who were barely shaving - writing numbers in the blues genre, one which is supposed to resonate with the experiences of American blacks and their only recently emancipated forefathers. "Actually, none at all," says Leiber. "In fact, we got a tremendous amount of support. We were sort of treated like pets, 'cos we were twenty years old or younger and most of the guys that we were writing for were between 27 and 45 (except for Little Esther). They treated us very nicely. This stuff about 'Can a white man sing the blues?' I never thought he could and when the white singers like Mick Jagger came along I was very sceptical - until I heard Bob Seger, and then I changed my mind." Stoller: "We felt black. Most of our time was spent in the black community and most of our friends were black. What we listened to at that time was just blues and jazz."

It's astonishing to think that while the pair were having their songs recorded and released, often by semi-legendary artists, they were literally still schoolboys. Leiber graduated from high school and began attending City College, where Stoller studied, and whilst there studied English lit, philosophy and sight reading. (He would eventually quit four months short of the end of the two-year course.) He asserts that none of his fellow students were particularly impressed at his and his partner's precocious achievements, although his English teacher, a would-be composer himself, most certainly was: "He was always trying to get me to take his song lyrics up to my supposed publisher. I tried to tell him I didn't have a publisher. He couldn't comprehend that was so since I had records coming out. What he didn't know was that Mike and I were short-circuiting the whole industry in that we were not going to Shapiro Bernstein and Leeds Music, we were going right to Modern and Aladdin Records and they were signing the songs up to their own publishing."

Stoller - who was a year ahead of Leiber despite being the same age as him due to the American policy of streaming pupils - dropped out of City College after a year. Because their songwriting was not yet bringing in any money to speak of, he obtained a job in the warehouse of Decca Records. "We were enjoying our success but we were not enjoying much income from our successes," he remembers. "In many cases, where the record company was also the publisher, they would give themselves a very favourable rate for the use of the songs, so what the songwriter ended up with was very, very little. A fraction of a penny."

This was despite the fact that in 1951 they had had their first hit, albeit a hit on the R&B chart rather than a national or main-chart placing. Said record was 'Hard Times', recorded by Charles Brown, released by Aladdin. Stoller: "I think they called it the Blues And Rhythm charts, in *Cash Box* magazine. We were somewhere on the chart." Stoller doubts that the pair received more than a hundred dollars for this achievement. Leiber reckons: "A few hundred bucks" but agrees that "the small companies didn't pay very well."

An interesting release from this period is 'Flying Home' by Amos Milburn, whose writing is credited thus: "Music: Goodman, Hampton/Lyrics: Leiber, Stoller". Explains Stoller, "That was a famous instrumental written by Lionel Hampton and Benny Goodman and it had the famous saxophone solo played by Illinois Jacquet. We wrote lyrics not only to the melody of the song but also to the famous saxophone solo. We got permission from Harry Goodman who was Benny's brother and he was the publisher."

In 1952, Little Willie Littlefield released a version of a Leiber & Stoller song which marked the point at which the pair began to move beyond the blues "inflections" Stoller refers to and started developing a style of their own, one which would result in some of the greatest songs in the history of rock music. The song in question was 'K.C. Lovin'', now better known as 'Kansas City'. It occasioned an argument between the collaborators. Leiber: "After it was finished, Mike said, 'You know, I'm bored with this kind of writing. I don't want to do shout blues. Any singer can make it up. I'd like to be responsible for composing a melody that is much more memorable'." Stoller: "It's definitely a blues but I wanted it to have a melody that you could recognize even if it was done instrumentally." The song was re-titled 'K.C. Lovin'' at the suggestion of an A&R man at King Records by the name of Ralph Bass who thought 'Kansas City' would be too square a title. Littlefield's record was a regional hit in a number of cities.

If 'Kansas City' was an artistic breakthrough for the pair, 'Hound Dog' by Big Mama Thornton was a commercial breakthrough. A phenomenal hit upon its release in 1953 on Peacock Records, it topped the R&B chart for several weeks and sold upwards of 500,000 copies. It was recorded in August 1952. Stoller: "Ralph Bass, who we'd met through Lester Sill, started calling us asking us to write songs for a number of blues singers like Little Esther, Little Willie Littlefield and others. The bandleader of these sessions was Johnny Otis. One day Johnny called me and asked if I was familiar with Willie Mae Thornton's style of singing. I wasn't, and Johnny needed songs for her for an upcoming record date." Willie Mae "Big Mama" Thornton was a blues singer with a voice as redoubtable as her frame and temperament. Stoller: "He asked that Jerry and I come down to a rehearsal at his house so we could hear her." Leiber: So we went down to Johnny's rehearsal garage and we sat in and we watched Mel Williams and Little Esther. And then we saw Big Mama Thornton and she was singing some soulful blues. I turned to Mike and I said, 'Let's get out of here and write our song - she's the one'. On the way to his house - which was only about twelve, fifteen minutes away - I was beating out this kind of rhythm on the roof of the car and I was singing some catch phrases to try and get the feeling for the song." Leiber was thinking of the spirit of a Furry Lewis number called 'Dirty Mother Furrier, Don't You Know?', which he describes as "insinuating and funky and kind of sexy", adding "I was looking for that kind of insinuation. She was so rough-looking and so tough-looking. I was looking for something nasty to put in her mouth. And out came 'You ain't nothin' but a hound dog'. And Mike said, 'Hey man, that's not bad'. I said, 'Oh that's so lame compared to "Dirty Mother Furrier". It just doesn't say anything'. He said, 'I think it says enough. "Dirty Mother Furrier" I don't think ever got played on the radio'. I argued with him for most of the ride to his house. When we finally got there he went right to the piano and he started playing this rhythm that I was beating out on the roof of his car. He had it down. He could do that. He could latch onto a nuance of an idea and bring it on home."

"We were kind of knocked out by her," says Stoller of Thornton. "She was a very formidable and tough-looking lady. She had some razor scars on her face. She was a big woman, very heavy. She wore army boots and overalls. Jerry had some stuff cooking in his mind and I started playing the piano and he started shouting and we started tossing lines back and forth and within ten minutes we had that song."

Thornton's recording of 'Hound Dog' was the first studio session Leiber and Stoller ever produced, albeit done unofficially. Thus was set in motion a producing career for which the pair have received as many, or possibly, more accolades than for their songwriting. Stoller: "We went back to Johnny's house and after Big Mama started to do the song and get the idea of how we wanted it done, Johnny sat down at the drums and was playing a kind of old southern style beat. He turned the snares off the drum, just using the snare drum as a kind of tom tom sound. Then when we went to the studio, which as I recall was the next day, Johnny was in the booth and he had the band start playing and it just wasn't happening. It didn't have the feel or the bite. Jerry said to Johnny, 'Johnny, it isn't happening. You have to play the drums, not your band drummer'. He said, 'Well who's gonna run the session?' So we said, 'We will'. He said 'Okay' and he went out and got on the drums. We did two takes, that's all. The first one was great, the second one was greater and that was it. Jerry was in the booth, I was working out on the floor, and I joined in with the horn players who barked at the end of the record."

Of course, running a session in 1952 wasn't as awesome a task for a couple of novices as the banks of buttons, switches and faders to be found in the modern recording studio would present today. "The mixing in those days was done as you went," recalls Stoller, "because it was mono. We came in after recording on wax so it was quarter-inch tape. It was much simpler, but you had to get it as it was happening. So the mix had to be done as the recording was being done. You couldn't bring up the voice at a certain point or bring up the guitar when the recording was over.

You had to bring it up during the recording if you wanted to emphasise something. Today sometimes it's six tracks on the drum alone."

When 'Hound Dog' was released, it actually bore the songwriting credit "Leiber/Stoller/Otis". Stoller explains that Johnny Otis had told Peacock Records owner Don Robey that he (Otis) was a co-writer: "He also told Robey that he had the legal authority to sign for on our behalf, which of course was nonsense." Otis later admitted he hadn't played any part in the composition of the song but Robey had already printed the record labels and, for monetary reasons, issued them with the incorrect credit rather than re-print them. Realising that the two songwriters were too young for their contracts to be legal, Robey flew to Los Angeles with a new contract, which the pair's mothers signed. "And he gave us a cheque," says Stoller. "I think it was for six hundred dollars. And then he went back to Texas and stopped payment on it. I guess we didn't have a very sophisticated attorney." Leiber and Stoller wouldn't see any money from 'Hound Dog' until the passage of several years, legal action and an Elvis Presley recording had taken place.

Another noteworthy L&S-penned record during '53 was 'Snow Is Falling', issued by no less an artist than Ray Charles. Unlike on 'Hound Dog', they were not present at the recording session. In fact, Stoller points out, they didn't even know the record existed until they came across it when browsing in a music store: "We saw this label that said 'Snow Is Falling' on Swingtime Records and, underneath, the writer's name in parentheses read 'Jerry Leiber-Stoller'. The song was actually a re-titled 'Gloom And Misery', which they had placed with Roy Hawkins in '51. "We were naturally thrilled," says Stoller. "We loved it. Obviously, we were big fans of Ray Charles."

In 1954, Leiber sang (under the pseudonym Billy Black) on a number the pair wrote with Sam 'Highpockets' Henderson (a pseudonym of Shorty Rogers) called 'Too Bad Sweet Mama'. "We were in the studio and the producer wanted Jerry to sing", says Stoller. "I think he was actually a pretty good blues singer but we felt at that time that even though we gave ourselves a path as writers, the fact that we were not black, which was evident when we passed a mirror, made it inauthentic to be a vocalist." Leiber: "I used to sit in when a singer was missing, a part was missing or someone was hoarse. I was never really trying to promote myself. As far as I was concerned, I was a songwriter. I would sing from time to time. I would sing on demos."

It was in this year that the pair first wrote for a white artist. "We broke ranks in 1954," says Leiber. "This kid was bothering me day and night. Pestering me: 'Please write for me and my act'. His name was Gil Garfield, and he's been a friend almost as long as Stoller and I have been partners. I said, 'Gilbert we don't write for white people. It's not that we are making a point of being racist but we are only interested in black singers'. Finally he got to me and I went to Mike. He didn't want to do it either. But Gil was persuasive and finally convinced us to do it. Ironically enough, we wrote two enormous hits for his group, The Cheers. The first was called 'Bazoom (I Need Your Lovin')' and the second was called 'Black Denim Trousers and Motorcycle Boots'." The latter song was later recorded in French by Edith Piaf and became the biggest-selling single of her career.

It was in 1954 that Leiber and Stoller, disillusioned at the fact that they had not received any money for 'Hound Dog' despite its tremendous success, set up their own record company, Spark. Stoller: "Lester Sill and a friend of his, who had a little bit of money, and my father, who had a little bit of money, pooled that money to start a little record company and publishing company. I think it was somewhere in the neighbourhood of three thousand dollars. And we started making records." On a shoe-string budget, Spark contrived to make some memorable, and occasionally commercially successful, records. "We were very under-financed but some of our records sold extremely well in Los Angeles," says Stoller. "Over a hundred thousand copies of 'Riot In Cell Block No. 9' and another record by The Robins called 'Loop De Loop Mambo'."

In addition to being successful, 'Riot In Cell Block No. 9' was an extraordinarily hard-edged record for the time. It - like another L&S-written Robins record, 'Framed' - portrayed a reverse of the clean-cut image that America then purveyed to itself through the media, a world of poverty, crime, violence and corruption, all of which people were far more susceptible to, as either victims or perpetrators, if they were black. Surprisingly, though, Leiber's lyrics were not based on real-life episodes. "Nothing's based on a true story," he avers. "All these things are more or less influenced by the 'Thirties, 'Forties and 'Fifties radio plays. 'Riot In Cell Block No. 9' was based on a show called 'Gangbusters'. In fact, it opened with a machine gun just like the one I used on the record. It's not one thing, it's a conglomerate of influences."

Despite successes like this, the going was tough for a small label like Spark. Stoller: "We were dealing with independent distributors and the general practice of independent distributors with independent record companies was, if they had a hit record they wouldn't pay until they got another hit record, then they'd feel that they had to pay. If you came out with a hit record and you didn't follow it with a hit you would always have trouble collecting your money on the first one." Because of these financial problems Stoller was still living with his parents. Leiber was forced to do day jobs, at one point teaching at a boy's school, where he lived part of the time.

Leiber says Spark was always doomed to relative failure: "We knew how to write songs and do arrangements and make records that were very good. But we did not know how to advertise, promote or distribute records so were never able to get any kind of saturation. There were other people who came along who didn't know how to write, who didn't know how to make records but they knew how to distribute and sell records. We just didn't know how to do a very important part of the process."

However, the artistic excellence of Spark's records ensured that it would transpire to be a springboard to greater things. Nesuhi Ertegun sent some of the Spark records he had heard to his brother Ahmet and Jerry Wexler, owners of Atlantic Records in New York. Stoller: "And they said, 'Listen, you guys make great records but you don't know how to sell them', which was true. Even though Lester knew how, we were just so totally under-financed that we couldn't sell outside of Los Angeles and they convinced us that we should give up the label and make records for them and they would pay us a royalty just for making them."

When Stoller says "Just for making them" he is, of course, talking about producing. The pair would have the same creative freedom they'd enjoyed with their own label, writing songs and supervising sessions to make sure they were executed in the way they had envisaged. Leiber: "It gave us greater liberty to do what we wanted. We had songs that were blues numbers in the early days at places like Capitol and a swing arranger would do an arrangement on the blues. Now that's ludicrous but you can't do anything about it when you're not running the session. If we're producing the session and we've got a blues and we've got a blues singer we're gonna get the right arranger and they'll do the right piece of work."

Though universally used nowadays, back then the word producer was not employed to describe the people running a recording session. It was, in fact, L&S who were the first to be given that title. Stoller explains, "They [Atlantic] came up with the title 'Producer' because prior to that there was no such title for the job that we did. A more appropriate title would have been 'Director'. What we did in the studio and in the preparation for the studio was really more or less what a film director does for a film. At any rate, they gave us label credit as producers from then on."

In addition, they were not tied exclusively to Atlantic, being free to work for other labels too. Leiber explains, "Other labels like Victor would assign us to *their* acts. Atlantic knew that they were getting the crème de la crème of the people we discovered and didn't need an exclusive contract." Stoller: "We got paid a royalty based upon the number of records sold." In addition, he says of Atlantic, "We liked the ambience, we liked the people and we got along very well with them."

Atlantic's first L&S release was the Robins' 'Smokey Joe's

Café' (October 1955). The record had appeared as the last Spark release. Atlantic leased the rights and released it on Atco, their new subsidiary. L&S actually remained in LA at first, where they recorded several records with The Coasters, including Atlantic's first million-seller, the two-sided hit 'Searchin'' b/w 'Young Blood'. Leiber and Stoller moved to the East Coast in the latter half of 1957.

Despite this exciting new deal with Atlantic, the record that changed Leiber's and Stoller's lives appeared on RCA and was, again, something they only found out about after it had been released. Elvis Presley was already a phenomenon following the chart topping success of 'Heartbreak Hotel' in early 1956 in the US (no. 2 in the UK). His rendition of 'Hound Dog' became his third US chart topper of that year. "I didn't find out he was gonna do it," says Leiber. "I found out that he had *done* it and it was already a hit. Harry Goodman called me and said, 'Hey man - you've got a big, big hit'. 'Big Mama Thornton all over again?' He said, 'No, Elvis Presley'." There was a delay before Stoller heard the good news. He had been travelling in Europe in the early part of '56 and the Presley phenomenon had completely passed him by. Returning from Europe, the ship he was on, the Andrea Doria, sank and it was a somewhat bedraggled Stoller who returned to America to find that his and Leiber's lives had been transformed. "We came back to New York where I was planning to meet with Jerry and Lester Sill and the guys from Atlantic," he recalls. "When the freighter that had picked us up out of a lifeboat finally arrived in New York, Jerry was waiting at the dock. He said, 'Guess what, Mike? We've got a smash hit - 'Hound Dog!'" And I said, 'No kidding! Big Mama Thornton?' and he said, 'No, some white kid named Elvis Presley'. And I said, 'Who?' I heard it the next day and it was number one already. It hit number one immediately after it was released."

Neither of the writers actually liked Presley's version, although Stoller wryly states, "As we've become used to saying: 'But after it sold seven million records we began to see the merits of it'." The reason for their antipathy was the fact that Presley had completely changed the mood, the nature, the beat, and the lyrics of the composition. Does Stoller feel Presley's version rather misses the point? "Oh sure. The point was totally different because it was no longer a woman singing to a man saying, 'You don't want a woman, all you want is a home'. The thing is, it still contained that aggressive anger in it with the line 'You ain't nothin' but a hound dog'. The original was better than the version that he sang but I'm glad he did it." Of the way Presley turned a slow, twelve-bar blues into an up-tempo number, Stoller says, "It sounded too nervous. The original record is insinuating and funky and this was some kind of fast, nervous, rockabilly version."

There were financial as well as artistic liberties taken with 'Hound Dog', with Johnny Otis making an unwelcome return appearance. Stoller remembers, "After Elvis's record came out, it seems that when Johnny was signing his name and our names (ostensibly on our behalf) as the songwriters to Don Robey he was under contract exclusively to another company that he co-owned with Sid Nathan of King Records in Cincinnati, Ohio. So after the Elvis record became such a big hit they decided they would come and claim that they owned it - or a third of it - because Johnny put his name on it. It was bizarre. It was thrown out of court. When he [Otis] went to court he said that he was a co-writer but he couldn't remember what he'd written on it and the judge more or less said to him, 'Do you know the difference between the truth and a lie?' because it was apparent that, number one, he hadn't written it, number two, he was claiming it on behalf of a company that he co-owned after he had claimed to have written it and signed it to somebody else." Stoller does add, though, "It was not an uncommon practice in the 'Forties and the 'Fifties for bandleaders to put their name on songs that they hadn't written but that they had recorded. For example, Duke Ellington's name is on some things - if one of his band members or Billy Strayhorn wrote something, Duke's name invariably went on it. What Johnny did was not that unusual. It's just that he didn't ask us, 'Can I put my name on your song?'"

'Hound Dog' was just the beginning of the phenomenon that

Leiber and Stoller's career now became. The Elvis camp, naturally
pleased with the success of 'Hound Dog', asked Leiber and Stoller
if they had anything else that might be suitable for The King.
There was one problem though, as Stoller points out: "At that
point we never had a big stack of songs. When we wrote a song,
we did it, we produced it usually with The Coasters or some other
group." Leiber suggested that Presley revive 'Love Me', a ballad
the pair had written for an act called Willy & Ruth in 1954. Though
the writers had been sceptical of his reading of 'Hound Dog',
L&S were ecstatic at the impassioned, lung-busting fervour that
Presley brought to 'Love Me'. "It was a wonderful recording,"
says Stoller. Leiber opines, "[Elvis's] 'Love Me' is one of the
best records I've ever heard that we've written. I think it's
absolutely beautiful." Released in late '56, the record reached
number 2 in the US national charts. And the snowball kept on
rolling. Leiber: "Colonel Parker and Jean Aberbach called us up -
the manager and the publisher - and asked us if we would consider
writing some new material for Elvis. We said we'd love to."

It's interesting that while it has become commonly accepted
in some quarters that the success of Elvis Presley and the explosion
of rock and roll his popularity engendered took black music out of
its ghetto (in fact, some even posit the theory that rock and roll
constituted the wholesale rip-off of black musical culture), neither
Leiber or Stoller view the Presley phenomenon in those terms. "I
don't think that we experienced Elvis as broadening the spectrum
for black music," says Leiber. "We always felt that he was a
great white Southern singer who had certain kinds of slight
coloration that were tinted black but we didn't feel that he was a
black singer at all. I thought he was a mixture of country & western
and somewhat gospel (but not necessarily black gospel - he sounded
white Baptist to me). To me, rock and roll was not black, rock
and roll was white. Black is rhythm and blues and rock and roll is
a hybrid. We have been attributed with inventing it and maybe we
have done things that might indicate that, but we have never really
experienced ourselves as rock and roll songwriters. For instance,
we wrote a song for Big Mama Thornton and it became a big hit.

And now comes the big transition: a white singer from Memphis who's a hell of a singer - he does have some black attitudes - takes the song over, does it and sells five or eight million copies compared to her half a million and saturates the world with his presence. But here's the thing: we didn't make it. His version is like a combination of country and skiffle. It's not black. He sounds like Hank Snow. In most cases where we are attributed with rock and roll, it's misleading, because what we did is usually the original record - which is R&B - and some other producer (and a lot of them are great) covered our original record."

In any case, says Mike Stoller of Elvis's breakthrough, "He wasn't the first one. After all, Little Richard's stuff was accepted. There were other performers who reached an audience beyond a black audience. There were white kids who were spinning the dial on the radio looking for something [other] than what they found on the top forty. But Elvis was certainly the culmination of that in one artist." Asked whether he considered rock and roll a new kind of music distinct from R&B, Stoller replies, "Not really, because it was evolving. I considered 'Tutti Frutti' a rhythm and blues record but I suppose in retrospect it's also a rock and roll record. I don't know what rock and roll really is because sometimes we use it as a term meaning a kind of rhythm and blues that wasn't so specifically ethnic but to the public in general I think rock and roll for certain people was any kind of popular music they liked and rock and roll for other people was any kind of music they hated."

Meanwhile, Leiber & Stoller were guiding the career of The Coasters, a vocal group that came into existence after a split in the ranks of The Robins when that band's manager set up a new label. Lead tenor Carl Gardner and bass singer Bobby Nunn opted to stay with L&S rather than sign to the new label. L&S recruited Billy Guy and Leon Hughes and renamed the act. The Coasters would record some of the wittiest and most innovative records of the era and have a string of national hits, among them 'Searchin''/ 'Young Blood', 'Yakety Yak', 'Charlie Brown', 'Along Came Jones' and 'Poison Ivy'. In contrast to the sepia tones of social realist records like 'Riot In Cell Block No. 9', The Coasters' records were infused with the bright colours of cartoons and comic books, their ambience much more one of levity. Stoller, though, sees a thread running right through from the Robins' records: "I think it was just a continuation. Jerry's a very funny fellow and I think it was just a continuum of comic material inspired by social situations, inspired by old radio shows and comic books."

The individual Coasters' singing styles were a superb range of comedy voices, from the doleful to the innocent to the wacky and often the members would sing succeeding lines in manners of precisely such extreme contrast. "We'd write them knowing what the voices could do," says Stoller of the material they came up with for the group. "It was like a little play act. A little acting troupe. A little comedy or vaudeville act and we had different roles for the different voices and they were like little plays, little comedy skits." Leiber notes, "I was designing the lyrics *and* the voices. I used to do the voices for them. I used to do line readings to demonstrate the way they were to be performed."

The Coasters took 'Yakety Yak' to number one in the US in late 1958. The song's lyric was the voice of a pompous and overbearing parent scolding a juvenile and nagging him to do household chores, something with which the young record buyers of America could easily identify. However, the song was not aimed at the teenage demographic. Stoller recalls, "I just started playing a rhythm on the piano that had a kind of country feel. It was a funny rhythm. Jerry just shouted out the first line: 'Take out the papers and the trash'." Leiber: "I was lighting a cigarette on the next line and he yelled out 'Or you don't get no spending cash'." Stoller: "We wrote it based upon the first two lines, which obviously sound like a parent and a teenager, so those lines were not thought out. We weren't discussing teenagers. It just came out. After the first two lines, we knew what it was about." With regard to writing for any demographic, Leiber says, "I never self-consciously constructed an idea in a song to appeal to any specific audience. The material came straight out of a very spontaneous impulse. It had nothing to do with 'Who will this appeal to?' or 'Who will this not appeal to?' That's something that we've never done. I would think that most good writers really don't design things that consciously. I don't think they think about the market."

A popular Coasters song, though not a hit, was 'Three Cool Cats', a tableau of teenage street life, which - with its images of girls sharing a bag of potato chips and boys eyeing up the talent - is no less observant for the fact of its funniness. "I remember when I was in junior high school", says Leiber. "There were three or four girls that would hang around together after school. Often they would be sharing a bag of pretzels or potato chips and walking down the street, giggling and showing off to some of the boys. That's sort of what this song is about." However, the song is not autobiography. "If it's based on anything it's based on an old Walt Disney song that I thought was very funny when I heard it as a kid - 'Three Caballeros'. You'll notice that the rhythm on 'Three Cool Cats' is very close to salsa."

Another well-known Coasters record that didn't become a hit was 'That Is Rock And Roll' (1959). Some have read this song as being a defence of rock and roll in the face of parental ridicule in the vein of Danny and the Juniors' 'Rock And Roll Is Here To Stay', The Showmen's 'It Will Stand' and a host of Chuck Berry numbers, but Leiber asserts that this is a misinterpretation. "This song had more to do with a tongue-in-cheek version of this kind of song," he says. "There are songs written about music: 'Strike Up the Band" 'Now You Has Jazz...' This song is a song about a song. The lyrics are rock and roll, but the music is Dixieland. It's a conceit, it's not an anthem." Leiber, incidentally, can be heard singing on the bridge.

The Coasters managed to take 'Poison Ivy' to number 7 in 1959 without anybody noticing that they were singing a lyric that was a sly allusion to venereal disease. Leiber: "I started writing 'Poison Ivy' literally about the plant. And then I began to make the story more ambiguous, and as I wrote it the story itself started to imply [V.D.]."

Leiber modestly disclaims any innovation in the lyrics he was writing for The Coasters, despite them being by common consensus leagues ahead in wit of the standard lyric of the original rock and roll era. Leiber: "I loved some of the early R&B song lyrics such as Rudy Toombs' 'One Mint Julep' and The Clovers' record of 'Your Cash Ain't Nothing But Trash'."

Innovative without doubt though are Coasters records like 'Along Came Jones' and 'Little Egypt', which can stake some claim to be rock operas - albeit mini ones - a decade before The Who's 'Tommy' supposedly kicked off that genre. Leiber himself calls them "playlets" and reveals how exhaustive, and exhausting, their creation could be. "They were more elaborate and more intricate and more complex because they had characters speaking words of dialogue and singing words of dialogue that were scored," the lyricist says. "That took a lot more fashioning in terms of lyric writing. The lyrics had to be absolutely precise because if something was off a syllable or whatever, it wouldn't work. And the same thing with the music." 'Along Came Jones' (US number 9, 1959) was the apotheosis of this style, a cowboy tale whose stops and starts echo the cliffhanger endings of movie serial episodes. It was actually based on the title of a Gary Cooper movie. Leiber: "We've got a white hero on a white horse. It's a combination of a cowboy hero and 'The Perils Of Pauline', because she gets tied to the railroad tracks." 'Little Egypt', about a belly dancer in a carnival, is similarly cinematic, with its droning tune and ululating sax invoking the exotic. "All these things are about a bigger than life kind of story that was often heard on radio," says Leiber. "It's a combination of soap operettas, pulp fiction, suspense stories, and cartoons."

The Coasters, incidentally, moved over to the East Coast when L&S relocated there in late 1957. Though living there, the composers had no proper office in New York until 1960. Stoller: "We would write at the offices of Hill & Range Songs 'cos we'd made a co-publishing deal with them, or we'd write up at Atlantic's offices or in a recording studio. Sometimes on the weekend we'd write at my house or we'd write at Jerry's house, on the phone, or wherever we happened to be. In 1960, when our contract was over with Hill & Range, we opened our own office on 57th street.

It was a small building over a corset shop." About a year later, the pair moved into the Brill Building, the legendary venue for songwriting whose name will crop up many more times in this book.

Stoller explains that though they were free to write for other companies' acts, this didn't always engender much record making: "When we got to New York, we had a one year contract to produce for RCA Victor but we stopped showing up there after a few months 'cos the place looked and felt like an insurance company. It didn't have the feel of a record company. It was antiseptic. We made about five or six records there. We got five or six picks in the trades and nothing ever sold because at that time the same outfit that was selling the records was selling refrigerators. Outside of Elvis Presley, it didn't seem to pay for us to do anything at RCA so we stopped."

Despite their groundbreaking work with The Coasters and the earthiness of much of the material they would write for Presley, L&S were capable of writing very mainstream material, as proved by songs like 'Dancin'', 'You Laugh' and 'An Open Fire', which they placed with Perry Como, Jack Jones and Johnny Mathis respectively between 1957 and 1960. "I don't know why we did that," says Stoller. "Jack Jones is a fine singer, so was Perry Como, but it wasn't our bag at all." Leiber suggests a reason for that line of work: "I think that we were so hot around that time that some of the A&R men from the major companies were reaching out to the younger sort of unconventional writers like ourselves." He even says, "We would have loved to have had a hit with Perry Como."

But above everything else in Leiber and Stoller's career was Elvis Presley. Popular entertainment had, due to the expansion of communications, probably never seen a figure like him: a man known to all society, whether liked or not. Through the medium of film, his fame was to spread even further than that which his records, stage performances and news media coverage had already brought about. Leiber and Stoller were commissioned to write two songs for what would be his second movie, *Loving*

You, released in 1957. One of them, the title track, was a ballad, and an exquisite one. Is it harder to write ballads? Leiber: "I think it was maybe for me back then. I had a tendency to avoid sentimentality and romantic material. I always felt more at home with humour and with irony and with some kind of action, a cliffhanger of some kind, and love ballads tend to be a lot more passive and not as rife with action."

Leiber and Stoller were asked to write the entire score for the Elvis movie *Jailhouse Rock*, also released in 1957. It was at this point that the pair effectively took over Presley's recording career, though Stoller points out "We weren't producing Elvis officially. We did non-credited production for the films *Jailhouse Rock* and *King Creole* and a few other recording sessions."

That the score to *Jailhouse Rock* is highly memorable is a tribute to the professionalism of the composers for they were never too impressed at the quality of the scripts they were asked to write songs to accompany. "I thought, 'Oh, the same old shit'," says Leiber of the script for *Jailhouse Rock*. "The script was just the same-old-same-old, but then you look for a nugget here and there where you can do something that might be exciting. I know that there was a moment in that script that called for a song and it outlined the kind of song. What I did was replace the kind of song that they indicated they wanted with 'Jailhouse Rock'. And completely contrary to what I was thinking, they loved it - 'cos they usually rejected those ideas." He describes what the film producers had originally wanted for that sequence as "very soft in the head and not very original and not very butch, not very tough. I remember it as being namby pamby and not believable as a guy in jail. I even found some of his choreography - sliding down the pole and going into that shimmy - slightly effete myself, even as good as it is." However, that choreography Leiber refers to - Elvis bumping and grinding in prison clothes in perfect synchronisation with the movie's title track - remains an unforgettable and iconic scene in rock (and cinema) history. That title track topped the charts on both sides of the Atlantic.

Another memorable song from the 'Jailhouse Rock'

soundtrack was 'Baby I Don't Care', whose lyric Leiber wrote with Presley's style in mind: "'Baby I Don't Care' had the sneer in it and Elvis Presley was very good at sneering. He was good at a certain kind of warm smile and he was good at a threatening or menacing look and he was good at a sneer and I was playing on those prototypical broad-based gestures." Presley actually plays the rumbling bass that opens the song.

It was while making *Jailhouse Rock* (in which Stoller can be seen playing the part of Elvis' piano player) that the pair got to know Elvis properly. "He was a nice guy," says Leiber. "He was a young guy and he was kind of like down-home, from the neighbourhood. He was rather unpretentious. A little bit self-conscious, not quite sure of himself in this big old star-ridden place called Hollywood. I liked him. And he worked like a Trojan. He was great in the studio. He could sing all day and all night." Did he ever make suggestions for arrangements? Leiber: "No, never, and he could have. We were not dictators in the studio. We were always very open. He *would* say from time to time, 'Can we do another take?'"

The following year's *King Creole* once again featured a memorable L&S title track, although the fact that it seems to refer to the notoriously swivel-hipped Elvis as a performer ("jumping like a catfish on a pole") is, according to Leiber, just coincidence. Whatever, it was a brilliant and breathless number. Possibly even better than that was the brooding, snarling 'Trouble', in which the narrator defies the world to take him on in hand-to-hand combat. That these two tough-minded numbers shared space on a soundtrack with the all-American corn of L&S's 'Steadfast Loyal And True' - about a man's memories of the "good old golden rule days" of the classroom - is something about which Leiber is unapologetic: "You can't do a high school anthem in rock and roll - it won't be authentic. It's like singing a marine corps hymn in rock and roll." But why write something like that for a wild performer like Presley? "It's always good to root things in a simple conventional, historically accurate statement," Leiber replies. "So you get a little anthem like that and all the wild stuff can play against it contrapuntally and make sense. But if everything's wild there's no contrast." The songs in *King Creole* also featured a lot of brass arrangements. "They were trying to indicate this small New Orleans band," explains Stoller, "which of course would have horns: a trumpet, a clarinet or saxophone and a trombone would be traditional Dixieland band and so they were trying to give it that flavour."

The audiences who were buying Presley's records were mainly white, something of a first for artists performing L&S songs (Gil Garfield notwithstanding). Did Leiber and Stoller, therefore, consciously write in a different style when creating material for Presley? "No, not really," says Stoller. "You know what? I don't think I've ever sat down and said 'I'm not gonna write this for a white audience'. I don't think I ever specifically said, 'I'm gonna write this for a black audience'. The thing was, we worked in that milieu [blues] to begin with almost exclusively and as things began to change, we just kept writing. I don't think we ever, ever said. 'We're gonna write this because this is what's happening in the market'. I wrote to amuse myself." The only alterations they made when writing for The King were in terms of personal idiosyncrasies. Leiber: "We considered his voice and what he did with his voice when we wrote for him."

King Creole is generally recognised as probably Presley's best movie. After that, they descended into a formula of cheesy scripts and cheesier soundtracks. Leiber knows for a fact that the story did not have to be that way. In the late '50s Leiber met an agent called Charlie Feldman who told him he had a project he might be interested in - a film of the Nelson Algren novel *A Walk On The Wild Side*. Feldman had persuaded Budd Shulberg, writer of cinema classic *On the Waterfront*, to write the script and the legendary Elia Kazan to direct it. Feldman said he wanted Leiber and Stoller to write the score for the proposed movie. Leiber: "And here's the crowning cherry: 'I want you to help me get Elvis Presley to play the lead'. I got so excited I couldn't sit still. I had to leave." Leiber and Stoller made an appointment with Presley's publishers, the Aberbach brothers. "I thought they were just going to jump for joy," says Leiber. "I told them the whole story. I finally said 'Presley' and the room got very quiet. [One of them said], 'I have to discuss this with the Colonel' and asked us to wait outside. We nervously waited, hoping for the best. The door opened and we were summoned back in. [they] said, 'You're very nice boys; we like you very much, we think you are very talented, but the Colonel wants me to inform you that if you ever dare try to interfere in the career of Elvis Presley, he will personally see to it that you'll never work in New York, Los Angeles, Chicago, London, or anywhere else in the world'."

Leiber likens this to a near tragedy. "I'll tell ya - Elvis would have wanted to do that picture more than anything," he insists. He is convinced Presley could have become as good an actor as he was a singer. "In the beginning he was what he was," says Leiber. "He was just a pop-rocker. A little better looking, a little better dance steps. He was just better than anybody else. That's what he was. He was not Marlon Brando. It would have taken some real work to get him up to snuff. You couldn't just give him *On The Waterfront* and expect him to do a great job of acting. But I think after a year or two of being with Kazan in the Actors Studio and top directors and screenwriters he would have finally emerged. I thought that Elvis could have probably become someone in a league with James Dean."

L&S also wrote some excellent singles for Presley, including 'Don't', 'She's Not You' and the raunchy blues 'Santa Claus Is Back In Town'. Their association with Presley ended in 1960. This termination was due to a business dispute, though not with Presley. Leiber: "Never had a disagreement with Elvis. Elvis and me and Stoller got along always famously. In fact, he relied on us to such a degree that at one time he would not record unless we were in the studio and that's what brought the problem to a head." Inevitably, the dispute was with Presley's notoriously philistine manager Colonel Tom Parker. Leiber had recently been hospitalised with pneumonia and had arrived home to find telegrams from Parker and the Aberbach publishers telling him he must be in Los Angeles in three day's time because a recording

session had been scheduled for Presley. There were also manila
envelopes containing contracts for Leiber to sign for the
forthcoming sessions and movie. "I called up Tom Parker," Leiber
recalls. "'How ya doing, boy?' 'Just got out of the hospital'. 'Well
I guess you're okay now, right?' I said, 'I'm pretty good but I
don't know if I can travel yet'. 'Oh why not? You can travel,
there's nothing wrong with you'. I said, 'Well I talked to this
doctor...' 'Jackasses man, they're just trying to rob you. I think
you ought to make it. I think you better make it'. And he got
slightly - not terribly, but slightly - menacing. 'By the way, read
your new contract. You'll love it. It's a great contract, boy'. So I
opened up the manila envelopes and in one was a cover letter
saying, 'Enclosed you'll find the contract for the forthcoming
picture and also the contract covering the recording dates...'
Signature page on the back: 'Please sign and return'. I looked all
over the place. There's a signature page but there's no contract.
So I thought somebody was delinquent in putting this together so
I called Tom's secretary and told her, 'I think there's been a mistake
here'. 'I'll get Tom'. 'What's wrong boy? We having trouble?' 'I
don't think so, Tom. I think it was just an oversight. I got a manila
envelope here. But Tom, there's a cover letter and signature page
but there's no contract'. 'Oh', he said, 'Don't worry about that.
You just sign it, we'll fill it in later'." Leiber was furious. "I said,
'Hey man' - and I never called him "man" before - 'Who do you
think you're talking to? One of your cotton-picking boys from
Memphis?' And he said, 'I think you're gonna be sorry you talked
to me that way'. I said, 'I think you're gonna be sorry you tried to
send me something to sign without a contract. If this gets out,
you're in a lot of trouble'." Leiber rang Stoller: "I told him what
happened. This is like burning up a couple of million dollars. I
said, 'So what do you think?' He said, 'To hell with him'. I was so
pleased because I was afraid he might say, 'You schmuck, what
did you do?'"

The pair never worked for Presley again, although the chance
did arise. "They really needed us so badly, they were willing to
compromise," says Leiber, "and I think I could have reinstated

the deal but after that we decided there was no hope. There was no way to do anything with Elvis that would amount to anything except very arch, commercial movies. We were not going to make James Dean out of him - which is what he could have been." He adds, "Actually, it's sad, because he really pined for us because we were his best producers."

Some years later, Leiber received a telegram at his office from Presley, inviting him to see him perform at Madison Square Garden. Leiber: "I took my wife and I went. I don't go to big concerts because I'm a little bit claustrophobic. We saw him and he was real good. I'd never seen him before - can you imagine? I was impressed. Just before the end I said to my wife, 'They're doing the finale. We've got to make our move now because if we wait to the end we're going to get caught in a bottleneck and you're going to have to call the paramedics to get me out'. We were in a box. I sort of skulked out and we got a cab and went home and my kids asked me about him and talked about it. I go to the office the next day, there's a note on my desk: 'Why did you leave before the end? Love, Elvis'. He didn't know I had claustrophobia. He probably thought I was walking out because I was bored or something. It was sad. Imagine him seeing me leave in an audience of 50,000 people."

Meanwhile, back in '59, L&S could do no wrong. As well as their huge success with Presley and The Coasters, they had an unexpected windfall when Wilbert Harrison decided to cover 'K.C. Lovin''. Released as 'Kansas City' (which, of course, had been its original title), it topped the US national charts. This in turn created a slew of other covers of the song - a slew which has become a tidal wave down the years. Stoller estimates that there have been more than a hundred, and possibly close to two hundred, versions of the song released. One of those recorded in the immediate aftermath of the Harrison record was that of Little Richard. Like Presley's version of 'Hound Dog', Richard's 'Kansas City' featured material not in the original song: he stretched and improvised the original structure, adding an infectious call-and-response segment. Leiber says, "I'm not mad for

Richard's version but I'm mad for Richard. The version he did kind of got lost." Little Richard later successfully claimed some of the publishing on his version of the song, a move probably prompted by the fact that one of the most lucrative versions of the song was that of The Beatles on their *Beatles For Sale* album (1964): they actually covered Richard's amended cover. Richard's version and the covers of it are now credited as 'Kansas City/ Hey Hey Hey Hey'. "The point is, it was an unauthorized use of our song," Stoller points out of Richard's tampering. However, he bears Richard no ill feeling for his proceeds from the publishing: "I consider him to be one of the greats. I think of him almost as highly as he thinks of himself."

And what of The Beatles' rendition? "I didn't like it," says Leiber. "I think it was kind of messed up. It wasn't the song. Too many liberties were taken with lyrics. The song got so fractured that it could have been anything. It was like a jam, and for that it's kind of fun and exciting. A jam is okay, but if you want to hear the song then you've gotta do the song." Stoller concurs: "I wish they had done it more like the original. Paul's done it a few times and the last version that I heard, he used a lot more of the original song than he did on The Beatles' recording of it."

So of the many versions of 'Kansas City' released, which do the authors like best? Stoller: "My favourite one is Joe Williams'. It has a little feel of Kansas City jazz, 'cos Kansas City was a magical place for us." He adds, "The first time we went to Kansas City was in 1986 or '7 and we were given the keys to the city by the mayor." Leiber also chooses the Joe Williams version but in addition nominates that of Count Basie. He says, "Wilbert Harrison's version is a straight-ahead take which has a good groove - the guitar lick is in the pocket - but it doesn't have any contour or flexibility. Joe Williams could sing the pants off of Wilbert Harrison." With so many covers, Kansas City ended up being recorded by many people the pair greatly admired but Leiber notes, "My favourite artists did it and none of them - the ones I loved the most as artists - did my favourite version. For instance, Little Richard, I think maybe of all time is the greatest blues singer for me. James Brown did not do it well. You know who puts them all away and he's not in their league? Little Milton. That's a killer record. It's very coherent."

In 1959, the pair secured a hit for longstanding vocal group The Clovers with the jump-style 'Love Potion No. 9'. Stoller reveals that the song had actually been written for The Coasters. "The Clovers' manager, who had just become the head of United Artists records, called us and said, 'Hey man, I need a hit real bad. I need a hit for The Clovers, they're gonna be on United Artists'. He was a buddy so we said okay."

1959 also saw the release of 'There Goes My Baby', a number two for the Drifters. It is possibly the most influential song with which L&S were ever involved, featuring two innovations on one record: classical strings and Latin rhythms, both of which were unthinkable for R&B/rock and roll artists. Despite the sweetness of the strings, there was a strange roughness to the ambience of the record, which came about by chance. Leiber explains, "The timpani player, who was a regular drummer, didn't know how to pedal the timpani properly, so it ended up being out of tune. That created this interesting abrasive rub in the record. Obviously, that wasn't planned. It was an accident. Sometimes you get these very fortuitous accidents." From unthinkable to commonplace: over the following few years, strings on R&B/soul records became almost de rigueur.

The Latin rhythms were the result of a recording by Silvana Mangano from the film *Anna* by which the pair had been impressed. Leiber: "Over a couple of years we put together an ensemble of Brazilian and other Latin percussion. It became the foundation of all The Drifters' records." Those rhythms were barely less influential than the strings. "Burt Bacharach was signed to us at the time", reveals Leiber. "Burt Bacharach started learning how to make records with us. He was always a great musician and a first rate conductor, but he came with us to learn how to produce records. Also, he didn't know how to write pop hits in the R&B genre. Burt has used the rhythmic stuff that we put together for every record he's made since."

Leiber & Stoller wrote more material for The Drifters but mainly restricted themselves to producing their records. Nevertheless, with their work for The Coasters, Presley and other more minor jobs, it was a huge workload. "There was a time when we turned out an enormous amount of material," acknowledges Leiber. "There was a time when we were doing one Coasters session every three months and a Drifters session every three months and a Presley picture." However, he says, "I don't remember it being a strain. 'Cos we used to work effortlessly. We would work eight, nine, ten, twelve hours a day - and love it. We were just so engrossed in it. We had so much fun doing it. The time when it became difficult was when it started to become boring - when it became so repetitious it wasn't fun to do any more. There wasn't anything to discover anymore, or learn. It was just the same old okey-doke."

The pair also wrote and produced for Drifters singer Ben E. King when he left the group to go solo in 1960. His 'Stand By Me' has been a top ten US hit twice over, first in 1961 and then again in 1986 when it was re-released after being used as the title song for a movie. (In Britain it climbed as high as number one as a result of said film.) The song actually bears the credit "Leiber/Stoller/King". Leiber: "The title was from an old gospel song. Ben E. King brought me a fragment of the song. It sounded like a church song. I said, 'I like the sound of that'. 'I like it too,' he said, 'but I can't get past the first four or five bars'. I said, 'Do you want me to write it with you? I can write it with you, we can get it finished today and we'll record it'. And he got very excited because he liked the song very much but he figured that he's not going to be able to write it. Then later Mike walked in and came up with the crowning stroke: he wrote the bass pattern." The result was a creation in which the tradition of supplication in gospel songs was married to the kind of expression of devotion more associated with romantic songs to disarmingly vulnerable effect.

Leiber had co-written another hit for King earlier that year, 'Spanish Harlem', although not with Stoller. His collaborator was a young wannabe called Phil Spector, who was working with the pair in the studio as a sort of apprentice. "Phil would ask me to write a song," says Leiber. "I kept refusing and turning him down. For two reasons. I didn't particularly feel like writing after hours when I came home and I also felt that if I had an idea, I really owed it to my partner, Mike, to do it. We didn't have a contract but we were very bound. Phil kept asking me and asking me and asking me and one night he caught me a couple of drinks down and after dinner and relaxing and he got his guitar and he put it on his knee and came over to my chair and he said, 'Come on man, let's write a song'. I gave in and I wrote 'Spanish Harlem'." Leiber wrote the lyric and created the contour for the melody out of 'Rhapsody Espanol'. It was an inspired move, the words and melody inter-twining and tumbling marvellously. Stoller laid out the arrangement, creating the counter-line played on the marimba.

It was one of the very few occasions Leiber has written with a different collaborator. Indeed, it is for this reason that Leiber's and Stoller's names are almost synonyms in the public's mind with each other's. Does it sometimes feel as though they're not even separate individuals? "I think so," says Leiber. "I don't think it's constant and I don't think that it's so intense but I think there are moments when what you describe seems to apply." Is that a good or bad thing? Leiber: "I think it could be either. There's something nice about it and something secure about it and sometimes it's a pain in the ass." Have the two ever fallen out so badly that it threatened the continuation of the professional relationship? "According to Mike, we're always falling out. We're in a state of falling out. It's been the longest argument on record in the music business."

Spector, incidentally, had actually been discovered by the same person who discovered L&S: Lester Sill. Spector had started out as a performer, having studied guitar with jazzman Barney Kessel, and had a hit with his own group, The Teddy Bears, 'To Know Him Is To Love Him'. However, he really wanted to be a producer. Leiber: "He told Lester he wanted to hang out with Leiber and Stoller. So Lester called me. I couldn't say no to Lester. I said, 'Send him out'. He sent him out. For about eighteen months, two years, he went to every session we did, he observed everything we did. One day I was approached by the Aberbach's cousin, Johnny Bienstock, who was running Big Top Records. He wanted us to produce an artist and we said we really didn't have enough time. But, I said, I would suggest someone I think is very talented and we'll guarantee his performance in terms of cutting, mixing, whatever." With Big Top Records artist Ray Peterson's recording of 'Corrina Corrina', so started Phil Spector's production career, one which would ultimately see him recognised as a genius.

'On Broadway' was a song which went through particularly complicated teething problems. It had actually been written by Barry Mann and Cynthia Weil and recorded by Phil Spector, who had thought it not good enough to release. Shortly thereafter, Leiber received a phone call from the song's publisher Don Kirshner. Leiber: "He said, 'Leiber, I've got an almost great song. I'm just asking you would you listen to it and tell me if the thing is worth re-writing, 'cos I think it's a hit.' I said, 'I'll tell you what I think of the song, but first you have to talk to Barry and Cynthia and ask them if they want us to rewrite it'. He said, 'Okay, I'll call you back'. He called me back ten minutes later. He said, 'They would be thrilled'. I got the acetate and put it on and I thought, 'This is a potential hit. No question about it. But it's gonna need some changes here and there'. I called Mann and Weil up and said, 'I think this song is a hit but I don't think it was finished right'. And they said, 'We know there's something wrong with it but we can't figure it out'. So all four of us sat around my house one evening and rewrote it together. Mike and I went in and we made the record with The Drifters and it was a stone smash." The resulting record - released in mid-1963 - was a slow, sophisticated song which simultaneously celebrated the neon charge of the bustling New York district of the title while at the same time pointing out that beneath the glitter lay grim scenarios of failure and disillusion.

Another hit for Ben E. King was 'I (Who Have Nothing)' (1963). This utterly melodramatic number was actually an Italian song to which L&S put an English lyric. The pair had had it suggested to them that they should completely remake the original record. Leiber: "It's the only time I've ever done this. I said, 'You're crazy - don't even try. You'll be in the studio for a year and it'll never be right. This soundtrack is a stroke of genius. Buy the master, we'll take the voice off of this, we'll write an English lyric for it and we'll do it with Ben E. King'. And that's what we did." The English title L&S gave the song was not an exact translation of the Italian and the rest of the English language record was merely in the spirit of the Italian one. "It's not a translation, it's an adaptation," says Leiber.

In 1963, Leiber and Stoller put the failure of their Spark label sufficiently to their backs of their minds to be able to set up the Tiger and Daisy labels. One would have assumed that their work rate would remain the same when records were coming out under their own aegis but the pair actually wrote very few songs for these and their successor labels, going into virtual retirement for several years. Leiber blames this on the changing audience demographics for popular music: "We signed a guy from New Orleans called Alvin Robinson and we made three or four records with him and he was a killer. We thought he was in the same league as Ray Charles. We got five-star ratings on records we made for him and we didn't sell two records. We thought maybe we just were deluding ourselves, that the records weren't as good as we thought they were. But after about four or five or six sessions, we started to concentrate more on less Leiber-Stoller-type sessions and more on things like the Dixie Cups. Little girl's groups rather than those blues things. I don't think we lost confidence. I think we lost a little bit of heart because we felt that the tastes were possibly changing and the demographics were changing and that the kids who used to buy the records we made were seventeen, eighteen, nineteen, twenty. Maybe some younger kids with The Coasters but by and large that kind of audience were now relatively young girls and they were like twelve and thirteen. As the years have gone on, it's gotten lower and lower. We felt the stuff that we were making was good, and also accepted too by the really tough badass critics in the trade who gave us nothing but three and five stars. They didn't stop doing that but we weren't able to sell records."

Leiber means the last sentence in both senses. As with Spark, the pair were finding that writing and producing was much tougher than marketing. After only a few releases, they were prepared to terminate the Tiger project. Then Leiber ran into George Goldner, a legendary music industry figure who had been the talent behind many famous labels - Rama, Gee, Gone, End and Roulette among them - and had lost them all through the debts accrued by his compulsive gambling. Leiber was so confident in Goldner's abilities that he offered him, for nothing, a third partnership in their record company. Goldner, who was broke and about to lose his house, readily accepted. Leiber: "I hired George Goldner that night. He said, 'Give me the keys to your office and tell me where the acetates are and how many you have'. I said, 'We have fourteen or fifteen unreleased records'. He said, 'Don't come back tonight'. I said, 'Are you gonna be here all night?' He said, 'Yeah'. I came back the next day at eleven o' clock and he was sitting in my desk, not a hair out of place, and he held up a record and said, 'Leiber, on my mother's grave, this is a hit'. I said, 'Play it, George'. And he played 'Going To The Chapel'. And I said, 'George, I hate that fucking record'. And he said, 'Who's running this company - you or me?' 'George' - long pause - 'I guess you are'. He said, 'That's right'. And he put it out." The record (actually called 'Chapel Of Love') was a saccharin tribute to the marriage ceremony written by Jeff Barry, Ellie Greenwich and Phil Spector and sung by the female trio The Dixie Cups. It was a million seller and a number one in the US in 1964.

That record - its female singers and the fact that Leiber wasn't too keen on it - was a symbolic pointer to the future of the label, which was renamed Red Bird (with Blue Cat as a more bluesy subsidiary). "He knew how to pick records," says Leiber of Goldner. "It was a good record - Mike produced it and did a lot of the arrangement - but it wasn't our taste. It's well made. The point is, it's not our kind of record and it's not something I could hear easily. I can hear Ray Charles, I can hear Wilson Pickett, I can hear Aretha Franklin, I can hear Smokey Robinson." Goldner was given his head and Red Bird became famous for the Girl

Group sound, acts like the Jelly Beans, the Dixie Cups and the Shangri-Las ensuring hit after hit for the label over the next two years. Many consider some of those records to be imperishable but it was a far cry from L&S' blues origins. Leiber: "It sounds like the records we put out, we didn't like. That's not so. They just were not our kind of records."

Leiber did have a penchant for the teen dramas that George 'Shadow' Morton constructed for the female vocal group the Shangri-Las, among them 'Leader Of The Pack' (a US number one in 1964 and a hit three times over in the UK) and 'Past, Present And Future' (a daring rape tale that was totally spoken-word and which Leiber helped write). "That's a soap opera all over again and it's speaking," says Leiber of the Shangri-Las' records, "and we invented single-handedly the speaking records with The Coasters. That's why Shadow Morton brought his stuff to us."

There was another element in the equation: the British Invasion. When The Beatles had hit America with a shock force even bigger than had accompanied Elvis Presley's emergence into public consciousness, they had a profound effect on what was referred to as the Tin Pan Alley songwriter, i.e., the non-performing, freelance popular music composer. In an era when it was fashionable for acts to write themselves - and uncool not to - the demand for songs from outside sources decreased accordingly. It is true that, had they had a mind to, Leiber and Stoller could have ridden out this storm - a partnership as talented as theirs would have been an exception to the rule in that self-sufficient era, just as were Bacharach & David. But the phenomenal success of The Beatles - at least in their early years - only served to confirm to L&S that the market for popular music was something they no longer understood. "I wasn't crazy about the British bands at the time," says Leiber. "Later on, I grew to really like them but also they got much better. The Beatles to begin with were not that great. We had three or four records of our songs [covered by] them and they weren't great, but The Beatles got to be stupendous. I think in the very beginning young kids really dug them because of what they looked like and everything else. I didn't like them 'til a few years later, but then I really liked them because I really felt with 'Eleanor Rigby' and songs like that, they really made their mark as writers."

Leiber and Stoller were pushed - or allowed themselves to be pushed - further and further into the background, leaving the writing of Red Bird's records to songwriters like Greenwich & Barry and Morton, who also tended to produce the songs they wrote. L&S could only take consolation in the great success of the label and their confidence in their role as executive producers. Leiber: "We were very good as executive producers because we know more on our left hands then most of the people out there making records. When it came to studio techniques - directing performance - I never saw anybody work better than me."

Still, there was a feeling of lack of fulfilment. "Part of it is how it affects your living," says Leiber, "and there was a tremendous amount of overseeing, supervising, consultation and not as much hands-on input that really gives you a jolt when you're working well and enjoying it." Ultimately, the pair sold the label. In light of the great success of Red Bird, it's hugely ironic that when they sold it in 1966, it was for the sum of one dollar. The buyer was George Goldner. Why the low figure? "That's the only answer that I'm gonna withhold from you," laughs Leiber. Stoller is more forthcoming, but only marginally: "Mainly, we were bored. Also George Goldner had some unsavoury associates or friends who would pop 'round all the time." Surely they could have sold the company for a couple of million? Stoller: "I don't think we thought it through that carefully. We just decided to move on."

Although dispensing with Red Bird did not mean a return to their previous high rate of productivity, the pair give the impression that they were able to enjoy themselves creatively again. They began working with The Coasters once more and, although not matching the success of the previous decade, made some good records with them. Mike Stoller recorded with his band The Stoller System in 1968. That same year The Monkees stirred memories of the days when recording a L&S song was a sure-fire recipe for success when they took 'D.W. Washburn' into the US top 20.

A new song, 'Is That All There Is?' recorded and produced by L&S with Peggy Lee in 1969, hit number 11 in the US. More importantly, from Leiber's point of view, it showed that the pair were not only back in the saddle composing-wise but that they were still capable of developing. "I had been a great deal influenced by Kurt Weil and Bert Brecht and we were kind of looking for a new avenue," he recalls. "We'd done an awful lot of rock and roll in all those years and we were also getting a little bit older and we wanted to do something that would appeal to a more mature audience. Although rock and roll is great, I think it's mainly a high-energy form for young people. So I started experimenting with different forms. I was looking to write something that was dramatic, theatrical and original. 'Is That All There Is?' was my first attempt at experimenting with a new form. I wrote a series of vignettes that illustrated the state of mind often referred to as ennui. Mike fell in love with them and set them to music. What was missing was a refrain to bind them together and make a whole. I said, 'I'm going to go home and try the refrain'. He said, 'I will too'. We both came into the office the following day and he sat down and I started singing the words that I'd concocted overnight and he started playing the notes that he had cooked up overnight and, of all the strangest things, the notes and the words fit. Absolutely perfectly. We've been partners over fifty years: that's the only time that ever happened."

He adds of the world-weary number with spoken verses, "When Peggy Lee heard it, she insisted that I'd written it for her." Leiber and Stoller had enough songs for Lee to follow up that hit with an album but she was too busy touring to record one at the time. Leiber: "In 1975, we did a Peggy Lee album where we finished a song cycle - songs that we were planning on the drawing board in about '68, '69. We were gonna do an album and put all these kind of cabaret songs on it but she went on the road after 'Is That All There Is?', it became such a big hit. In '74 she called us and said, 'Hey, how about that album?' We said, 'Peggy, it's five years later, who knows if anybody wants it anymore?'

'Oh they'll want it'. So we went and we made the Peggy Lee album *Mirrors* and it became kind of an underground hit but it did not become the kind of smash that it could have been on the heels of 'Is That All There Is?'"

In the mid-Seventies, L&S signed a deal with A&M Records whereby they would produce albums by up-and-comers on the label's roster. The first was a folk-rock group called Stealer's Wheel, featuring future solo superstar Gerry Rafferty on vocals. Their 'Stuck In The Middle With You' - a record which sounded uncannily like a Bob Dylan number in structure and execution - was a Transatlantic top tenner in 1973. The other A&M artist whose career the pair boosted was a sort of English Janis Joplin, the gravel-throated Elkie Brooks. Unlike with Stealer's Wheel, the pair contributed songs to as well as produced her project, the album *Two Days Away*. One of them, 'Pearl's A Singer', was an achingly sad number which reached the top ten in the UK charts in 1977. It was actually a slightly rewritten version of a song the pair had composed with Dino and Sembello, an act they had recorded in '74. Leiber: "'Pearl's A Singer' is kind of a pathetic story about a nightclub entertainer who's in her mid- or late-thirties and who doesn't really have the looks or the chops anymore but she's got a lot of heart." Was it intended as the single from the album? "I always hoped so because I always thought of it as the best or most interesting song on the album", says Leiber. "I thought it was gonna be a hit in the US as well and I was very disappointed when it wasn't." In between the Stealer's Wheel and Brooks projects, L&S produced *Procol's Ninth* for pomp rockers Procol Harum, released in 1975 and generating a UK hit in 'Pandora's Box'.

A glance at Leiber and Stoller's published songs from the mid-'Seventies onwards seems to reveal a dramatic slowdown in their songwriting. "Our stream of productivity is kind of strange and kind of unpredictable", says Leiber. "We started off writing like machines. We were writing five songs a day for the first seven or eight or nine years. And then we slowed down somewhere, somehow, for whatever reason. It's been very spotty in a way".

However, the pair were busy, having transferred their ambitions from the rock arena to that of the stage musical. "Strangely, it was sort of always there", Leiber says of their ambitions in that direction. "We always hoped that we'd one day be able to write for the theatre. We've flirted with it off and on through the years".

At one point, Leiber had actually been involved in an abortive attempt to write a stage musical with Leonard Bernstein. "I spent about eight or nine months working with Bernstein", he recollects. "We got along famously. We wrote some good stuff but the project never got produced. Bernstein at one point came to me and said, 'It's not easy for me to write, I don't have a lot of time, I conduct a lot. If this show doesn't go, do you mind if we separate our interests and you take your words and I take my notes?' I said, 'Absolutely fine with me'. And when we both found out that the show was not going to be produced, I took my lyrics and he took his music. And I was just as happy because I felt Mike wrote better songs for the lyrics than Leonard had. I don't know whether there were any hits but they were some songs Mike and I both prize very much."

The first actual tangible fruits of the pair's desire to write a musical was called *Smokey Joe's Café: The Songs Of Leiber & Stoller*. It came about almost by accident. "It grew out of two productions in London", says Leiber. "One was called Yakety Yak and another was called *Only In America* and each one had some really great things in it but neither one was consistent enough and had the going distance for an entire evening. They had three, four, five good numbers and we'd say, 'Jesus, if we only had 25 numbers like that, we'd have a show'. A couple of years later, I got a call from a director of a Seattle repertory company who said, 'I'm so-and-so and I'm a director. I'm leaving next year. We all love Leiber and Stoller songs. We grew up on them and we'd like to do a musical. We don't know what kind of evening it'll be. It could be a concert, it could be a recital, it could be dramatized, but we can't afford to pay you anything so if you give us the rights to the songs we'd be happy to send you free tickets when it opens'. I was charmed by the guy's effrontery and I told him he could have the songs for nothing. He spent six or eight months putting it together and invited us up. The day we were supposed to go, I had the 'flu. I couldn't go. Mike went and he saw it and he called me that night. He said, 'You didn't miss anything. It's terrible. They can't sing, they can't dance, they can't play their instruments and the story is terrible. I don't know what the hell to think of it - but one strange thing that kept occurring all night. I can't stop thinking about it. The audience stood up, standing ovation, and applauded after every number'."

So began the idea for a show that would feature uninterrupted Leiber and Stoller classics. It was a slow and complicated process, with the pair paying for workshops themselves after early hiccups. The end result - with the title taken from the record they had written for The Robins in '55 - was a show that played to packed houses on Broadway (it became the longest running revue in Broadway history) and in London's West End. Leiber: "There was no book. Just a very delicate juxtaposition of material that created a sense of continuity."

The pair are still asked to write pop songs, as witnessed by their 1995 composition for Frank Sinatra, 'The Girls I Never Kissed'. Leiber: "I think it's one of the best songs we've ever written. Frank was not at the top of his game when he recorded it but we're thrilled that he did. It's the only Frank Sinatra recording of one of our songs."

Leiber's comments on that song begs the question of what he thinks are the very best songs for which he's ever been responsible? "'Hound Dog' - and of course I mean Big Mama, so it's not just the song, it's the record - and 'Is That All There Is?' [by] Peggy Lee. I think in a funny way that covers the whole spectrum. I could say 'On Broadway' and 'Spanish Harlem', 'Kansas City' and some others." Stoller: "The best songs that we wrote, we wrote for The Coasters and for Peggy Lee. In the case of The Coasters, 'Searchin'', 'Young Blood,' 'Yakety Yak', 'Little Egypt'. For Peggy Lee, things like 'I'm A Woman', 'Some Cats Know', and of course 'Is That All There Is?'" And their worst songs? Stoller: "The worst songs we wrote I'm not gonna tell you because I always insult somebody who finds it to be their favourite song." Leiber is not so unforthcoming: "'That's What The Good Books Says' and 'One Bad Stud'." Of the latter, he says "It's funny, everybody picks that out as some kind of real find, a nugget that's hidden in the hills. It's one of the worst songs I've ever written."

What do the pair think of the state of songwriting today? "I think there are a number of people who have the talent and have the craft," says Stoller, "But I think that the advent of the televised music promotions have really made the craft and the artistry of lyric writing in pop music atrophy to some degree because it's all about the visual. Of course, in the case particularly of Jerry's writing, the visual is in the audio. By listening, you get the picture. You don't need to do that today: you just show a video. So I think that has cost a great deal in the sense of the lack of necessity to create visual images from lyrics. I think oddly enough that has affected melody. Sure, there are some fine writers and occasionally you'll hear a fine melody, but I don't think as often as one used to. The accent on hip-hop and rap music has not been on melody."

Leiber says, "I think that the keynote and the focus of today's songwriting is virtuosity in the studio. I think it depends upon great playing of instruments, et cetera. I think it also depends upon great virtuosity vocally. I think the dimension of lyric writing has gotten kind of slim and I think there've been many reasons for it. You see videos where there're all kind of images going on while a guy is singing. When you have images going on you don't really need the images provoked by words, and a tendency to let down your guard and go easy on the lyric writing is there. It's not there musically, 'cos you need the music but you're really not dependent that much on the word, and I think the tendency in today's songwriting is to go with this almost ulterior, subliminal flow of what is needed and what isn't, and that all the kids that are writing songs know that the stuff is eventually headed for the screen, and I think they act accordingly. I think that the lyric writing has gotten thin. There's nobody around today writing like The Beatles. One of the only guys left out there writing anything that is literate, funny, insightful, philosophic is Randy Newman."

Asked whether modern computer programs that allow non-musicians to construct a melody will have a detrimental effect by reducing the incentive to learn traditional instruments and thereby reduce the talent pool, Stoller evinces a lack of concern: "I suppose it could but I don't even think about that 'cos that's not the way I write. I still write with a keyboard or piano and a pencil. And an eraser!"

Considering that the pair are now of pensionable age, do they never think of retiring? Leiber: "If we write songs, we meet four times a week for three or four hours a day. If we've got anything we really have to do we can go seven or eight but I consider myself semi-retired now because I'm not making records. But I don't know what I'd do with myself if I stopped writing songs." What would tempt them to go back into the studio? "I would consider it if it were a good artist," says Leiber. "I'd go in the studio with Mick Jagger and I'd show him how to get a hit!"

2
MANN & WEIL

The songwriting partnership of Barry Mann and Cynthia Weil is responsible for a remarkable feat. 'You've Lost That Lovin' Feelin'' - the song they wrote, with some input from Phil Spector, for the Righteous Brothers in 1965 - is the most broadcast song of the twentieth century.

Just as impressively, of all the subjects of this book, their partnership has achieved more continuous chart success than any other. Admittedly, this is partly because some successful writing partnerships have been distracted from the task of securing chart placings by other ventures (Leiber & Stoller), some have been terminated for non-professional reasons (Greenwich & Barry) and some are simply too young to be able to compete in the longevity stakes. Nevertheless, that the Mann & Weil partnership has scored chart success in all decades of its existence is highly remarkable. Just as remarkable is that their marriage has remained intact while those of other married writing teams like Goffin & King and Greenwich & Barry fell by the wayside.

Barry Mann was born in Brooklyn, New York on 9th February 1939 and raised there. He played piano as a child. "I was not a great schooled musician," he says. "I took regular piano lessons for about a year-and-a-half and then I took some popular piano lessons. I would take sheet music of the hits of the day and there would be chord symbols above them and I would learn chords that way. Then I picked up the ukulele to learn how to play that. The ukulele tuning is like the last four strings of the guitar so I learned chord progressions from that also. It taught me a lot." Mann is proof of the theory that one does not have to be a great instrumentalist in order to write great melodies: "I had a good ear but not a great ear but it was good enough. I'm not the kind of piano player that can go sit and play a melody. I will sing accompanying myself."

Despite his musical skills, composing was something that Mann came to via a circuitous route. His professional ambition as a young man was to be an architect: "I had no intention of being a songwriter. Before I studied architecture, in order to make money for college I worked up in the Catskill mountains during the summer and also on vacation. I used to perform. I had started writing songs when I was about fourteen or so. I had written about eight or nine songs and when I was working up at the mountains in Catskill there would be talent shows and I would perform in them. When I performed in one of them, one of the guests happened to be a publisher. Lowell Music was the name of the publishing company. After I performed, he gave me his number and said, 'If you ever decide to become a songwriter or you want to get into music, just give me a call'. For some reason, I don't know why, I kept the number." Of the songs that impressed the Lowell employee, Mann says, "Some of them were doo-wop, four-chord songs and there was a song called 'The Ecstasy Of Love'." At variance with Mann's future song writing technique, he at that point wrote lyrics as well as melodies.

After completing high school, Mann went to Pratt Institute to study architecture. After a few months of his second year there, he realised that he had no passion for the subject and decided to leave. This put him in something of a quandary. "I thought, 'Well - help'," he remembers. "I kind of got depressed and wasn't quite sure what I wanted to do and my parents were worried about me. And I thought about songwriting.. I ended up calling this guy at Lowell Music and I played about five songs I had written. He ended up publishing them. He said he liked my stuff and he said, 'Go cut a demo'. I didn't know what he was talking about so he ended up hiring musicians and he cut the demo of this song, 'Ecstasy Of Love'." By remarkable coincidence, at this juncture while Mann was in the Brill Building vicinity, he bumped into one Jack Keller, an aspiring songwriter he had first met in the Catskills. Keller had now made the jump from the aspirant to the success: "Jack Keller had just had a hit with a group called The Chordettes, 'Sitting In The Sand'. He was hooked up with a publisher named George Paxton. He said, 'Why don't you come up, I'll introduce you to George Paxton, you'll show him some of your stuff'." In the close-knit Tin Pan Alley community of the early 'Sixties, fortuitous meetings and path-crossings were commonplace, as illustrated by another stroke of luck for Mann that occurred around the same time: "After Lowell Music took some of my songs, I said, 'You know, I have some other songs', so I figured I'd go down to a recording studio there. I ended up putting all my other songs on tape. Maybe nine. While I was there in the recording studio, a guy named Lou Stallman walked in and he happened to hear me. Lou Stallman at the time was writing with a guy named Joe Shapiro. Lou and Joe had a bunch of hits. They had written a song called 'Round And Round' for Perry Como and they had written a song called 'The Treasure Of Love' that Clyde McPhatter had recorded and some other stuff. Sid Jacobson, Lou Stallman and Joe Shapiro had just started a publishing company called Round Music. So Lou Stallman says, 'Why don't you hang around the publishing company? You can write with Joe Shapiro and with Sid Jacobson'."

Cynthia Weil was born in New York City on October 18th 1940 and raised in Manhattan. Her first ambition was to be a dancer but that career avenue was closed off at an early stage when she injured her back. She set her heart instead on being a singer. "Then I started re-writing - the audacity, I can't believe it - re-writing Cole Porter lyrics and adding verses and doing a little club act. I would just drop one of his verses and put mine in. It was so bizarre. Now that I think of it, if someone did that to me, I'd go shoot them! I auditioned for a manager who said, 'You shouldn't be singing but who wrote those lyrics?' I said, 'I did'. He said, 'You ever think of writing songs?' When I was a kid, I had written poetry. I had always been, in a sense, a writer: stories and whatever. Often school people had said, 'You should be a writer'. I thought, 'Being a writer is so lonely, I don't want to sit in a room all by myself'. Then I suddenly realized that songwriters sit in a room with somebody else. That sounded like a good idea. So anyway, he said, 'If you write some lyrics, Frank Loesser's music publishing company is in this building and I know him and if they're good enough I will show them to Frank Loesser'. So I went home and I remember during commercials of *Playhouse 90* I wrote lyrics. They were just freestanding lyrics to, like, melodies in my head, really bad trite melodies in my head. I came in with them and he actually set up a meeting for me with Frank Loesser. I showed them to Frank Loesser and he was very encouraging, amazingly enough. What a generous, nice man - he met with us at seven o' clock in the morning. He would have his meetings at breakfast time so he didn't waste time: so he could be writing the rest of the day. He sent me up to his publishing company." In reference to the publishing company through whose aegis Weil would later make her mark, she says "It wasn't like Aldon Music: these guys were not getting the kind of really commercial pop things. It was a little more going for the older artists, a little more traditional. But it was the first time I actually met people and collaborated with them. I was learning how to work with another person."

Weil's first meeting with the man who was to become her lifetime partner in both a domestic and composing sense came when a friend of Weil's aunt transpired to know Kenny Greengrass, the manager of pop artists Eydie Gorme and Steve Lawrence and suggested she show him some of her lyrics. "So I went up there," she recalls, "and his associate was a guy named Stan Catron and I showed Stan my lyrics and he said, 'We have a young writer-singer here named Teddy Randazzo. I'd like you to

try writing with him'. So I was writing with Teddy and these two
guys came in to play a song for Teddy and one of them was
Barry Mann. He came in with Howie Greenfield and he sat down
and he played a song called 'Way Of A Clown' and I thought he
was *really* cute. So when this was all over I said to the receptionist
there, 'Who was that? Does he have a girlfriend? Do you know
him?' So she said, 'He's signed to a friend of mine named Don
Kirshner. Why don't I call Kirshner and I'll send you up there
and, who knows, maybe you'll run into him again'." Kirshner, in
his role as head of the up-and-coming Aldon Music (publishers of
Sedaka & Greenfield) was already well on his way to becoming
a living legend in the publishing business. "So I was like a stalker
in my own way," says Weil of Mann, "and I stalked him up to
Kirshner's and got an appointment and showed Kirshner my lyrics.
Kirshner said, 'Oh, I know who you should write with'. And I
thought, 'Here comes the cute guy'. The next thing I know this
little girl walks in. He says, 'She's really talented but she writes
with her husband and he's working as chemist during the day so
she can only write at night. You could write with her during the
day." The "little girl" in question was a young lady named Carole
King, an individual who, like Weil, was destined to become one of
the most famous songwriters of all time. King played Weil a melody
at the piano with which Weil was very impressed and the two
agreed to have a bash at collaboration: "I schlepped out to Brooklyn
to write with her. No sign of Barry in the meantime so I figured I
got to keep writing with this girl so I can keep going back up
there. Carole and I had our first writing session, which was the
beginning of a 39-year friendship. She gave me this melody and I
didn't get any ideas while I was there. I said, 'I read music: could
you write it down and I'll take it home and I'll work on it and call
you back'. When I got home, the phone was ringing." The caller
was King, with the news that her husband - Gerry Goffin - had
just come back from work and was upset that the melody had
been given to Weil "'...because he really wants to work on it. He
has some really good ideas'. I said, 'Oh yeah? What's the great
idea?' She says, 'It's called "Take Good Care Of My Baby".' It

ended up being a number one song for Bobby Vee. [Gerry] could think faster than I was thinking. I hadn't even gotten anywhere with it." Despite that unpromising start, the three did collaborate. Weil: "She and Gerry actually came over and wrote with me and we wrote a song together. I don't even know if it was ever recorded, but the guy who cut the demo was named Paul Simon. It was called 'Echoes'. He was Jerry Landis then."

Weil's repeated visits to the Aldon offices finally led her Mr. Right to notice her. "At the time," explains Mann, "I was kind of breaking up with an 'older woman'. She was 24, I was 21 I think. But I really liked Cynthia and the more I was with her, the like started to turn to love. We didn't start writing right away. We were going out. I would sleep over once in a while - which was very daring in those days."

Weil's haunting of the Aldon office with her ulterior romantic motives led her, not a natural pop or rock 'n' roll consumer, to begin appreciating the kind of music Aldon was peddling. "At the time I had no interest in [it] whatsoever," Weil says of pop and rock and roll. For his part, Mann says, "I was brought up on pop music. I started to like doo-wop so I came from that. I was never into really guitar blues stuff 'til later on. It was basically a kind of New-Yorkey sound that I was into." Weil quickly came round to perceiving the merits of pop and rock: "I was really impressed with what Carole and Gerry were doing. Because you'd sit in Aldon Music and you'd hear all the music coming out the walls, I just knew that this was something new and that this is what was happening. It was the music of its time. Then when Barry and I started seeing each other, he kind of educated me and told me what to listen to because I was really coming from a Broadway school of theatre. If I'd gone any direction, I think that's the direction I would have gone."

"I asked to look at some of her lyrics and I really liked her lyrics," Mann says of the beginning of the couple's artistic collaboration. "I always felt her lyrics were different for the market. There was a sophistication that I think combined with what I was doing melodically [made] something very fresh. I always think that Carole and Gerry and Cynthia and myself and people like us - at least in that period of time - bridged Tin Pan Alley into the rock and roll era."

Before that collaboration could really take off, however, Mann embarked on one of many abortive attempts to achieve success as a performer. "Don Kirshner and Al Nevins, besides having a publishing company, were a production company," he recalls. "They started producing records. They thought that I could be an artist also, if I sang my own material. I was signed to their production company and they made a deal with ABC-Paramount." Under his own name, Mann put out 'Counting Teardrops', a flop in the US although a hit in the UK in 1960 for Emile Ford and the Checkmates. He enjoyed greater success with a song he co-wrote with Gerry Goffin as a spoof of the doo-wop genre, 'Who Put The Bomp (In The Bomp, Bomp, Bomp)'. "It was a very hip song 'cos it was a put-on of all those records that were out there," Mann says. "It was not really a putdown. It was a satire." Weil adds, "I would say that eighty per cent of the people who bought that record never realized it was a satire." Mann recalls that Goffin was initially unconvinced that the song had potential: "We were writing the song. He said, 'I don't wanna do this'. I said, 'Gerry, it's a hit song'."

The record reached the top ten in the charts of both *Billboard* and *Cash Box* in 1961. (Bobby Vee's version of 'Take Good Care Of My Baby' was then sitting at the top of the *Cash Box* chart.) Additionally, it was twice covered to top forty effect in the UK, first by the Viscounts, then in the Seventies by Showaddywaddy. Mann, however, never really capitalized on that initial success as a performer, something about which he is ambivalent. On the one hand, he notes, "As a songwriter, I wanted an outlet for my material and I wanted to cut out the middle man. To this day, I hate having to play songs for people and sit there and wait to see if they liked it or don't like it. I don't like rejection." Weil observes, "I think it also would have allowed [him] to be more experimental. Once you have a hit, then you can throw a couple of things on the next record that no-one in the world would ever let you write or record." Mann: "Basically what The Beatles ended up doing, I would have loved to do that. If I had made it as an artist. Just started to kind of broaden and grow and experiment. Of course part of it was, I'm sure, ego." Yet Mann adds, "Underneath it, I never really had the temperament back then to be an artist. I had too much fear performing in front of an audience: forgetting the lyrics, all that kind of stuff. I think I had much more of a temperament to be a songwriter. More of a behind-the-scenes kind of a guy."

Though Mann started composing with Weil, he initially maintained his professional relationship with his other collaborators, mainly Larry Kolber, Gerry Goffin and Mike Anthony. (He also wrote 'Come Back Silly Girl', a US top twenty for The Lettermen in 1962, by himself.) Weil, on the other hand, having found the perfect musical foil for her lyrics, was reluctant to work with anyone else. "I think I was afraid of other collaborations," she says. "I just didn't know if I could write as well with anybody else. When Carole and I wrote together, we never even did it seriously. We'd start writing and then we'd go shopping. We were never really trying. I think we wrote one or two songs that we really tried. We had one Andy Williams record or something."

Yet the fact that the Mann and Weil songwriting team achieved success immediately and that they were lovers (they married in August 1961) probably meant that it was inevitable that they would become each other's main collaborator. "We got a record on our first song we ever wrote, 'Painting The Town With Teardrops', Vinny Monty," Mann recalls. Nor was it very long before they had their first chart placing, the pleasantly saccharine 'Bless You' climbing to number 15 in the hands of Tony Orlando in 1961. "It felt very natural and once you start clicking with somebody it inspires you to keep going," Weil explains, adding, "If we hadn't gotten that kind of response to the material, who knows what would have happened?" Of their early writing technique, Mann says, "I think we probably started by sitting down together, at the beginning." Weil adds, "We'd sit together and it would happen together. Sometimes it comes from a title, sometimes it comes from an idea, sometimes it comes from a melodic riff."

Quite quickly, the pair settled into a method that they have stuck with their entire lives: melody first (though sometimes in conjunction with an idea of a lyric or theme). "Once you have a great melody, I think it's easier to have a hit," opines Mann. "You can have a terrible melody with great lyrics but if that melody isn't good, forget about it. You can have a mediocre lyric with a great melody and still have a hit. I think also, it was more inspirational for [Cynthia] to write a lyric to a melody that [she] loved." Weil says, "The only time I can remember writing a lyric first was 'I Just Can't Help Believing'." Mann adds, "She did that to prove something." Changing times have served to vary the method slightly but not make it redundant, as Weil points out: "As the technology became more sophisticated, Barry could go to a studio and create a real track for me to write to. Other times I'll give him a title and he'll go in and create something."

Not that inspiration was the sole reason that would lead the pair to create. Mann: "We were writing for artists too. Aldon Music would tell us certain artists would be about to record and everybody would try to write for that artist and we would try to tailor a song for that artist. So we did have those kind of constraints. It was school really. We were learning all different idioms. We were writing for character. Those artists were characters and we'd try to come up with an idea that would be right for each one. A lyric that would be right for each artist." Mann also notes, "Sometimes, you'd write a song for one artist, another artist would record it - it would work for that artist too. We wrote 'Blame It On The Bossa Nova' for Bobby Rydell and Eydie Gorme cut it." Asked which they preferred between writing to order or writing off their own bat, Mann replies, "They both had their good points. Sometimes it would be good to have a guideline. Sometimes it was good to have total freedom."

The pair found the atmosphere at Aldon incredibly invigorating and conducive to inspiration, something helped by the fact that their talents were explicitly appreciated by the company. "We were the main teams: Goffin & King and Cynthia and myself," says Mann. "There was Neil Sedaka/Howie Greenfield. There were other songwriters like Jack Keller, Larry Kolber, Helen Miller, Mike Anthony were all around. You'd hear other people writing in some of the cubicles but we wrote 60% of our songs at home and maybe another 40% there at the offices. Our world was Aldon music and we were self contained. We were such a hot publishing company." However, he says that they were not only inspired by those with whom they rubbed shoulders at Aldon: "We [knew] Jeff [Barry] and Ellie [Greenwich]. And Leiber & Stoller of course because we ended up writing with them. They were doing a lot of producing so we came in contact with them that way. We were aware of some of the black writers like Otis Blackwell and some of the Hill & Range writers: Bert Berns. Burt Bacharach also."

Mann and Weil are generally described as Brill Building writers, i.e., part of a 'Sixties scene centered around publishers' offices in New York's Broadway area where young songwriters would sit in cubicles turning out songs which adhered to the short and catchy nature of traditional pop music but which acknowledged both the sonic and cultural overtones of the more hard-edged rock and roll. However Weil points out that they didn't actually work in the famous Brill Building at 1615 Broadway itself: "Our offices were at 1650 Broadway, which is a block away from the Brill Building, but it's the same kind of building." Mann: "There was a recording studio in the basement in both places."

Mann and Weil's promise brought them to the attention of Phil Spector. "Phil wanted to write with us, so he asked Donny Kirshner about us," says Mann. Before Mann and Weil began composing with the producer, a Spector recording of the Mann-Kolber composition 'I Love How You Love Me' was taken into the US top five by the Paris Sisters in 1961 while Mann-Weil songs 'Uptown' and 'He's Sure The Boy I Love' were hits for the Spector-produced Crystals, reaching number 13 and number 11 in 1962 and 1963 respectively. 'Uptown' was a song about a man who finds solace from the petty humiliations and tedium of his job in the arms of his lover, narrated by the woman. It was one of the first signs of Weil's then-unusual propensity to inject social commentary into her songs, one that would become more pronounced as the decade wore on.

Amongst others, Mann and Weil co-wrote 'You, Baby' and 'Walking In the Rain' with Spector in this period. Clearly, the Mann/Weil/Spector combination was a winning one. Before long it was to achieve success literally greater than any other, before or since.

Before that however, there was a collaboration with producers - and songwriters - every bit as legendary as Phil Spector when the pair teamed up with Leiber & Stoller for the 1963 hit 'On Broadway', a song with a fame far greater than its number nine US chart placing (and no chart placing in Britain) would suggest simply due to the fact that it's a virtually *de rigueur* staple of soundtracks to documentaries about that famous NY district. Mann and Weil are both insistent that the version of how the song came to be finished as told by Jerry Leiber in the first chapter of this book is slightly cockeyed. "By the way, we tell you this story as Mike and Jerry's friends," Weil says. "I think it's like *Rashomon*: everybody has a different memory of how this thing happened." Mann: "I think Jerry got that mixed up with something else he must have written because it's so clear to us how this happened."

Mann and Weil's version of events goes like this: "The germ of the song started with me," says Mann. "I wanted to write something that I felt had a Gershwin-esque feel to it that could be a rock and roll hit. I wrote a melody, it's slightly different [to the familiar one]. It had this kind of Gershwin-esque note in it." Weil: "With my whole Broadway [obsession]. I always wanted to write a tribute to Broadway." Phil Spector proceeded to cut a track with The Crystals using Weil's original lyric. "It's not exactly my feel," Mann reflects of The Crystals' rendition. "My feel was the feel of the [Drifters'] record. He put his own feel to it." When Spector decided not to release the track, the pair played it to Jerry Leiber and Mike Stoller in the hope that they might place it with The Drifters. "They said they really liked the song but they felt the slant was not right for The Drifters," Mann recalls. "So they said, 'If you want, continue to try to write it for The Drifters or try to write it with us'. And we said, 'Great, we'd love to write it with you' - 'cos if we ever idolized anybody, it was Jerry and Mike. So we went to Jerry Leiber's apartment, all four of us. I sat down at the piano. I remember some of the contributions. I remember Mike changed a few notes, which made the melody very commercial, and he also suggested we modulate three times, which was very good, very important. And then, we all sat and wrote the lyric. Basically Cynthia and Jerry - and a lot Jerry, by the way. It was very exciting writing with them. Being in the room and watching Jerry's process, which was so different from Cynthia's."

It was in this session that Weil achieved a breakthrough in her writing technique. "I felt like I was going to school because I had always started writing a lyric and felt you can't move on until you get the next line, then you gotta get line three, and then you gotta get line four," she says. "Jerry would write a couple of lines, then he'd try for a while on something else, then he'd skip to another verse and we'd do that. Then we'd go back and get the first one."

Weil's original lyric had idealised Broadway and its status as a beacon light for those wishing to pursue the American dream in the field of entertainment. With Leiber's input, the song took a much more cynical look at Broadway and, by extension, the American dream. "The lyric got much ballsier and one thing that I do well is I can pick up on somebody else's creative process," says Weil. "I could get where Jerry was going and it's like he took me along for the ride but I got it and I started to write like him. The other one was more like, 'I've gotta get out of this place: I can't stand this small town, I've got this dream, I've got to get to Broadway' and his was more of the underbelly of Broadway and his was a much better way to go... I don't want to try to remember who wrote each line, but it was definitely a very 50-50 collaboration. I actually remember that Mike's contribution was the idea of playing the guitar."

In 1964, Mann and Weil wrote that song with Phil Spector that

would not only top the chart either side of the Atlantic but would
go on to rack up enough airplay to make it officially the most
broadcast song of the twentieth century. Of 'You've Lost That
Lovin' Feelin'', Mann says, "[Spector] played us this group called
the Righteous Brothers out of Orange County and he wanted us
to all write for them." Weil: "They were singing Sam and Dave
kind of stuff." Mann: "We thought 'Well, it would be great to do a
ballad'. We loved 'Baby I Need Your Loving' by The Four Tops
and it was kind of an inspiration for 'You've Lost That Lovin'
Feelin''. Cynthia and I started the song and we wrote a verse and
a chorus and we played it to Phil over the phone and he really
loved it."

Mann and Weil, incidentally, are happy to dispel the whiff of
payola that for some hangs over Phil Spector's numerous co-
songwriting credits, acknowledging that he made significant
contributions to their songs. This is perhaps nowhere more so
than on '..Lovin' Feelin'', one of whose most famous parts, Mann
says, was Spector's handiwork: "'Gone, gone, gone - whoa-oh-
ohhh'. That was Phil's idea. And then Phil came up with the idea
of doing that middle part, the Latin riff leading into the bridge
["We had a love, a love you don't find every day.."]. Very important,
by the way, because it really was very different for a song in that
period. When we finally wrote that, then we all sat together and
kind of completed the end of the song. For that time, it was one of
the great records."

The song was one of the first - possibly the very first - to be
given the description "blue eyed soul". However, though the pair
had been initially inspired by the Four Tops, they had not intended
to create a form of soul for white people. "We just wrote a song,"
says Mann. "There was no thought behind that at all. Just wanted
to write a great song for that artist." Weil: "Those voices really
turned us on. Those two guys in that kind of harmony." Mann:
"They had a huge range and a lot of songs that I've written have
very wide ranges and it worked great for them." Mann adds, "I
really thought as a song it was a great combination of soul and at
the same time there was, I wouldn't say sophistication but it was

melodic and soulful."

'(You're My) Soul And Inspiration' was another Mann-Weil-written Righteous Brothers US number one in 1966 and it was the Righteous Brothers that the pair had in mind when they devised 'We've Gotta Get Out Of This Place' the previous year. Mann, however, was so pleased with his demo of the latter song that he decided to release it as a single under his own name on Leiber & Stoller's Red Bird label, to whom he was signed as an artist. Unfortunately, as Mann explains, "Somehow we had given the song to Mickie Most and forgot about it." Weil says of the British pop impresario and producer of The Animals, "He never said anything. Next thing we knew, it was number 2 in England, so that killed Barry's record... Had Barry's record come out and been a hit, our whole landscape could have changed."

To add salt to the wound of Mann's solo record having to be aborted was what The Animals had done with the song once the producer had delivered the demo to them. Though they were almost exclusively cover merchants, the rhythm and blues band prided themselves on spurning carbon copy performances in favour of re-jigs and rearrangements which put their own personal stamp on a song. In the case of 'We've Gotta Get Out Of This Place', this meant not just tweaking with the melody but dropping an entire verse of Weil's lyric. "I just felt that what they did was right for themselves but I think a lyricist deserves the respect of being consulted," laments Weil. "If they had said, 'Look, this doesn't work for us... We'd like to change it to this... How do you feel about it?' I think we could have worked together and gotten something that might have pleased both of us. I felt that it was great disregard for what I did to just drop a verse and change things and not even say anything. 'House Of The Rising Sun' is one my favourite records ever so I was so thrilled that he was doing it and then when I just heard this I just felt so bad." The fact that The Animals took the song into the top ten in Britain and - strangely, via a different recording - the top twenty in the US softened the blow a little for the pair. With the passage of time, they have also gained enough distance to see The Animals' recording the way many others do: as a brilliantly gritty evocation of the working class experience with a soberingly authentic vocal performance by their frontman, Eric Burdon. "It was a terrific record," Weil concedes. "He's a great, great, great singer." In a bizarre postscript to the whole saga, Burdon recorded the song again in 1990 with Katrina and The Waves in which he sang Weil's original, unexpurgated lyric. "Listen to that - you'll hear the right lyric," says Mann. "He made up for it."

The social realism of 'We've Gotta Get Out Of This Place' was continued with 'Kicks', a crunching anti-drugs anthem that Paul Revere and the Raiders took into the American top five in 1966. "Someone that we knew was really getting heavily into drugs and was screwing up their lives," remembers Weil. "We tried talking to them and they wouldn't listen to us and out of, I think, just frustration we wrote this song thinking, 'Maybe he'll hear the song'." Mann asserts that in no way did they think the aggressive, denunciatory tone of Raiders singer Mark Lindsay was - from their own perspective - over the top: "I'm sure we felt that way about it, because of the effect it had on this guy. It wasn't only him alone. I saw so many people freaking out in that period who got into acid. You can see some of the repercussions today."

Weil's willingness to confront issues like this in pop songs is now recognized as groundbreaking: though people like Dylan had addressed the political issues of the day in the folk genre, pop at this point still primarily revolved around romantic love. That she was a revolutionary was something that didn't occur to Weil, however. "You know, I never thought of it as trying to do something different," she says. "I simply wrote about things I was interested in and I was interested in changing the world.

Commenting on it and drawing people's attentions to situations, thinking that maybe songs could change the way people think. I was very young and naive." Though the chart success of these political songs vindicated them commercially, did she not think at first that she was taking a risk by assuming that people wanted to buy material that reminded them that life could be less than sweet?

"We just did it because we wanted to do it," shrugs Weil. "And if someone liked it, great. If they didn't like it, that's okay too - we did it anyway." She does admit that the reaction of publishers could be suspicious: "Kirshner didn't get 'Uptown' at all. Then when it was a hit, he came to me and he said, 'Write more of these songs I don't understand'. Because he was really very traditional: 'It's got to be a love song, it's got to have a happy ending'. I felt that Kirshner always had his commercial hat on as a publisher and so he always thought about what had been written before as opposed to creating something that had never been done." Mann adds, "But Kirshner really didn't sit on us. We just did what we wanted to do. We just wrote what we wrote. There were no restraints because of Kirshner."

Yet despite barriers being smashed not just by her own lyrics but the increasingly progressive subject matter explored in songs by artists like The Beatles and the Rolling Stones, Weil points out that freelance songwriters never reached the point where they had free rein: "I feel that the only people who could really write about anything they want would be writer-performers because you always as a writer had to go to somebody to have them say, 'Okay'. So that restricted things."

Nevertheless, it was seldom that Weil's lyrics were considered too extreme to be put in the marketplace. One of the few occasions was near the beginning of the couple's career when they penned a caustic ode to a country with both the most patriotic inhabitants on the face of the earth and inhabitants most blind to their country's shortcomings: 'Only In America'. "We had a thought," remembers Mann. "A concept. We didn't sit down and do it. As we were doing it, we started doing the complete opposite: 'Only in America/ Where they preach the golden rule/Do they start to march when my kids try to go to school/Only in America/Land of opportunity/ Do they save the seat in the back of the bus just for me.' We were writing it for The Drifters and I really wanted to do it and Jerry and Mike said, 'You'll never get it played'." Weil: "We had such respect for [Leiber & Stoller] that if they said, 'Listen, don't do this kids, it's not gonna work, you're shooting yourself in the foot..' I didn't have the courage to argue with them."

Weil re-wrote her words so that the song took on the very opposite meaning to that which had originally been proposed: a flag waving song. The Drifters issued a recording of the song with the altered lyric, with, as Mann points out, ironic consequences: "What happened is exactly what would have happened if we wrote it the other way: black disc jockeys would not play the record because it was a lie. And they were absolutely right. It was a lie for any black artist." The Drifters' vocals were subsequently taken off the track and substituted for those of white artists Jay and the Americans, who took it to number 25 on the *Billboard* chart in late 1963.

The political content of many of the couple's songs didn't prevent them blanching a little at the way that rock and pop musicians, as the 'Sixties progressed, became a group whose views were solemnly sought by reporters. They expressed their ambivalence about this in the spectacularly titled 'Young Electric Psychedelic Hippy Flippy Folk & Funky Philosophic Turned On Groovy 12- String Band', a single release by Mann in 1968. Weil: "It was the period when all the groups had opinions on every political issue and they were just a bunch of kids who could sing and reporters were standing around asking them about the war in Vietnam." Mann: "Like they were experts." Weil: "So we wrote a song about this group with that title who had an opinion about everything."

With them having produced both simple love songs and profound sociological statements and having had hits with both, the question arises of which of the two is more difficult to write. Weil says, "I never thought in terms of writing that way." Mann adds, "Trying to write sometimes is like trying to solve a puzzle: 'Will this work for this artist?' Sometimes it's not just about the song, it's about solving the problem." Weil: "But when you're just writing, sometimes it just comes from a creative urge: 'I wanna try putting these chords together, I want to see where this takes me. I have this great idea and I want to explore that'."

Though The Monkees, the pop group manufactured in the mid-

1960s as America's answer to The Beatles, was a project supervised by Don Kirshner, one of Kirshner's most successful writing teams was actually reluctant to get involved in it. "We were one of the groups up there that didn't write for The Monkees," says Mann. "We didn't want to be part of that whole [situation where] everybody was scrambling to get a Monkees record." Though the Monkees did in fact end up putting out some Mann-Weil songs, Weil points out, "We wrote those songs for other people and The Monkees recorded them." A case in point was the beautiful and world-weary 'Shades Of Gray'. (First line: "When the world and I were young, just yesterday".) An ornate rendition of this song was included by The Monkees on their 1967 album Headquarters. It was a song that the pair had originally written with The Byrds in mind, thinking that though the Byrds wrote much of their own material, their connection with them through their producer Terry Melcher - producer of Paul Revere and the Raiders - might give them a chance of placing it. "And, also, even if we weren't writing it for them, we were inspired by them," says Weil of this hope-against-hope mentality. "We loved what they were doing. I think we played it for Kirshner and he wanted it for The Monkees."

The couple recall the early-to-mid-'Sixties as a whirlwind of activity and a period when they were completely immersed in their art. "It's all we did," says Weil. "All we ever did was write and demo and write and demo and then Carole and Gerry and Barry and I would go away on weekends together and so we were always together. It was very close-knit." Mann: "Our life was that. That's all that mattered to us: were we on the charts? Donny Kirshner would make our lives great or bad: did we get the next record? All that kind of stuff." Mann adds, "Although there was a competitiveness [amongst writers], there was an excitement when we think back. When you're in the middle of doing it, you don't think to yourself, 'Man, this is really exciting. thirty years from now I'm gonna think about this and say, "Hey, we're having a great time"'." Weil and Mann are in agreement that producers and record company owners got just as excited by the music they were involved in producing as the songwriters. Weil: "What was really great was that we really loved what we were doing and everybody felt really passionate about it... You'd go over and play something for [producer] Jerry Wexler and he'd get really excited. It's just so completely different than the whole corporate A&R thing now where no-one wants to make a decision. Everyone's scared. A song has to go through five people before it even gets considered to be put on hold." Mann also points out, "The music was very diverse back then. It's just a whole different market now. The diversity was incredible. There were many labels, so there was more opportunity to expand." Weil: "And producers like Leiber and Stoller were always interested in trying something new. It wasn't like, 'Let's reproduce the last record.' [It was] 'Let's stay true to the character of this group but let's do interesting things'."

At the height of all this, the pair were turning out fifty completed songs per year: writing a song roughly once a week and demoing it the next, by which time they would be writing another. Mann: "All these creative juices had to be released." Weil marvels, "The stuff was pouring out of us. And I think we all stimulated each other. So that I don't know if we would have been as productive if Carole and Gerry hadn't been around and we were seeing how productive they were: 'Oh my God! If they can do it, can we do it?'" Mann: "And they felt the same way too." This hothouse atmosphere is one no longer available to songwriters. "I think most songwriters today feel somewhat isolated," says Weil, "Especially with the advent of the home studio and everybody being so self-contained. They get really hungry to share musical thoughts with other people."

Mann and Weil are an exception to the general rule that sees songwriters drift into production as their careers progress. Though they have dabbled with working behind the mixing desk, they have been generally content to hand over their songs to third parties and let them do with them what they will. "I tried to produce but I just never got into it," says Mann. Weil says, "I hate it. I find that studio time so wearing and boring and awful. I can't wait to get out of there." She adds, "The stuff with Leiber and Stoller, we were at the sessions 'cos it was New York but when we wrote with Phil we came out to California and then we left and then he cut the record. You knew when you left it with Phil it was in good hands... I think when Phil came on the scene he really brought a new way of producing and making records." Mann does point out, "I didn't realize that I was producing when I was producing my demos. We were known to cut great demos: Carole and Gerry and Cynthia and myself." Weil: "You're giving them a template." Not that artists necessarily stuck to that template: "It was all different," Mann says. "I wrote a song called 'Patches'. My original demo was like a Marty Robbins record. I wrote it with Larry Kolber. It had a lot of verses to it and the record was totally different. I never thought it would be a hit and it was. They were all different. Sometimes the records were close to the demos, sometimes they weren't."

Both Mann and Weil are of the opinion that the record of their song 'Hungry' by Paul Revere and the Raiders was an improvement on the arrangement on the original demo: "Terry Melcher took what I gave and made it better," says Mann. "Absolutely made it better. What they did instrumentally was better than I did. They came up with a vocal part going 'Ahhh-ahhh-ah-ah', which was great. It just had more guts to it. It had more weight than what I had done with it. I think 'Kicks', the other song we wrote that was a hit with Paul Revere and the Raiders, was closer to my demo but they made it better."

Asked how many songs of their 'Sixties songs were rejected by publishers and artists, Mann says, "I think we had more taken than rejected but I don't know. A lot of them, we didn't even try to get records on." Weil: "We don't keep track of that stuff but when we look back we forget the really bad ones so it seems like everything got cut but I'm sure it didn't."

Every golden age comes to an end and the golden age of Brill Building songsmiths was drawing to a close as the 'Sixties did. "It was really kind of like a four-year period," says Weil. "It seemed endless. I think [Kirshner] sold after three years. The atmosphere changed once we moved out of 1650." Mann: "Then it became very corporate." Weil: "He sold to Columbia Pictures and Screen Gems and we moved into a building on Fifth Avenue in which they built all these cubicles that nobody wanted to write in. It just wasn't the same feeling."

Another thing that caused a kink in the Tin Pan Alley tradition was, of course, The Beatles and the inspiration they gave to other performers to write their own songs. However, like several subjects of this book, Mann and Weil insist that the effect of The Beatles on freelance composers has been exaggerated. "When I think about it, some of our biggest songs were in the later 'Sixties," says Mann. "We were nervous about it but when I look back it didn't really shake us up that much, it didn't affect our writing that much." Weil: "But it did give us less outlets." Mann does note one major difference: "Before that, a lot of keyboard-oriented songs were written. Once the Beatles hit, songs became a lot more guitar-oriented. So it was more difficult for a keyboard player. There is a difference." Did he try to change his writing style because of this? "Always tried. You were always affected by what you heard. There was always going to be a core of who I was - that's what's always there - but you do try to change your style a bit." Weil: "You have to. Then also, as you evolve as a person, your style changes."

Though the Brill Building's golden age might have gone, it didn't mean the end of Mann and Weil's career nor of their capability of fulfilling more of their own professional dreams. For their generation of writer, one holy grail was having a song covered by Elvis Presley. In 1970, the pair were very pleasantly surprised to find out that *That's The Way It Is*, a documentary about The King's live work in Las Vegas, featured Elvis performing both 'You've Lost That Lovin' Feelin'' and a newer Mann-Weil composition, 'I Just Can't Help Believing'. (Both songs also featured on the accompanying soundtrack album.) The latter was an exquisitely tender creation in which the narrator marvels at how much he loves his woman - and how much he hopes that this relationship doesn't go the way of all his previous ones. Mann had recorded it himself in 1968 and had it had subsequently been covered by Bobby Vee and B J Thomas (for whom it was a US top tenner) before it attracted Presley's attention. "You know, we didn't hear about that until after," recalls Weil. "Someone told us about it and then we went to see that film. The funny thing is, he keeps forgetting the lyrics and he starts writing them on his hand or on his jacket or something and I was always so notorious for screaming at people who didn't get lyrics right that I just always wondered if my reputation had gotten away from me!"

As mentioned previously, the song was one of the few where Weil didn't wait for a melody from her husband before setting pen to paper. "It's always sounded too short to me," she observes of her lyric. "I felt like I should have written more but I think I just kind of said everything I had to say and records were much shorter in those days." Asked whether it is difficult to compose a melody when a lyric already exists, Mann says simply "No, very easy." Weil adds, "He wrote 'Sometimes When We Touch' that way. You can hand him any lyric." Presley's version was released as a single in the UK and climbed as high as number six. "I really like that version," says Mann. "I never had like a new song done by him. I would have loved to have had that happen but I'm glad he did those two songs. Before I was ever signed to Aldon Music I tried writing for him. I wrote one song I tried to get to him, 'Cream Puff', but he never cut it."

Another musical giant to unexpectedly cover a Mann-Weil song in the Seventies was Dolly Parton, who took the pretty but distraught 'Here You Come Again' into the American top three in 1977, thus securing a national chart breakthrough in her native country that her own considerable songwriting talents had previously failed to achieve. "We wrote it for B J Thomas," says Weil. "And then Barry recorded it. Then the guitar player on Barry's session arranged the Dolly Parton record, Dean Parks." Of Parton's version, Mann says, "I thought it was great. It's a little faster. My record should have been that speed too. My record almost came out but - I was on Arista at the time - Clive Davis wanted to get a TV show for it before he put it out."

The fact that two men recorded the song before Parton is intriguing: 'Here You Come Again' has come to be considered a female anthem, a song similar to Gloria Gaynor's 'I Will Survive' (written by Freddie Perren and Dino Fekaris) in nailing down romantic heartbreak from a distinctly female perspective. "Actually, it probably suited a female because I wrote it about an experience of a female friend of mine," says Weil. Asked whether she has ever considered her lyrics to be gender-specific, she says, "The best songs are the ones that can be sung by either sex." She also points out that although her songs have not changed, general perceptions about male and female perspectives have: "We wrote a song called 'I'm Gonna Be Strong' that Gene Pitney did and then Cyndi Lauper sang it. There's a line in it: 'I'm gonna be strong and take it like a man'. I thought, 'Is she gonna sing "Take it like a woman"?' No, she sang, 'Take it like a man'. So I think the gender lines are far less strict than they ever were." Mann: "But there are certain songs that you know are female songs. We just wrote a song, 'I Wanna Be Somebody's Angel'. You're not gonna have a male sing that song."

As their career progressed, Mann and Weil became more amenable to the idea of working outside their professional partnership. Weil acknowledges that this is partly because of the danger of a married couple being in each others' pockets for prolonged periods: "I think there was a period when we felt that and then we didn't do it for a while and then we came back together with a perspective that whoever wants to write with somebody else, that's fine. We encourage each other to do it. Sometimes people want to write with both of us, which is always very interesting: to put a third party into the mix with the two of us... I also think that creatively I feel so comfortable with Barry that in the past I would feel that it would shake me up a little bit, kind of get me on my toes again, get me a little nervous about a writing session, which is good and kind of like [what] actors say: that it helps them. Each new collaboration is very stressful. Dan Hill calls them creative blind dates." "It's always good to get other input from a different creative source," acknowledges Mann, before raising another, more practical, reason for outside collaborations: "I think it's much easier to get a record if you're writing with the artist." Weil is quick to point out, though, that her collaborations in the 1980s with Lionel Richie - 'Running With The Night' and 'Love Will Conquer All', both US top tens - were not borne out of this kind of compromise: "He was a major artist and a really good one and I was thrilled to have the opportunity to work with him. But when we have been asked to write with people who are not really writers and kind of do the work so that the singer can put their name on it and get it in their album, we just don't do it."

Mann has written with Al Gorgoni (for the soundtrack to the 1969 movie *I Never Sang For My Father*), Dan Hill (with whom he secured a 1978 US top five and a UK top twenty with 'Sometimes When We Touch'), Leo Sayer and Curtis Stigers. Weil has collaborated with Tom Snow (their 1980 song 'He's So Shy' was a US number 3 for the Pointer Sisters), David Foster & Tom Keane, Keith Thomas and Tommy Lee James.

The 1987 animated movie *An American Tail* featured songs the pair wrote in collaboration with James Horner. One of them - 'Somewhere Out There', performed by Linda Ronstadt and James Ingram - was a Transatlantic top ten. It is also a song Mann believes proved that some compositions can defy fashions: "'Somewhere Out There' could have been written in the 1960s just as well as 1987. There are certain songs that can span time." Ironically, he adds, "By the way, I don't know if a song like that could ever be a hit now at all. It's just not the way the market is. It'll never go back." Weil, referring to a 1981 hit they wrote for Quincy Jones (featuring James Ingram), says "I don't think it'll ever go back to the 'Just Once' kind of thing either. The changes are far too complex, the idea takes too much thinking. That was one of our great writing experiences: writing that song and working with James."

Those who think it ironic that Mann and Weil should assign such a sophistication to 'Somewhere Out There' - part of a soundtrack to a film about talking mice - will receive short shrift from them. The pair insist that the soundtracks they wrote for *An American Tail* and the 1996 movie *Muppet Treasure Island* involved a creative process just as difficult - if not more so - than that attending their more 'profound' songs. "Actually, when you analyse the Muppet movie, those characters all have different voices and different points of view," says Weil. "It's very theatrical. The Henson people know those characters inside out and when you are writing for Kermit or writing for Piggy or any one of those characters in ...*Treasure Island*, I would say to Brian Henson, 'How would he look at that? What would his attitude be?' I had to learn these characters and they had to have complete logic in that world. It's a world with its own set of rules and you have to follow the rules. Writing something that is funny and that is hip and that makes sense for the characters and that moves the story forward - that's really tough. But it's so much fun."

Mann also has fond memories of this venture into cinema: "*An American Tail* was an amazing experience and the Muppet movie was probably the most wonderful creative experience we had in films, working with the Henson organization and Hans Zimmer, the scorer. Just writing for those characters. Because you could be hip and funny and use rhymes that you'd never think of using. It's one of the things I'm proudest of that I've done. I love that movie. I love what we did. Writing for Muppets is not the same as writing for *Sesame Street*. It's just a whole other thing. It's so hip. It really goes above the heads of the kids who are gonna see it." Weil adds: "They enjoy it on one level but their parents get the inside jokes on the other. That's what's fun."

Despite their film ventures, Mann and Weil maintained their pop scene relevance into the 1990s with, amongst other things, their collaboration with Hanson, a trio of young musicians all of whom were brothers and none of whom were of the age of majority. "Steve Greenberg, who discovered Hanson, called me up," explains Weil. "He had recorded a song that I wrote a while back, so I met him that way. He said, 'I've found this new group and I'd love you and Barry to write with them. They're out in

California for the summer and I'm having them write with good songwriters'. He sent us the demo of 'Mmmbop' and we just thought, 'This is a smash'. Mann: "And we loved Taylor, the lead singer. Just a great singer. We just felt the guy really had it." Weil: "So we went in to work with them and we were lucky enough to come out with a song that went on the record. We wrote 'I Will Come To You', which was the third single."

In 2000 Mann released *Soul And Inspiration*, an album that saw him revisit some of the songs he and various collaborators had seen other artists securing hits with. "It was really an historical album to just put those songs down the way the songwriter wrote them," says Weil. Mann adds, "Something on record of me singing those songs. It was a one-shot kind of a deal. I'm sure if it did something - if it by chance got lucky, sold a lot of albums - I'd have probably done a second one." Weil: "But there's really no marketplace on radio to play those songs because oldies radio won't play them and contemporary radio won't play them."

When the author spoke to them, Mann and Weil were working on a stage musical based on *Mask*, a true story of a mother's love for her deformed son, memorably made into a motion picture starring Cher in 1985. They were also writing a separate show based on their catalogue. "We love this project so much," enthused Weil of *Mask*. "We're so excited about the work we've done for it. It's very combination rock-Broadway. It's a new direction and it's been a joy working on... For me, this is what I always wanted to do. I just kind of took a detour for some thirty-odd years."

The couple did actually try to branch out into stage musicals as far back as 1969 when they worked extensively on a proposed Broadway musical version of the movie *A Face In The Crowd*. "It never happened and it cost us a year of our working lives and it kind of scared us because we were out of the marketplace that long," says Weil. "So it was always, 'We'll get back to this when we can afford to and have time and don't have to worry about making the guarantee and all that'. We decided around five years ago (1996) that if we're gonna do it, 'Now's the time to do it'. Then we thought of this property and it really lent itself to what we wanted to do."

The pair admit that after forty years their enthusiasm for making pop records is now decidedly less keen than once it was. "I think it's a young person's idiom at this point," says Mann. Weil adds, "And are you interested in writing those kind of songs? At a certain point you're not as interested as you used to be."

Does this mean they feel they've written everything there is to say? Mann: "In the pop market, I would think." Weil: "I don't know. I'm afraid to say yes because then I could feel differently tomorrow." Mann: "Also it depends on the market you're writing in." Weil: "When you're talking about the pop field, it amazes me when I do come up with something new but I think that a lot of what I would like to write now is not really particularly viable for this marketplace. The songs [on the charts] are pretty much rehashes of stuff that has been written before. The Backstreet Boys kind of thing, they're sweet young songs - they're the kind of songs that if we were twenty years old now we'd be writing too - but the great writers - Marc Cohen, people like that - are not getting played on the radio. One of the reasons that writing for theatre is so interesting is because you can write about so many other subjects that you would never in the world write about if you were writing in the pop music field."

Mann also notes, "The biggest problem for me - my end of this - of writing stuff for the market now is not writing the melodies, it is the presentation. There are sounds that are commercial now and you got to know how to do that. There are certain drum sounds that are commercial. and I'm not into that now. We wrote a song and I did my demo of it - it was very good, a nice demo - but then we gave it to somebody else who programs for the market and he took it and really brought it to a whole other place. I could never have programmed it that way. And it's so much more commercial-sounding. The melody was fine. It's just that I didn't present it right."

Salvation has been offered to the pair, up to a point, by the country market. "Chord-wise, it's not enormously challenging in most places but certainly lyrically you can at least talk about something meaningful and try to get a new slant on something," says Weil. "I think Nashville's a really interesting songwriting town." 'Wrong Again', a collaboration by Weil with Tommy Lee James, was taken to the top spot on the country chart by Martina McBride in 1999. "It was a pure country song," she says. "It was the first song we wrote. It went to number one. I thought, 'Gee this is easy'. Now I realise how fortunate I was. You kind of have to be down there [Nashville] in the mix. It's a social-professional thing that gets all mixed up. People hanging out and playing songs for each other. If you're not there and you're just sending them down, you have a chance but I think your chances are a lot better if you're walking into that office yourself and holding that demo."

With four decades of writing songs that would ultimately be acknowledged as classics behind them, both Mann and Weil admit that they genuinely do not know when one of their compositions is going to go on to be one of those accorded entry into the ranks of the evergreen. "Back then we didn't think about that," says Mann. "All we did is we wrote a song. We didn't know the history that was gonna follow it." Weil says, "Also, so much depends on that. You can write a great song and if you don't get the right record or the right artist and the right production and the right promotion, it doesn't matter. So the song is so dependent on so many other things." Have they ever been surprised that songs they considered slight have been acclaimed as great works? Weil: "I don't want to mention them because sometimes they're people's favourite songs but there have been a couple that just got lucky. They really did. They were just okay and they happened to get the right artist at the right time." The pair also assert there is not even a set pattern to when songs get covered a lot. "It just seems arbitrary," says Weil. As evidence of this, Weil cites 'None Of Us Are Free' a song of theirs covered by both veteran bluesman Ray Charles and Southern boogie band Lynyrd Skynyrd: "When they called me up and said, 'Lynyrd Skynyrd are doing it', I said, 'Are you sure you got the right song?'"

When it comes to the issue of the state of songwriting today, the pair's opinions diverge. Weil is convinced that depth of talent

amongst lyric writers still exists but that people are constrained
by what the market requires. "Someone rang me up and he said,
'Do you think that the writers today who are writing for all the
Britney Spears and the Backstreet Boys and those things are
kind of like the new version of the Brill Building?'" she recalls.
"And I said, 'Absolutely not. They don't have any freedom'. Not
only do they not have any freedom but a lot of those writers,
certainly the ones in America, are mostly in their thirties and forties
and they're having to put on their 18-year-old hats. They're not
writing for their contemporaries. They can't." She also notes,
"The whole cultural attitude now is far more superficial than it
was in the 'Sixties and 'Seventies. Everything is about appearances,
sex and how people look and boyfriends and girlfriends. There's
very little thought about changing the world or dealing with facts."

Mann feels the problem is not the market but the mindset of
the current generation of composers: "In the past.. there was
more talent and there was more intelligence when it came to
writing a lyric. There was more depth of feeling. They can't write
it. It's a generation that was brought up on TV. They didn't read
as much as our generation did. They don't have the depth of
feeling. There are some that do - there are some alternative artists
that do have that kind of depth. There are a lot of lyrics written by
lyricists who don't know how to put ideas together to make the
point of the song. They just kind of slap phrases together that
sound good to the ear and then they put it out as a song. There
are exceptions of course. Probably the hippest thing is rap. Rap is
a sociological kind of phenomenon. That is the protest songs of
today. Whether I like it or not it doesn't matter, it is what it is."
Mann also detects a problem with the talent pool when it comes
to people able to devise an original melody: "It's the sampling that
can take bits and pieces and paste them together to make up a
song. That is what contributes also."

As to their favourites of their own compositions, Weil says
"They're all like your kids and they're different but I would say
that some of my favourites are: 'Just Once' and '..Lovin' Feelin'"."
Mann says, "I agree with those two so far. For me, also

'Sometimes When We Touch' I love. And I wrote a song by myself that I love called 'There's No Easy Way'." The latter was recorded by James Ingram and released in 1984.

Weil nominates one last composition of which she is proud: "I think that 'Somewhere Out There', for what it was, was very classic in a Harold Arlen kind of way and I always loved those kind of songs. Great old composer. He wrote all the songs from *The Wizard Of Oz*."

The couple are less forthcoming when it comes to songs of theirs that make them cringe. Weil: "A lot of them but I think they should remain nameless." Mann: "One was a hit that we never mention. The guy who recorded it is a really nice guy and we like him a lot." Weil: "Talking about those things always hurts somebody, whether it's the artist or some person out there who loves that song and it's their wedding song."

Now that '..Lovin' Feelin'' is almost part of the wallpaper of our lives through Gold radio saturation, there arises the issue of hearing a song so much it makes one cringe despite its high quality. Both Mann and Weil are perplexed by the suggestion. Weil simply considers the song's status as most-broadcast-of-all-time as a "compliment" to both the song and the Righteous Brothers' performance. Mann says, "I don't sit and think about it. Not at all. It's nice they're still playing our stuff on the radio."

3

GREENWICH & BARRY

If ever the songs of a writing team seemed ubiquitous, it was in the early-to-mid-'Sixties, when the parenthesised publishing credit of "Greenwich/Barry" seemed to adorn the label of every second or third single that passed through the hands of the average pop consumer. The apparently effortless hit-making propensity of husband-and-wife team Ellie Greenwich and Jeff Barry was only underlined by their strike rate for Leiber & Stoller's Red Bird label: of the first 20 Red Bird records, fifteen charted and all of those fifteen were the handiwork of Greenwich & Barry. Such iconic classics as 'Leader Of The Pack' and 'Chapel Of Love' came from their magic pens. They subsequently triumphantly transcended the break-up of their relationship with their equally iconic collaboration with Phil Spector, 'River Deep, Mountain High'. This sophisticated song also transcended the perceived musical limitations of pop and proved that the couple were capable of writing classics for adult ears as easily as great records for kids.

Jeff Barry was born in Brooklyn, New York on April 3rd 1938. He was given the name Joel Adelberg but changed it when he began recording records, feeling he required something more "showbizzy". "Barry" came from a family friend's surname while "Jeff" was probably inspired by the actor Jeff Chandler. He describes his background as, "Kind of middle class parents until they got divorced when I was seven and after that it was much more lean. My father was blind, my sister is retarded." Despite the hardships, Barry had one advantage many in his income group lacked: a readily available piano: "My father played piano. When I was a teenager, I took lessons but never continued. I took a couple of lessons on drums and one piano lesson and enough lessons on an upright bass so that I could play with this band in the Catskills Mountains of New York and sing with the band but I was never much of a student where I could start with it and practice and learn." Nonetheless, Barry gained the proficiency on piano needed to become one of the greatest songwriters of all time - which, as it turns out, is not much: he describes his piano skills as: "..enough to write, but I don' t do it in public." As his guitar ability is even more rudimentary ("in the key of 'E'") he almost always composes on piano.

"I've always loved it," Barry says of music, but adds, "I didn't realize it was a viable and honest way to make a living until I was well into my teens. I've always been writing songs. My mother wrote one down when I was seven because she was impressed by it. When I first started out I wanted to be a singer. I didn't know that songwriting was a choice." Barry had a brief stint in the army before going to college. ("There was a program you could go in for six months and then serve on inactive status. You go to meetings and things like that for a few years after.") He dropped out of college in his second year when he obtained a job as a songwriter almost by accident. With a view to becoming a professional vocalist, he approached a friend named Arnold Shaw who was in music publishing. The material he sang for Shaw was some of his own compositions. "He was more interested in the songs I was singing," recalls Barry, "even though he did set me up with Hugo and Luigi at RCA and they made a record with me as an artist. But the publisher signed me as a writer. I had a specific offer to be a staff songwriter at D.B. Marks Music."

Barry was earning a weekly wage as he learnt his compositional chops, almost always in collaboration. Beverly Ross (who co-wrote 'Lollipop' for the Chordettes) and Ben Raleigh (who wrote the lyric of Johnny Mathis' hit 'Wonderful! Wonderful!') were among his earliest partners. "Usually I would write with people who were really proficient at music," he explains. "For me there are three parts to the song, not just the lyric and the music. It's the lyric, the melody and the chord bit. I like to write the part the singer sings - which is the lyric and the melody - so I work best when someone other than myself is guiding the way chordally speaking. When I write myself, the chords pattern and structure, sequences, usually are more basic." Writing on his own is something Barry has done down the years but he prefers not to: "It's easy enough. It's not as much fun and it doesn't get done as quickly. You can tend to put it off more easily."

By 1960, Barry had notched up his first hit with 'Tell Laura I Love Her', written with Raleigh. This rather morbid record was a man's message to his titular sweetheart as he lies dying after a stock car crash. "I didn't even own a car when I first got the idea for the song and even though I lived in Brooklyn I was always interested in horses," Barry recalls. "So the first lyric, instead of seeing a sign for a stock car race, he saw a sign for a rodeo and was gored to death by a bull. The publisher thought that was a little over the edge so I changed it to the stock cars." The song was a US top ten for Ray Peterson and a UK number one for Ricky Valance in the same year. Barry's career was up and running but despite their joint success it was not Raleigh who was destined to be his long-term writing partner but a young lady from his hometown who was also destined to be his partner in the romantic sense.

Ellie Greenwich was born in Brooklyn, New York on October 23rd 1940 and lived there until the age of eleven, when the family upped sticks and relocated to Levittown, Long Island. "I was born to a Jewish mother and Catholic father so I had the best and the worst of both worlds!" she notes. "My dad was an artist. He used to draw but he couldn't make much money at it so he was an electrical engineer. And my mom, she had business management so she was one of the main managers of the J.C. Penny store. She also was a nurse and a doctor's assistant, so she was a woman of many trades."

Greenwich's father played the balalaika and the mandolin, mainly by ear. "It was a family that just loved music so there was always singing and records and things playing in the house", she recalls. Greenwich's own first instrument was the accordion. "I had to be about ten years old and my parents had some friends that were in Germany or something and they sent a little accordion. Very feminine," she notes wryly. "It really wasn't so bad but it wouldn't have been my choice. Just that it was there. I just picked it up and was fooling with it and he minute my mother saw that, it was like, 'Would you like some lessons, dear?' I was technically very good but I didn't much like what I was doing." However, it was on the accordion that Greenwich first began the composing craft that would become her livelihood. Her first songs were written around the age of thirteen: "I'd be in school and I would have a crush on somebody. So I would write a song called 'The Moment I Saw Him' or 'Be My Valentine'. They were cute little ballads, nice little two-part harmony, kind of like the Maguire Sisters. Pretty ballads. I was able to get my feelings across in song."

At fourteen, the age at which Greenwich started to dabble on piano, her songwriting skills prompted her mother to arrange a meeting for her with Archie Bleyer of Cadence records: "He took the time to see me and talk to me." Bleyer told her she had talent but advised against putting all her eggs in one basket: "He goes, 'School won't always be there for you but the music business will be'." Despite her dabbling, Greenwich didn't take the piano seriously until after she attended an audition at the Manhattan School of Music, aged 17: "I brought my accordion and I auditioned with that and they said I was technically very good but they did not consider an accordion a major instrument. I did immediately go and take piano lessons and learnt to play the piano."

Greenwich studied English in college but only as an insurance policy should she fail to succeed in the field in which her true passion lay: "I always knew in my heart of hearts that somewhere along the line I would just have to try. I would give it 'x' amount of months or a year and if something happened, great, and if not I would fall back on my teaching degree. I just had to try."

Her musical ambitions were given a boost when one night, while still at college, she met Jeff Barry. It wasn't their first meeting: the two are actually related, Barry, being the cousin of a woman who was Greenwich's aunt through marriage. "We happened to get together for a particular Thanksgiving dinner and that was that," Greenwich remembers. "He was filling me in on what he was doing and I actually brought my accordion with me to play some songs at this dinner. We just hit it off because we were both so in love with music." However, the pair became partners in a romantic sense before they became songwriting partners.

Fortune fell into Greenwich's lap in 1962 when, still at college, her path crossed with that of one of the most famous and powerful songwriters in the world, Jerry Leiber. "Somebody in my block knew somebody who knew somebody who knew somebody and this particular man's name was John Glove Jnr and he was one of the writers of 'It's my Party', the Lesley Gore hit," she explains. "So I called him and he goes, 'Why don't you meet me at 1619 Broadway? Meet me in room 902'. I met with John Glove, who literally had to leave to go to a demo on one of his songs, and he put me in one of the cubbyholes in room 902. Room 902 happened to be Jerry Leiber and Mike Stoller's office. I was sitting in there and I was dibbling round a little bit on the piano and Jerry came running in and he just said, 'Oh, Carol?'" Leiber had expected to see another young female writer, Carole King. The two introduced themselves. Greenwich: "He said, 'I haven't seen you around'. 'Well, I'm rather new to the business'. And he goes, 'How new?' I said, 'Like - right now. This is it. Just starting now'. We talked for a bit and everything else became history. I played him a couple of things and he goes I was welcome to come up there and just hang out there if I wanted to. The only thing he really would like, for me to be able to use his offices, all that stuff, would be that I would give he and Mike Stoller first refusal on all the songs that I wrote."

It couldn't have been a more auspicious start to a songwriter's proper career and Greenwich remains aware of both that and of the fact that the now defunct informality and friendliness of the industry that existed then made such a chance encounter possible: "It was such a wonderful business. Today, it's like the music business, with the emphasis on business and back then it was the music business. You can imagine being signed to Trio Music, which was Leiber and Stoller's company: what wonderful people to work for. Talk about getting constructive criticism. Here you're working with some of the top creators."

Amongst people with whom Greenwich would collaborate creatively in this period were Mark Falcon and (ironically) Ben Raleigh, plus.. "..a couple other people that I sort of met at one o' clock and by three o' clock we'd finished the song and then we would play it for Jerry and Mike. If they liked it fine, if not we were free to go and sell our stuff." Amongst the earliest songs she managed to place was 'I Wish It Would Rain All Summer', recorded by Jo-Anne Campbell. She adds, "I had a couple of little things that were kind of floating out there but the ones where I was really getting serious and getting covers and stuff was with 'This Is It', 'He's Got The Power'." Those songs were minor hits for Jay and the Americans and The Exciters respectively. Greenwich's main collaborator became, for a while, Tony Powers. Their 'Why Do Lovers Break Each Other's Heart' was a top forty US hit for Bob B. Soxx and the Blue Jeans in 1963.

Jeff Barry, meanwhile, had seen Gene McDaniels take his 'Chip Chip' (written with Arthur Resnick and Clifford Crawford) into the US top ten in 1962. He had also recorded a dozen or so singles under his own name, though none with significant success. His main writing collaborator was lyricist Resnick, whose credits included the Drifters hit 'Under The Boardwalk'. However, as the relationship between Greenwich and Barry deepened, they decided to be exclusive collaborators. "Within a short period of time, we both spoke to those people and just said, 'Look, we're gonna get married'," says Greenwich. "We're gonna be living together. The most natural thing would be to write together'."

Asked whether they made this decision because they were lovers or because they were genuinely each other's best writing partners, Greenwich says, "I think it was a little bit of both. We really were in synch. And it worked. We liked the same kind of music, we had the same kind of rhythm, our hearts beat at the same time. It sounds very romantic but it was true. We sounded good when we sang together. It sort of all fit. The fact that we were married, it was like 'We can write in the bathroom, we can write in the kitchen, we can write in the bedroom, we can write in the cab..' The availability for writing was just, like, right there."

Unlike with writing partnerships such as those of Leiber & Stoller or Mann & Weil, there was no demarcation of labour with this pair. "As a matter of fact, I think that was the beauty of our relationship and at the same time might have ended up being the problem," Greenwich says. "Both Jeff and I did the music, we did the lyric, we did both produce, so there was maybe too much oneness."

Nevertheless, while the very intensity of their partnership may ultimately have led to its rupture, while they were working together Greenwich and Barry truly did seem to have that proverbial golden touch, pouring out a stream of songs which not only became hits but which have endured both in popularity - making the transformation from hits of their day to golden oldies - and aesthetically, becoming recognized as pop classics.

One of the duo's earliest hits was 'Da Doo Ron Ron (When He Walked Me Home)', a US number 3 and UK number 5 for The Crystals in mid-1963. The title phrase, now unquestioningly accepted due to millions of radio plays, was not originally intended to be part of the finished song. "It was a nonsensical riff but it worked," recalls Greenwich. "We jokingly tried to fill in with some words. It didn't work. 'Da Doo Ron Ron' literally just worked. It just felt right so we kept it." Barry offers, "I think it was calculated to be interesting and somewhat kinda cute. In other words, everybody can fill in the blanks." This type of nonsense vocal refrain became a trademark of the pair's writing for a while, although there were no hidden meanings or particular reasons for the formula of words chosen. Greenwich: "How about 'Do Wah Diddy'? That was cute too. What the hell was that? People always say, 'So where'd you get that?' Beats me. We were young, we very happy, it was still relatively innocent. We didn't really think about, 'Well is this gonna be bubblegum?' Nothing was labelled then to us. We just [wrote] what we were feeling; we were feeling giddy and happy. We would just do that and not even think about what it might mean. Also, who knew it was gonna last all these years?" Indeed, this ostensibly meaninglessness song proved meaningful for another generation when Shaun Cassidy took it to the very top of the US charts in 1977.

Also in 1963 came the Raindrops project. "We made a demo of a song called 'What A Guy'," says Barry. "It was nothing more than a demo. I did the bass voice on it and the demo had a certain charm and ended up on the charts." Greenwich (who, in 1961, had released a single called 'Red Corvette', credited to Ellie Gee and The Jets which didn't get anywhere) sang the lead vocal. Though the single was a top 30 hit in the R&B charts, it served to mark a watershed for whatever performing ambitions Greenwich or Barry had left. "When the act went out to perform, I did not perform as the bass voice, so I guess my desire to do it wasn't that great," reasons Barry. The Raindrops would notch up five more medium-sized hits, 'The Kind Of Boy You Can't Forget' - a number 17 in the *Billboard* chart in '63 - being the most successful. They also released an album. Bizarrely, the most lucrative results for songs connected with the Raindrops project were accidents. The first such accident was 'Do Wah Diddy Diddy', another of the pair's nonsense creations: "We had done it with The Exciters," remembers Greenwich. "It was funny 'cos nothing really happened with the Exciters record." The pair decided not to waste the track. "Jeff and I were in the studio and we were doing an [Raindrops] album and that was one of the songs. That was gonna be our next single. Then we get notified from Jerry Leiber that he had just gotten a telegram that Manfred Mann was putting out the song and it was gonna be their next single. From what we understood, they had found a copy of the

Exciters record." Though unfortunate from the perspective of the Raindrops project, the fact that Manfred Mann's impassioned rendition went to number one on both sides of the Atlantic in 1964 softened the blow somewhat for the writers.

Even more bizarre a story is that of 'Hanky Panky', a throwaway (Barry: "I'm sure it sounds it as well") they'd knocked off simply to occupy the B-side of another 1963 Raindrops single, 'That Boy John'. As if to prove how unforeseeable the ripples can be when writers throw a song into the pool of the public consciousness, it became a US chart-topper three years later. "Tommy James bought the record, flipped it over, heard it and decided that he was going to cut it," recalls Barry. "Total accident." By the time Tommy James and the Shondells' rendition was climbing the charts, the pair were sufficiently well established for Barry to approach Morris Levy - head of Roulette Records - and attempt to hide their involvement with what he considered a piece of juvenilia: "I said, 'Morris, that's terrible. That song is horrible. You gotta take our name off the label. It's gonna hurt us. It's just terrible'. And he said, 'Okay, on the next printing I will, but we shipped about 80,000 this week'." Barry thought this over for a moment. He then decided he had a different complaint: "I said, 'Morris, why does it say "J. Barry and E. Greenwich"? Don't you have enough ink to put the full name in there?'" Barry, incidentally, is puzzled when it is suggested to him that the title must have been daring for the period: "I was very conscious that we were creating musical entertainment for young people so I was conscious to keep it all clean. I always considered that just kinda cute and not even risqué. 'Hanky Panky' doesn't mean anything. You can put any meaning to it you want. Just kind of means fooling around to me."

In late '63, Greenwich and Barry's 'Be My Baby' was recorded by The Ronettes under the supervision of Phil Spector and went top five in both the US and the UK. Though Greenwich and Barry were to become renowned producers in their own right, Greenwich is certainly convinced that Spector deserves his status as production legend, citing the finished record as one of the most gratifying experiences she has had when handing over a song and hearing the finished record after having played no part in its production process: "It's interesting because sometimes you're very pleasantly surprised and go, 'Wow, that really worked, that sounds great'. Other times you go, like when Melanie was singing: 'Look what they've done to my song!' I think the most pleasant, I guess it would be 'Be My Baby'. I just felt that that, with Ronnie's voice throughout that entire thing, all that stuff was so street and that whole record with that drumbeat, just the whole record, the whole performance was very thrilling." In contrast, Greenwich was less than overwhelmed with John Lennon's later interpretation of the same song on his 1975 *Rock 'N' Roll* album. Excited to find out that a version by the ex-Beatle was to be released, she says of the finished product, "I don't even wanna discuss it. I don't even know what that was. Real slow... It was just so out there. He could have done a really good job on it."

As well as producing their songs, Spector began to collaborate with the pair in the writing process. Three certainly didn't turn out to be a crowd with this trio as they embarked on what would be a phenomenally successful partnership. "He certainly had a vision to the kind of record he makes and he would invariably be at the keyboard so his contribution was his style and his chordal input," says Barry of Spector's contribution. He adds, "Melodic as well. It was kind of a general mish-mash." As for himself, Barry says, "When someone other than myself was at the instrument, it would fall to me to do my favourite part which is lyrics and melody. It's hard for me to write lyrics without singing them. The songs seem to start that way so I tend to do that. If I don't hear a better melody - or someone can't come up with a better one - I'll just start singing."

The magic combination of Greenwich, Barry & Spector was employed on 'Baby, I Love You', the Ronettes follow-up to 'Be My Baby', in early 1964. As sweet and devotional as its predecessor, It only reached a modest number 24 Stateside but went as high as number 11 in Britain. The song was revitalized twice, once by Andy Kim, who had a US number 9 with it in 1969 (produced by Barry, who also provided the drumming on it). In Britain, meanwhile, it has been a hit no less than three times, for the Ronettes ('64), Dave Edmunds (number 8 in 1973) and punk band The Ramones. The latter was a surprisingly effective rendition with a lip-trembling emotional vocal which reached the UK top ten in 1980. Phil Spector once again acted as producer. "It wasn't as bad as I thought it was gonna be," says Greenwich of the Ramones' unlikely take on the song. "They made it theirs and it was the same but different enough. Actually I was pleasantly surprised, I must say. Then again, Ronnie Spector singing [it] - that's it. Nothing will ever beat that. There are certain records [where] that's what it is."

In 1964, Greenwich and Barry started working at Leiber & Stoller's Red Bird label. Interestingly, one of their first songs for Red Bird, 'Everybody Come Clap Your Hands' by Moody And The Deltas, showed a black influence not previously detectable in their work. Yet Greenwich says, "I really think so much of the stuff that we wrote, so much of the roots were R&B. It was a very natural thing to do more of the R&B stuff." That record, recorded in 1963, was one of the first examples of the fusion of R&B and gospel that would become known as soul. It wasn't a hit but Barry cites this period as the beginning of the pair's golden age: "When we first started in a partnership with Leiber and Stoller and Red Bird records - Ellie and I had a small piece of the label as well - that seemed to just open the floodgates."

It was Red Bird who put out another Greenwich/Barry song Spector had recorded with The Ronettes but had failed to release, possibly because the record was the kind that, according to Greenwich, "Was either gonna be a number one record or nothing at all." A lush, slow paean to the glories of matrimony, 'Chapel Of Love' was rescued from the vault when the word was put out in the industry that a new girl trio called the Dixie Cups reacquired songs. "A guy named Joe Jones that came up from New Orleans with a whole bunch of acts, one of them being these three girls," Greenwich explains. "They needed material because most of the time back then with the different labels, a lot of the singers and acts were like moving vehicles for the songwriter and producer's ideas and records. I said, 'Well they could sing this - enough to get the song out'. Real girl next door song: like, 'Hey, going to the chapel'. Little bit of harmony. Mike Stoller took it and made up these New Orleans kind of horns, and what he does is bring it up to a slightly other level. Jerry Leiber was just going, 'Ugh! God, what is this?' George Goldner felt the same way I did: it's gonna be a biggie or nothing and he opted to chance to put it out and see." The result was a single that stayed at number one in the US for three weeks in mid 1964 and will probably stay in the public consciousness forever more, it now the inevitable lazy choice of television programme producers looking for background music to a wedding scene, as well as the aisle-walk choice of women who will imminently be brides.

Greenwich cites this record, incidentally, as proof of the fact that the notion that Beatlemania somehow ended the Tin Pan Alley tradition is something of a myth. She notes, "When 'Chapel Of Love' came out and went to number one, the headline in *Cash Box*, and *Billboard* I think, was, like, '"Chapel Of Love" invades the British Invasion'." Another enduring song the pair wrote for the Dixie Cups was the following year's chant-like 'Iko Iko'. "That's a new Orleans marching song or something like that," explains Barry. "They used to sing that in parades, walking with umbrellas."

In late 1964, a Red Bird act called the Shangri-Las, who had had a US top five hit that year with the melodramatic 'Remember (Walking In the Sand)', recorded a Greenwich & Barry song called 'Leader Of The Pack'. The record was, at the time, shocking, glorifying the kind of leather-jacketed, motorcycle-riding youth still considered a threat to civilization by many. It also blew apart the moon-in-June/happy endings convention of pop by climaxing with the youth's gory road death. One other innovation was its construction: a narrative told from the point of view of the youth's former girlfriend after being accosted by a group of friends and asked about her love life, its several distinct sections - spoken word opening leading into conventional melody leading into a sound effects-laden crash scene (including screams, motorcycle engine noises and squealing breaks) leading back into melody - have some of the attributes of an opera several years before the release of the Pretty Things' *S.F. Sorrow*, the album widely recognized as the first rock opera. As if that isn't enough, it's a song which features several of the most memorable phrases in pop history: "Is she really going out with him?", "I met him at the candy sto-ore.." and "Look out, look out, look out, look out!"

The idea for a story song came from George 'Shadow' Morton, a hustler on the fringes of the music industry who had followed the smell of success Greenwich & Barry had generated at Red Bird and turned up and declared himself to be a producer. Greenwich: "When Shadow first came to Leiber-Stoller's office - 'cos I had known him from years before and we had lost touch - he had a tape of 'Remember (Walking In The Sand)'. That went on forever and forever and a lot of it was talking. That's where I first realized that this guy is very much into creating these little stories on record." Barry concurs: "They were mini-operettas. Teen operettas. The intent would belong, credit-wise, to Shadow Morton (who I named by the way - because he would disappear for days at a time; very elusive. Still is). Once we started working on the Shangri-Las, most of them had some kind of sound effects. Tried to paint a sound picture and these little operettas. He was the soul and inspiration for that song. Created most of it."

Of the gossipy, spoken word opening, Greenwich says, "If girls get together, they start yakking: 'Hey, so what's going on? Are you going out with him? Is she really this?' The songs were like everyday slice of life. You meet somebody, you don't say, 'How you doing today?' You talk to them." The actual idea for a story centred around motorbikes came from close to home. "At that time everybody had a motorcycle," says Greenwich. "They had their Harley's, their BMWs, the Hondas, the this, the that. It became like the big thing. And of course there's always somebody who's the head of the gang or the leader of the pack or whatever term you want to give it." The song's narrator was a middle class girl smitten by a rough and ready head of a - it is implied - group of louts. Greenwich: "It became like this little vignette. [Morton] wanted all the emotion and all the heavies and all the different stuff so it would kind of make sense to have, 'Here's a good girl from one part of town liking the bad boy from the other part of town' and 'Oh my God, look what's just happened: he's died and...' Ah, what a sad song."

Asked whether it would even have been possible to tell story without the sound effects, Greenwich says, "Yeah but I don't think it would have been as effective. I think that whole thing, it just works. People look forward to hearing the 'Look out, look out, look out!'"

Nowadays, such is the changed climate that this once shocking number has gained an almost camp patina. "How seedy was it, compared to what goes on today?" says Greenwich. "That was whitebread. I don't know if the song was as shocking as it was with the whole picture of the Shangri-Las coming out with tighter pants and the whole attitude. Now I laugh at it all but at that point it was a little different. Please. Bad? These people were like little babies in kindergarten compared to what goes on now... I think the Shangri-Las had taken a very sweet song and made it sound like a bad song."

Morton soon got Barry into the biking fraternity: "After 'Leader Of The Pack' was a hit, he bought me my first motorcycle." This act of generosity has been somewhat spoiled in recent years by Morton claiming that he wrote 'Leader Of The Pack' in its entirety, something which causes no little irritation and bewilderment to Greenwich: "Oh, please. Yes I know he does [claim he wrote all of it] but no he did not."

Morton aside, there can be no disputing that at this point Greenwich & Barry were in their pomp, without question amongst the most in-demand composers in the business. That they were able to keep up with this demand without sacrificing quality is almost as stunning as their resume. How fast did they tend to write? "There were some songs that we knocked out in an hour and then were other songs that we would really get stuck on,"

Greenwich says. "Very often there were songs that you would start and you weren't thrilled with it and all of a sudden you ended up coming up with this one particular line or melodic phrase and go, 'Ah ha!' Then that would become the song. It really did vary."

Another thing that varied was the technique with which the pair wrote: "It would either be a title or a hookline melodically, that would be the start of a song for sure," says Greenwich. "Most of the songs that I can recall, we'd start with the chorus and then we'd fill in the verses and stuff. But we definitely would have the hookline first and most of the time there was a title, going right to the hook, which would generally be the hook." Barry adds, "It happened any way it could happen. Start with a title or not. I have written so many songs that I'm sure I've done it every way you can do it. I don't think there was any pattern. We could start with a blank page and come up with something or come in with an idea or just a title or a riff or something." Riffs were a very important part of the song. Greenwich: "Working with Phil Spector too, 'Then He Kissed Me', 'Da Doo Ron Ron' - they really are songs to me that are more like records than songs per se. There was a riff that would run through it or a certain kind of a feel and those things were written as much a part of the song as the song itself."

Barry points out that there are two kinds of inspiration when writing songs: "There's the kind that you get in the middle of the night and get up and write down and there's the professional inspiration - you come up with it 'cos you have to. We were always writing about the same subject and it's just a new way to say, 'I love you'. Most songs I write are positive-lyric love songs so it's more professional than inspirational." Asked whether there is a difference in quality in songs brought about by the "middle of the night" inspiration as compared to those borne out of "professional inspiration", Barry says, "I think they may be the more interesting. Not necessarily the bigger hit. For me, songs like 'I Honestly Love You', which I wrote with Peter Allen, that's more gathering from life. A song I wrote that several people have recorded called 'Walking In The Sun' came from having a blind father." Those songs were the exceptions: "I would say the vast majority were just created for the entertainment of young children."

Greenwich and Barry, particularly Barry, were by now producing almost every record they wrote. "It was just a natural progression from making the demos on the songs to realising early on that some of the records I was getting weren't as good as the demos or at least I could certainly do that if I had a decent budget," explains Barry, who says he "dabbled" in producing before Red Bird. This natural progression led to almost complete control over the way their songs turned out. "Most of the hits I produced or controlled or knew where the song was going," says Barry. "Very rarely were they ever demos and hawked. Anything that was recorded outside of Red Bird or Phil's label - like Lesley Gore, 'Maybe I Know' - that just happened, she's in the building. People would come up to our office and see if we had songs. Those were accidental records." Barry's production philosophy was quite simple: "I've always as a producer looked at the song in the record as the stone in the ring. The record needs to be created around the song because that's what I was always presenting. Decorate the song without over-decorating." The fact that Greenwich and Barry were producing added another element to their writing process: "When you're actually writing the song, the riff and certain basslines and certain things, part of the record - you wrote the record," says Greenwich.

Once in a while the pair would write something specifically for an act. Greenwich: "I was very big on doing demos for publishers and what would happen was they would call and say, 'Oh, do a demo for Lesley Bush, who's looking for material'. So I would be hired and I would do this. 'Maybe I Know' was written specially for her." Greenwich didn't find it noticeably more difficult to write to order in this manner: "I think you know what their voice sounds like, you know where they're going with what they are saying and whatever, although I haven't written for all that many people. When you write something, [you think] 'Oh this person's very big on doing ballads' so you write something in the kind of range that they sing in and you try to construct it close to what you feel that they have been doing. Or you do a whole 360 and say, 'Now this person can handle it, they've never done something like this before. Gonna take a chance with that'."

Despite their phenomenal success, Greenwich claims that the pair had no great intuition as to which of their songs would be hits and which misses. "We would take bets as to what number on the charts this particular song might go to and most of the time we really weren't sure if it would even make the charts, except for two of the songs which I said would either be number one records or nothing at all: they were 'Chapel Of Love' and 'Leader Of The Pack'."

Despite their incredible success at Red Bird, Greenwich doesn't recall the period as being the exhilarating experience an outsider might assume it to be. "You know what, it's very interesting but I am learning more about that time now from interviews, because I didn't even think about it much back then," she says. "Don't forget also, along with all the wonderful times and all the good stuff that happens there's also the stuff that's not so terrific. Arguments and 'It's not gonna come out and this will come out'. There were several songs that we liked but they didn't sound like the ones that were the hits so they wanted us to do something that was more geared to the same sounds and the same feeling and the same flavour. Sometimes we would rebel against it." However, Greenwich does concede, "Every now and then, we'd go, 'Whoo, this is pretty cool'. In '63, I remember Jeff and I had seven in the top 20 on the charts, which was amazing. I think that was one of the first times that I actually sat there and went, 'Oh my God - this is pretty cool!' And then of course the next thought is, 'Oh God, I'm never gonna top this, what do I do now?' But we never thought what was happening - we just did it." Barry says, "It was certainly fun - and awfully, awfully busy, when you consider we were doing Red Bird, there was much activity outside of that, plus having a life."

With Leiber & Stoller taking a backroom role at Red Bird, the pair could be said to have taken the company over but Barry says, "We didn't even think about it. We were just doing our thing and that seemed to be working. There was Blue Cat as well, which was considered the R&B label. I think they might have had more interest and activity in that. It only went on for two years. It was all over pretty quick. We were just very prolific. If it ain't broke, don't fix it."

It was while at Red Bird that Greenwich and Barry discovered a young singer-songwriter named Neil Diamond for whom they secured a deal with Bang Records, producing him themselves. Though Greenwich & Barry had ridden out the British Invasion with ease, Diamond heralded the start of a trend which - though it was not to reach its full fruition until the early Seventies - was far more of a threat to their livelihood. Greenwich: "The singer-songwriter type came in and that wasn't what we were working with back then. There was Jeff and I, the writers and the producers, and then there was, 'This is the artist' and 'This is the head of the label' and 'This is the publisher' and everybody had their own little department. Then all of a sudden here's now the era of the singer-songwriter and everyone's writing their own songs. That's where the trouble came in. Why would they wanna do one of our songs when they write their own? It was hard for we independent songwriters. It was like, 'Okay what do we do now?' I found Neil Diamond, so even though Jeff and I produced him and had some of the publishing with him, so what happened was, we kind of had our own little singer-songwriter that we were dealing with." Greenwich states that this situation led to a blurring of line between producing and writing: "Even though he was the writer, I remember certain things: we would come up with the riff lines of 'Cherry Cherry'.."

During all this time, Greenwich - amazingly - found time to sing back-up on a lot of records. Says Greenwich, "I split a lot of my time up. That was a fun thing for me to do. I could pretend I was a girls group. I would take on all those sessions."

The beginning of the end for the Greenwich & Barry songwriting team came when the pair's romantic involvement ended in the mid-'Sixties. However, though they divorced, their artistic collaboration did not cease immediately. 1966 saw the release of 'River Deep - Mountain High', one of the most famous and celebrated of all Greenwich & Barry songs. Written, as so many of their great songs were, in collaboration with Phil Spector, it came about when the production genius needed some new material for his acts. Greenwich: "Jeff and I were already split up and Phil I don't think even knew it. He called for us to get together again and do some writing. The three of us had been on our own for a while and we all came in with different pieces of songs. That's why that song actually sounds like so many different sections."

The song's title phrase stated the intensity of the narrator's adoration of her lover. Greenwich recalls, "I think it might have been Jeff that was singing, 'Do I love you, my oh my..' and we're throwing different lines in and all of a sudden,.." When someone suggested the phrase that became the title, it seemed perfect. Greenwich: "It sort of expressed to us the intensity [of] the feelings... It sang well and it painted a nice image."

The song's sentiment, structure and repeated melodic crescendos gave Spector the perfect excuse for a grandiose arrangement - and Tina Turner, who ended up singing it, the perfect excuse for a nigh orgasmic vocal performance. "I was impressed by it and I thought it was a great record," says Barry of the finished 'River Deep - Mountain High' (actually credited to "Ike and Tina Turner"). Greenwich had a somewhat different reaction. "When I got that, I went, 'What the..?'" she recalls. "It was so, to me, overloaded. I appreciate it much more now. When I put it on, I went, 'Hello? Where has Phil *taken* this?' Not that Tina didn't do a great job on it but I wasn't used to hearing her like that and I just thought Phil had really gone to the limits. I had a little temper tantrum initially and then that kinda dissipated. It kind of threw me."

The record was a top three in the UK but, to the distress of Spector, who considered it his masterpiece, failed to chart in the US. It is reputed that Spector's retirement (temporary, as it turned out) in the late 'Sixties was due to that distress. "He stopped making records," says Barry. "In fact, when Ronnie Spector needed another record, he asked me to produce her because he was gonna show American radio and not produce. So I produced 'I Can Hear Music' with her. He was, the psychological term is, pissed. He was just angry at American radio. I've heard so many different rumours about why it wasn't a hit here, like he insulted some disc jockey so all the disc jockeys decided [not to play it]. 'The American Network of Disc Jockeys'. I don't know if they're that well-connected to one another where they decided they're not going to play his next record. It's just silliness."

Time has certainly vindicated Spector's work: Ike and Tina Turner's record re-charted in Britain three years later. In addition, the Supremes & The Four Tops took a cover of it into both the US and UK charts in 1971. Nonetheless, Greenwich points out, "It really hasn't been that major a hit. In England with Tina Turner but never here. It wasn't as big as the song is itself. It kind of amazes me. The same with 'Christmas Baby (Please Come Home)' - it's never been a hit but it's been covered. Everybody knows the song and it's become the anthem on the David Letterman show. It's kind of a privilege that I'm a part of those kind of things: 'River Deep..' is so revered by people." Barry isn't particularly surprised that the record made the shift from flop single to legend: "It just seems logical to me. If a record over decades starts to have a story attached to it, people play it. And it is genuinely a great record, so I'm not surprised it's become a classic without ever being a hit initially."

The contrast between 'River Deep - Mountain High' and the nonsensical refrain songs like 'Do Wah Diddy Diddy' couldn't be greater. "I think it's harder to write the silly ones," says Greenwich. "Because they are so silly that you almost go, 'Naaah. We can't possibly keep this line'. Or, 'What does *that* mean?' It isn't even so much the writing of it as to in the writing of it to make it work. And when you get done you say, 'Yes, it is inane and it is silly but it feels right and it works'. When you're writing more of a profound song, I think it's easier because you're making statements and you're covering different grounds and you can get a little amplified on what you're saying and take it further. These others songs, what are you gonna say? It is kind of like a nursery rhyme with a little riff at the end of it. They have to be records. You have to see how they're gonna feel. 'Be My Baby' and 'I Can Hear Music', you can sit at a piano and just sing it and it sounds good. 'Do Wah Diddy' and 'Da Doo Ron Ron' don't exactly sound so right." Barry disagrees, saying of the nonsense songs, "I suppose there is less a degree of craftsmanship necessary."

Though 'River Deep..' had proven the old Greenwich & Barry magic could work even though they were no longer personally involved, the atmosphere could be uncomfortable. "I can't say I recall any specific incidents or emotions from the time but I'm sure it couldn't have been as comfortable as before," says Barry, adding, "I'm sure the professional part, which I suppose you could call talent, doesn't go away. When you're immersed in writing, everything else seems to go away. Tunnel vision." Greenwich has more acute, and awkward, memories of that period: "It was weird. It was strange. We were producing Neil Diamond. Most of the sessions would be held at night. It really got uncomfortable so all of a sudden we switched them to the days. We were out of the studio by the time the sun went down. It was stuff like that. It's very different when you're that intimate with somebody and you're writing all the time and whatever and it would happen and it was easy and simple and all of sudden, it gets complicated. Now you're like: 'Well I'll meet you at one o' clock'. Just awkward. And I go to play the 'C' chord and he goes to play the 'C' chord and our hands touch - it's like, ooh, ooh, ohh."

Whatever aesthetic and commercial success they were having, things were clearly not destined to last. Greenwich: "We were producing Neil Diamond and we wrote a couple of things. Then we had our nice little surge with 'River Deep..' and then we really went our separate ways and I got very involved in doing jingles and commercials."

Greenwich is sufficiently older to now perceive her three-and-a-half year personal relationship with Barry as "very short lived". However, the perception on the part of the public that their names are inextricably linked is, she acknowledges, not too far from the truth. She says of their songs, "Jeff and I never had children so I always look at it like, no matter what, these are our kids we had together. The business thing that will come up and there's the orders that has to be done or the selling of a copyright, whatever it is, we have to talk and be in touch. And we'll always be linked [through] those songs, no matter what."

Around the time of the final split, Barry set up his own Steed label and acquired several new songwriting collaborators. "I was writing with a lot of people," he says. "I was writing with a lot of my artists on Steed records: Bobby Bloom and Andy Kim and Robin McNamara. Concentrating on that a lot. I think that the evolution was very natural. I do essentially the same thing. It kind of doesn't really matter who I'm doing it with." Steed was not a label for which Barry had a specific artistic vision. "I was just gonna do my thing and see what happened," he recalls. "Can't say I was looking for a particular kind of artist or trying to create any kind of record or write specifically any kind of songs. At that time I was firmly into writing for myself to produce. It just never occurred to me really to just become a songwriter and try to get outside records."

It was with Bobby Bloom that Barry wrote 'Montego Bay', which Bloom took into the US top ten in 1970 (though it was not a Steed release). In the UK, the record went as high as 3. Barry: "Montego Bay is in Jamaica. Ellie and I went there on our honeymoon. And Bobby Bloom had been there many, many times. Basically, the lyric is a story of a typical trip that he would take to Montego Bay. I said to him, 'What happens when you go to Montego Bay? Just write it'. And he said, 'Well, I would take British Overseas Airways' - BOAC. And he would go so often that the hotel he stayed at would send this guy Vernon down with a car for him to drive around. That's what the lyric is all about. It starts off: 'Vernon will meet me when the BOAC lands/Keys to the MG will be in his hand'. There's another guy at the hotel. The second verse is, 'Gillian will meet me like a brother would/I seem to remember that it's twice as good/How cool the rum is from his silver tray/I thirst to be thirsty in Montego Bay'. So both Vernon and Gillian are in there."

Straightforward though the lyric may have been, there were problems getting a satisfactory record. "We sat in my office and wrote the song," Barry remembers. "He would be on the guitar and I would be tapping on something and I absolutely loved the way that felt: when he was singing it and playing it on the guitar and I was banging and doing the harmonies. We went in to cut it, I used those same musicians that I would use on everything else - best players in town. They came out with an absolutely personality-less record. It didn't capture the setting for that particular stone in that ring." Barry abandoned that recording and instead hired a band in their early twenties: "I brought them in the studio and put the chord sheets in front of them and they were kind of not sure what to do. It had a little more personality but still I said, 'Bobby - there's something wrong. When we're in my office, you're playing and singing and I'm doing the harmonies and tapping on my desk or on my guitar - I love *that*. Let's go back in the studio'." Barry and Bloom booked a studio and proceeded to cut a third version on their own: "We hung a microphone, went over to the piano, got the key and started clapping our hands in front of the mike for the length of the intro. Then we sang the song while we clapped our hands all the way through and that was our click-track basic. Then we put on the earphones and he and I overdubbed every instrument on there one at a time to that vocal. And the last thing we did was erase that vocal handclap track and then he put on his vocal. It finally fit the song." The resulting record was like a mixture of reggae and calypso, though Barry points out of the authentic-sounding percussion: "That is me tapping on the sides of a metal snare drum which I discovered had different sounds. Just making a record as opposed to trying to make a reggae record. I'm sure that whatever knowledge I had of that kind of music was in my head."

Back in '66, Barry had produced several tracks on the second album by The Monkees, *More Of The Monkees* (released in January '67). At the end of the 'Sixties he was approached by Monkee-maestro Don Kirshner about a project in a similar vein. This time, though, the manufactured group with their own TV show would be cartoon characters and the targeted demographic would be almost certainly the youngest in pop history. The project was The Archies and Barry would be writer and producer. "My interest in that is I wanted to create songs and records that would fit a pre-school audience show but yet could sound like radio hits," Barry explains. "I felt if I could do that, we didn't need to get airplay to reach the audience. [The songs were] going to be on the show - definitely - so that would be a big asset. And it was a bit of a challenge and interesting, fun. I also had three- and four-year-olds at the time. My oldest son and daughter were about that age so I kind of felt that I knew what they liked and was aware of what was available then to them. It sounded like an interesting, different, new kind of project." Though aimed at little kids, Barry - who wrote the Archies material with childhood friend Andy Kim - didn't make any profound changes to his writing technique: "I just had to make sure the lyric worked for the audience. That they would understand it and the parents would accept it and like it as well. I don't tend to write anything that my own children couldn't hear so it really wasn't that big a challenge... I obviously had to keep it young, things that they can understand, but I've always given kids credit for understanding."

As producer, Barry was responsible for selecting the people who would provide the singing voices of the animated characters. For lead character Archie Andrews - a wholesome, red-headed, freckle-faced high school boy - he selected Ron Dante from the auditonees. "He was Archie," smiles Barry. "He looked like Archie and he sounded like Archie to me. It was perfect casting."

After a couple of reasonably successful singles, The Archies suddenly smashed out of their intended demographic with 1969's 'Sugar, Sugar'. A glorious confection of sighing vocals and lilting melody, it reached number one in both the US and the UK. "I'm quite sure I had 'Sugar, dah-dah-dah-dah-*dah*-dah' before I went in the studio," says Barry of the refrain. After knocking the song together with Kim ("Invariably, he'd be picking up the guitar and I'd be tapping on the desk and away we'd go"), Barry arranged for ultra-slick backing (with Barry playing the organ riff) that helps explain the song's brilliance: "I used the same musicians I used on most of the other records that I cut. I would call the same musicians for Neil Diamond as I would for The Archies. Great musicians can play anything."

Kim was also a successful recording artist and his 'Shoot 'Em Up Baby' - a collaboration with Barry - was a minor US hit on Steed in 1968, with a little inadvertent help from a crusading journalist. "Somebody wrote an article about it in Seattle, Washington saying that 'Shoot 'Em Up...' was a reference to drugs, which I wasn't then and never have been involved in," recalls Barry. "'Shoot 'Em Up' is a saying regarding old western movies. It's like on a Saturday night the cowboys would go to town and fire their guns in the air and get drunk and just kind of have a crazy old time and that's what 'Shoot 'Em Up' meant to me. But this guy wrote a big article on this record saying what a bad person I am and horrible to do to kids. I wrote him a nice thank you letter because the record broke out of Seattle. It brought so much attention to it that it became a hit." A Kim single from the following year, 'Tricia Tell Your Daddy', is notable for being one of the few protest songs Barry was ever responsible for. Written in collaboration with Marty Sanders, it was a plea to the daughter of then President Richard Nixon to see the error of his ideological ways.

Another successful Steed artist was Robin McNamara. His chirpy pop number 'Lay A Little Lovin' On Me' - written by Barry, McNamara and Jim Cretecos - was a US top 20 in summer 1970.

It was in 1970 that Barry went back to producing for The Monkees. He also for the first time, (excluding his 'She Hangs Out', which had been on their fourth album) wrote for them. By now the Monkees were down to two members, Micky Dolenz and Davy Jones, and had not had a top 10 hit for two years. In retrospect, Barry thinks the project, which resulted in the album *Changes*, wasn't destined for any great success. Though he says the album (comprised of songs mostly co-written by him with Kim or Bobby Bloom or alone) was "Okay. Everything but a hit in it", he also says: "It really wasn't The Monkees. It wasn't The

Monkees situation and time had passed. You're creating for a different situation. Maybe somewhere in my psyche I was trying to update it and upgrade the age level, feeling that I was going to try to now appeal to a fan who was a couple or three years older." The album was the first Monkees album not to chart. "It was basically a challenge that I accepted - and failed at, actually," Barry sums up.

Somewhat more successful was 'I Honestly Love You', written with Peter Allen: "I wrote that with Peter in two three-hour sessions. Worked three hours one afternoon and three hours the next afternoon, it was done". The song was a 1974 US number one for Olivia Newton-John but that wasn't what was meant to happen. "I wrote it with Peter for him," Barry explains. "I made a little piano voice demo with Peter singing it so I could work with an arranger. And somebody heard that and brought it to Olivia - didn't know what my plans were."

Greenwich, meanwhile, collaborated with Mike Rashkowl, with whom she wrote for the TV show *The Hardy Boys*, and Jeff Kent. She also made solo albums, including *Let It Be Written, Let It Be Sung*, which despite critical plaudits failed to do well commercially, partly due to a stage-fright that prevented her promoting it properly. Though she would continue to write songs (she composed for Ellen Foley, Cyndi Lauper and Nona Hendryx) much of Greenwich's energies after the split with Barry were spent writing jingles for commercials.

This new avenue was opened when a company was hoping to secure the services of Neil Diamond to write a jingle. Greenwich informed them that he would be unable to do it because he was in the UK at the time. "They wanted him to do a spot for Cheerios," she recalls. "So they said, 'Do you think you could do it?' I said, 'I don't know. I certainly could try'. Which I did and out of eighty people competing, I got it. They gave me this lyric and they said, 'Do this all in 28 seconds. It's a 60-second spot but you have to fade in and fade out'." Of course, somebody of Greenwich's proven abilities was going to have ideas of her own to contribute: "I went, 'I can't even say what you have written down here, much less put it into some sort of a song. Can I just take it and do what I wanna do with it?' Which I did and it came out really, really great."

Greenwich became a prolific, in-demand jingle writer in the years that followed, writing the music to commercials for the First Union National Bank, Macy's, Sassoon Activewear and many others. Though Greenwich was able to bring her pop savvy to jingle writing, she acknowledges that writing jingles is a different art form to composing pop songs: "Very much so. You have to say something within a certain period of time. And they have their own ideas of what they want. They want you to write something that's fluffy." Asked if writing jingles is as fulfilling as writing hit pop songs, she says: "No, no, no. Except when you're able to get something out in that short period of time that really happens. That really sounds good and you say what you had to say and the track is fabulous and the singing is terrific. It can be exciting. I never thought I would ever say that but there have been many a time that I went, 'Wow, that is really a good spot'. But is it the same as a record? No."

It wasn't just Greenwich's newer compositions that found their way onto the soundtracks of commercials. Many of the classic Greenwich & Barry songs from the Red Bird era were given clearance to be used by advertisers. There are many who think this tends to cheapen worthy songs. "Not necessarily," Greenwich counters. "I think it depends on what they use it for. They once wanted to use 'Da Doo Ron Ron' for a toilet bowl cleaner and I said, 'Mm. I don't think I like that idea'. But they've used 'Be My Baby' for [when] someone's pregnant. I think there's something very sweet about that."

In the early Seventies, Barry also learnt a new discipline. After a move to California, he received a call from TV producer Norman Lear and ended up providing the themes to several of his shows, including *The Jeffersons, One Day At A Time* and *A Year At The Top*. His success also earned him jobs writing themes for other producers. This new discipline necessitated new techniques. "I would go to the initial taping of the pilot just to get a feel of really what it was, and read the script of course," he says. "I needed to know what the characters were and what their situation was." Barry considers the principles behind writing TV themes significantly different to those employed in pop records: "Because you have the subject matter and you have 45 seconds and it has to be timeless. It needs to be able to go on for years if the show is successful. So it has to have some kind of universality as far as the sound of it and what it's saying. It can't be of the moment." Yet he considers TV themes in some ways to be easier than songwriting: "I've done lots of TV and I kind of have a lot of confidence in my ability to capture the show in 45 seconds, so it's really a lot of fun as far as the ego and the show-off thing go. I'm always very confident - more so - that I'll come back with a song that the producers will make than I will that any given song or record is going to be a hit." He adds, though, "Songwriting is still the most fun."

The next step up from writing for television is, of course, writing for the movies. Barry had already scored a picture for Ivan Torres in the late 'Sixties called *Hello Down There*. In 1980, he provided both the score and songs for the movie *The Idolmaker*, a story based on the life of Bob Marcucci, who was the manager of 'Fifties pop idols Fabian and Frankie Avalon. Phil Spector had already been commissioned by the producers to provide music and called his old colleague to get him on board. "I wasn't sure if I really wanted to get involved with Phil again," Barry recollects. "He's, at best, difficult to get along with socially and I certainly had lots of other stuff to do. But at the same time, when we're working, I really enjoy working with him. I thought it was an interesting script and committed to the project and we started working on it. We started on two songs. Something happened between me and Phil and I told Phil, 'You know what? I just can't deal with you anymore' and that was the end of our relationship." There was a strange twist in the tale: "Some time passed and I got a call from somebody whose name sounded vaguely familiar. It turned it was the producers of the film. They told me about it and I took a meeting with them. I hadn't discussed anything with them and they told me that they were starting to work with Phil Spector and they said, 'But we couldn't get along with him and it's unfortunate because he was really doing a great job'. I said, 'I was working with him on it'. I was curious about what he had delivered to them: he had taken the songs that we had started, finished them and brought them as his. So I said, 'Well I think you'll be happy to hear that it was me who was working with him on those songs'. So I ended up writing and producing it all myself. It was a fabulous year I had working on that because I like the movie industry." Not so fabulous was the task of composing the incidental music: "I don't really like scoring. First of all, they say a good score is not heard. And it's more musically technical, which is not my forte, so it's a bit of a struggle for me."

One occasion when Barry felt his gifts were too rudimentary for him to flesh out an idea occurred in the early Eighties when, having started a song called 'The Last Time I Made Love', he felt compelled to call fellow tunesmith Barry Mann, with whom he'd been friends since the mid-'Sixties. "I had the beginning of the song in my head and something told me it needed more chordal expertise than I could come up with," he says. "I said, 'Barry, I started on a song, the hook is, "The last time I made lo-o-ove/I made it with you..."'" He said, 'Get over here and let's write!' The song, finished with the assistance of Mann's wife Cynthia Weil, was a US top forty for Joyce Kennedy and Jeffrey Osborne in 1984.

It was in that very year that *Leader Of The Pack*, a stage play based on Ellie Greenwich's life with which Greenwich had co-operated, was premiered. By the following year, the show had graduated to Broadway. The idea for *Leader Of The Pack* originated with Arnold Pepper, one of the owners of New York's Bottom Line club. "When he was working with Nona Hendryx and this and that, they would do shows down at the Bottom Line," Greenwich explains, "I would go see them and Alan Pepper would always say, 'Why don't you do a show here with the musical?' He finally convinced me. He goes, 'You don't have to be in it but just work on it with us'. It came together for a three-night little run. I was in it for a bit: act two, I did a little connective tissue telling a little bit of a story. It went over so well. All of a sudden it became this bigger-than-life thing. Never was intended. It was so exciting and the reviews on it were so terrific. There were these two Broadway producers that came to see it and they took it."

The play, of course, featured many of the classic hits from Greenwich & Barry's writing heyday. These were interspersed with biographical details. Greenwich: "It's snippets. I call it a lot of connective tissues so you can get from one song to another." The show was nominated for a Tony award for Best Musical and the cast album received a Grammy nomination.

Greenwich admits that she is slightly bewildered by today's music scene, which, she feels, for the first time doesn't seem connected to the traditions of popular music: "There was the disco. Still in all there was songs. There might have been harder rock, there might have been this and that and the other thing. I don't think I ever felt the change as much as I have the past number of years with the rap and the hip-hop. I don't fully understand that music. I know it's big, I know it's necessary, I know it's part of a culture and all that stuff but I think the song was a lot more important in the days before even when I came in the business and still held its own when I came into the business and even after that for a while. Now I think it's so much more the video and how this one looks and how that one doesn't. It's become the package is so much more the important thing than the song. Back in the days that I was doing it, there wasn't a video really to speak of. It was just like, make that record, get it played and hope for the best."

Barry has no particular problem with the music on contemporary records ("It's the same twelve notes. The rhythms are good, the kids are dancing") but is scathing about modern lyrics. "Well I guess whoever was down on Elvis Presley was right," he says. "There's some pretty ugly stuff out there. I don't care what MTV says, they're still selling music to nine-year-olds and fourteen-year-old girls and the quality of what they're hearing and the lyric content of what they're hearing has degenerated. Some people might say, 'Well it's more sophisticated than the stuff you're writing'. Well, you know what? A five-year-kid today isn't a whole heck of a lot more sophisticated than they were in the 'Sixties. So I think that today's music - an awful lot of it - is negative and is having a negative influence on our youth." Barry partly attributes this to the philistinism of record company executives: "The biggest difference if I look at the 'Sixties - which I call the Wright Brothers days of pop music - it was all exploratory and new and fresh and creative and people got excited about titles and riffs and about the music. Then it started to become more big business. Certainly in the Seventies it tried to get sophisticated. And if I were to look at the 'Sixties and the Nineties, the big difference to me is the people who run the industry, and that's always worked as a control - not the kids, it's the people who put the records out. The big difference lies there. Creative people are still creative people and they're gonna write love songs. But the people who run the labels are the biggest change to the negative. They don't care anymore about the titles and the riffs. They're interested in selling records: Get 'em out there. That's always been of an interest but there still was the love of the product. I wouldn't be surprised if some label heads don't even hear the product. Why would they?"

Greenwich lists her personal favourites of her own compositions as 'Maybe I Know', 'I Can Hear Music'. 'River Deep - Mountain High' and 'Be My Baby'. As to her worst songs, she says: "I think one of the worst songs ever written was 'Hanky Panky'. 'Da Doo Ron Ron' was fun and 'Do Wah Diddy' was fun - I think 'Hanky Panky', that I consider silly. I thank God for it every day 'cos it did very well but that I would put in the bottom category." The latter is something on which Barry concurs with Greenwich. As for his own favourites, Barry says, "I think 'I Honestly Love You', perhaps. 'River Deep, Mountain High' is a good song. 'The Last Time I Made Love' - I think that's a good quality song."

As well as her pride in having written songs considered classics, Greenwich is delighted and surprised at the way her and Barry's joint compositions have become synonymous with a specific time and climate. "They were a major part of an era," she says. "I see what happens with the show *Leader Of The Pack*. I see what goes on with people and how it evokes such memories. It takes them back to a simpler, easier time. It's unbelievable."

4

HOLLAND-DOZIER-HOLLAND

"The Sound Of Young America".

It was the slogan adopted in the mid-1960s by Motown Records, the independent record label operating out of Detroit. Such a slogan would be considered an unremarkable piece of marketing self-aggrandisement from just about any other company. From this label the audacity was almost breathtaking. For Motown was a black label. In an era where segregation in America's deep south was still a burning issue and Northern cities would sometimes explode into race riots, this would have been unspeakable effrontery to many of the white population. A couple of years before it would also have been demographically nonsensical: black kids bought records by black artists, white kids records by white artists. Motown, though, changed all that, shifting records by the likes of the Supremes, the Four Tops, The Miracles, The Isley brothers, Martha and the Vandellas and Marvin Gaye in such numbers that it was obvious that there could be only one explanation: audience barriers were collapsing. In the vanguard of this social revolution that Motown were - accidentally - instigating were the team of Brian Holland, Eddie Holland and Lamont Dozier, writers of songs for all those acts. Their two-and-a-half minute paeans to romantic love may not have chimed much with the rhetoric of the militant black movement but certainly struck a common chord with white and black adolescents and in their own small way ensured that black and white would never be so far apart again.

Eddie Holland (born October 30th 1939) and Brian Holland (born February 15th 1941) grew up in Detroit and for the most part were raised by grandmother Ola Everett and their uncle James Everett. "It was a poor background," recalls Brian. "We could eat and go to school and get clothes but didn't have a lot of money. We didn't have a father at the time. My grandmother worked day work and my uncle worked at Ford Motor Company. My mother couldn't afford really to keep us at that particular time. She worked at Ford Motor Company also."

Of the two of them, it was Brian who showed an aptitude for music. He began teaching himself piano at the age of nine or ten. Brian: "I learned how to play because I was interested in knowing what songs the lady played in church. She was playing the white keys and the black keys and I was interested in knowing how she knew how to play the white keys rather than the black keys. So what I would do is wait 'til after everyone would leave church and I would go up and start plucking out notes and eventually I just learned how to play a little melodies, a little chords from there. I would do that every Sunday. No lessons. Trial and error. I kept it up."

Ironically, though, it was Eddie who first landed a job in the music industry. "I sort of just fell into it," Eddie recalls. "I was going to school for accounting and a friend of mine wanted me to go to an audition with him, a gentleman by the name of Teddy Johnson." Johnson was attending an audition held by a Mr. Jones whose first name is lost in the mists of memory. Mr. Jones mistakenly assumed Eddie was also there to addition and asked to hear him sing. Eddie duly obliged with 16 bars and to his surprise got himself a contract. Eddie started auditioning songs for Mr. Jones, who suggested that he should see another industry figure with whom Eddie was not familiar: "He said, 'See if you can get some songs form Berry Gordy'." Though he had set up the Tamla label in 1958, Gordy was at that time just as well known as a songwriter as a record label boss. "So I went to Berry Gordy's to get these songs," Eddie recalls. "Berry Gordy wasn't expecting me. Berry Gordy's position was that he only wrote for people he managed. So he said, 'Well, let me hear you sing'." Eddie obliged with a Jackie Wilson song and Gordy expressed interest in managing him. "I said, 'I'm under contract to Mr. Jones'. He said, ''I know him and I'll talk to him and I'll get you out of the contract'."

Gordy was as good as his word and before long Eddie had notched up a minor hit with 'Jamie'. 'Jamie' appeared on Gordy's own Tamla Motown label in 1962. (Gordy had merged Tamla and his newer label Motown to form Tamla Motown in 1961.) Eddie saw the opportunity to help out his brother. Brian had left high school but was not particularly thinking of a musical career. "Edward told Berry that he had a younger brother that was interested in music," explains Brian. "So Berry said, 'Well bring him in, let me meet him'. My brother introduced me to Berry. I sung a couple of songs. Didn't play anything, 'cos I couldn't play that well at that time. He got me into a group. I tried to sing a solo at the time and I was not that good of a singer but he was interested in me 'cos he said I sound like I had a good ear for music... He found out later that I could write melodies so he had me start writing melodies to different lyrics. One person in particular was Janie Bradford. She would write lyrics and he would give me lyrics and told me to try to put melodies to 'em... He came up with a group called the Rayber Voices, which was with Berry's ex-wife Raynoma Gordy and a couple of other people." Brian started a production and writing partnership with Motown colleague Robert Bateman and achieved considerable success with him in the shape of 'Please Mr Postman', a plaintive number directed at a delivery man who failed to bring expected love letters. It was a US number 1 for the Marvelettes in 1961. it topped the US charts again in 1975 in a rendition by The Carpenters. Between those two chart toppers was a quite possibly even more lucrative album cover version by The Beatles. "I thought it was good," says Brian of the Fab Four's rendition. "They did basically the same thing. The Carpenters had a number one record I thought was good too. I thought they were all good. They was just different, singing-wise. Production-wise they was basically the same."

It was at Motown that Brian first met one Lamont Dozier. Dozier, born on June 16th 1941, had already met Eddie Holland when they were fellow Anna artists. As with Brian Holland, much of Dozier's early musical knowledge stemmed from the church. "My grandmother was a choir director there," says Dozier. "A lot of the training that I got was from that experience, being that that was something that we had to do, my siblings and I." He adds of his family, "We were music lovers, of course. My father sang pretty well but it was just a dream in the back of his mind but he never pursued it. My father's brother played piano and my mother's younger sister used to put me on her knee when I was very small and play all the classics: Bach, Beethoven and those people. So I grew up appreciating the old classics. My uncle would play the boogie woogie. He played that quite well on the old upright piano." Dozier would also watch an aunt play piano. However, Dozier spurned the opportunity offered by his aunt when he was six to take formal piano lessons after being horrified by the sight of her aunt's piano tutor punishing wrong chords by rapping her fingers.

Dozier points out that it wasn't just an interest in music that played an important part in his destiny as a songwriter: "By the time I was eleven years old, I started writing poems, thanks to a lady named Edith Burke at Edgar Allen Poe Elementary in Detroit. She was the English teacher there and social studies and she had this challenge that she gave everybody to write a poem and the best poem would be displayed on the blackboard for a week or two. In my case I submitted a poem called *A Song* and it stayed on the blackboard for about a month because she thought that was so poignant, what it was saying about what a song does to the human psyche. It did something for me, just by having that poem on the blackboard for that length of time. It encouraged me to keep writing poems. I would take those poems a few years down the line and try to apply music to it. I think my first song from those poems came when I was around thirteen years old." Despite his lack of formal lessons, Dozier had acquired sufficient skill to set those poems: "I plunked out melodies on the piano. Self-taught."

At junior high, Dozier and a friend started a vocal group called the Romeos. A local white businessman named George Braxton was setting up Fox Records and expressed interest in the ensemble. Dozier: "Lo and behold, after a few months of sorting out contracts and getting together material to record, we went to record on a Sunday in 1957 and recorded my first song, which was 'Gone, Gone Get Away', which was the worst song I have ever heard. My wife [recently] found it in some old, old obscure shop in California - a mint copy of it. It was so awful." The record was a flop but Dozier could at least claim that he had a record under his belt while still only fifteen. The second Romeos release was another Dozier composition, this one called 'Fine, Fine Lady'. It was a local hit and attracted the attention of Atlantic Records, to whom Braxton sold The Romeos' contract. Dozier, however, spoiled a good opportunity for the group: "I felt that we should have an album out," he says. "I [was] the lead singer and the writer of the group as well as the spokesman. I called Jerry Wexler at Atlantic Records and couldn't get any response so I wrote him a letter giving him an ultimatum of sorts. They sent back a very tidy letter saying that they wished us well and we were free to continue our career somewhere else. That was not the response that I wanted. Needless to say the group was quite pissed off at me. That was my first experience of big business. Shortly after that the group and I broke up."

Aged 18, Dozier auditioned for a Detroit group called the Voice Masters. The group, residing on the Anna label, were about to lose members to the draft. He recorded a couple of singles with them, plus a solo record called 'Where Is My Baby?' He thought he had secured his big breakthrough when he released a song called 'Popeye' under the name Lamont Anthony. Dozier: "It became a huge local hit but the people that owned Popeye wouldn't give us a license and we had put this record out without getting permission to use the name. I was really sick. This was my first sure smash - it took off like lightning. We had to pull the record." Dozier re-wrote the track as 'Benny The Skinny Man' and re-dubbed the lead voice but it was to no avail: "The record just didn't go. It was awful, it was like a joke. It just fizzled out. Nobody wanted to hear it that way and the potential top ten song I had just seemed to fizzle away. Shortly thereafter, Anna Records fizzled out too."

The demise of Anna left Dozier free to sign with a different label and he joined Tamla Motown in 1961. It wasn't the first time that Berry Gordy had expressed an interest in Dozier's talents: "He had heard me sing and knew of me before I even got to Anna records. When I was in the Romeos I had had a short meeting with him and we had talked about him being involved with us but it never amounted to anything." Initially at Motown, Dozier was still thinking of a career as a performer. "Berry let me put a record out on myself on the Melody label that they were trying out for their more pop-type of releases but it didn't do so well," he recalls. "A thing called 'Dearest One'. Afterwards, about a month, he called me in the office and asked me did I really want to make some money in the business: 'Your singing is fine and everything but you're a hell of a writer and you should be doing that. We have a lot of artists here. Why don't you try that first and if you really want to get into your singing thing you can do that later, but right now the company needs writers of your stature and producers'. So I said, 'Fine, I'll do that. Whatever comes first'."

Dozier and Brian Holland have different recollections of how they teamed forces.

Brian: "His wife Ann Dozier was working at Motown at the time and she told me she had a husband that writes and sings songs. She said, 'I want you to meet him'. Then what happened is that Lamont was down in the studio one day writing a song and the song was 'Forever' that we eventually did on The Marvelettes and Marvin Gaye. I said, 'Man I like that, I like that. Let's try to

finish this song'. So we joined in and we wrote that together."
However, Dozier recollects that their union was engineered
by Robert Bateman, who also happened to be a neighbour of his.
Bateman was disenchanted with Motown. "But before he left, he
thought that Brian and I would be a really great chemistry, could
do things together, 'cos we were two of the same sort, as he put
it" says Dozier. "So he invited Brian over for dinner one afternoon
and he sort of put us together. The following day, Brian and I
sorted out what we had song-wise and we decided that we could
work together, that we did have a chemistry of sorts together. We
started writing."

What would ultimately become a multi-million dollar industry
was beginning to take shape - although the trappings of wealth
were nowhere in sight at those early writing sessions. Dozier's
ideas were stored on brown paper shopping bags: "I was saving
every penny I could get 'cos I didn't have much money. I wouldn't
throw anything away. I had a lot of little songs started on paper
bags. I had some ideas for 'Heat Wave'. A lot of titles mostly.
They weren't songs yet. 'Come And Get These Memories' was
one I had just about completed."

Dozier recollects the latter song being, officially at least, the
first work by the team that would become known as Holland-
Dozier-Holland. After Brian and Dozier had tasted some success
as writers, Eddie Holland expressed interest in getting in on the
action. "I wasn't that interested in singing," explains Eddie. "I did
not really care for the performing part and the travel. I only did it
because I felt you could make money." He had realised that this
was in fact a misapprehension, as his brother explains: "He wanted
to join in to write songs because he said when he looked at my
writer's statement, he said, 'Man, wait a minute. What am I
doing?'"

Eddie duly joined the team. The arrangement was that while
Brian and Dozier would come up with the initial ideas and titles
and compose the music, Eddie would devise the lyrics and teach
the song to the artists who would be recording them. In the context
of Motown, this was the most logical way to go about things.

"The competition was really fierce with a lot of producers and writers being there," says Dozier. "And the policy is that the best song would get the release on the artist, whoever it may be. So the writing that I had to do was extensive being that Brian didn't write lyrics. He and I would produce a song as well, would sit at the piano, often side by side, and finish off the music as well. Then I would have to go off somewhere and finish off the lyric. So after a while it became tedious for me because I was very meticulous about what I was writing. Eddie did not want to sing anymore and he said, 'Hey, look, I can fill this void that you all have for lyrics. I can come in and I can do that'. So we decided that he would come in and act as another lyricist and we would be a writing team, a factory-within-a-factory type of thing. That's how we were able to get out so many things." This new team adopted an all-for-one, one-for-all approach. Dozier: "We would split everything that we write together, whether I did most of the writing or [Brian] did."

Intriguingly, Dozier reveals that that famous team could conceivably have been, but for Berry Gordy's idiosyncratic methods, Holland-Dozier-Gorman: "Freddie Gorman, for a moment there, was trying to fill in that space as a lyricist but he was unable to come and meet Brian and I because he had a job. He was a postman." Gorman had helped Dozier and Brian write 'Someday, Someway' and 'Strange I Know' for The Marvelettes, relatively successful singles. "Brian and I would be there at nine o' clock. We had to punch a clock from, I think, nine to six. It was a thing that Berry [did] I guess to create some sort of stability or working environment. He worked at Ford's and that's what they did at Fords so he figured that's what we'll do. So he just more or less copied the operational situation at Ford's for his own, like having quality control and what have you."

While this proved unfortunate for Gorman, it turned out for the best for the other three. The new team had an instant chemistry. Dozier: "There was no doubt about it that we had something very hot. It worked so well and we blended very well. Not that we were people that hang out together but our working environment was superb, I would say one of the best ever, and we got along so well in that working environment."

The team soon settled into a consistent pattern of working. Usually, a song's initial impetus came from Dozier. Dozier: "The idea man - that's basically what I was called, because I came up with a lot of the ideas and titles." Brian: "Lamont was a lyric-melody man and producer. Lamont could do everything. Lamont was a very, very highly talented person that I was in awe with at all times. He impressed me very much from the beginning. I could do everything too but I was not that good with writing the lyrics but I could produce and I could write melodies and I was good with engineering also." Dozier and Brian would then work on a melody. They would go into the studio and record a proper backing track - telling the musicians precisely what they wanted - before handing it to Eddie to provide the words. This did not always come easily to this then novice. Eddie: "Basically, when I started writing songs with them, I was actually learning. I had never written songs before so I was teaching myself as I was actually doing these songs. It would take me a considerable time to write the lyric. Now, what would take me two or three days, it may take me a week or two weeks then." After securing Dozier's and Brian's approval for his lyric, Eddie would then teach the song to the vocalist of the group with whom the song had been placed. With the vocal dubbing completed, Brian would supervise the final mix.

Though 'Come And Get These Memories' scraped into the national top thirty in 1963, Dozier says that it's a toss-up between Mary Wells' 'You Lost The Sweetest Boy' and The Marvelettes' 'Locking Up My Heart' - *Billboard* numbers 22 and 44 respectively the same year - as to the first true collaboration by the trio.

Though the Holland-Dozier-Holland writing credit has become so familiar from so many millions of record labels as to now seem unremarkable, it seemed bizarre at the time. When each of the three is asked how this billing (which was actually swiftly abbreviated to H-D-H, though the complete rendering is more famous than the acronym) came about, three different answers emerge.

"That's a very interesting and good question", laughs Brian. "I don't know!" Eddie offers: "It was 'Holland & Dozier' and then when I started working they just added 'Holland' to it so it became 'Holland, Dozier and Holland'." Dozier says, "It was just apparent that it sounded right, instead of calling ourselves Dozier-Holland-Holland or Holland-Holland-Dozier. It had a nice little ring to it."

The instant chemistry referred to above translated almost as quickly into sales. In '63, the team secured two top tenners for Martha and the Vandellas, 'Heat Wave' and 'Quicksand'. Brian is particularly proud of the production - with prominence given to dramatic drum rolls - on the former: "As I listen to it now, I marvel at the production work that we did. We did that on the spot." Also that year, they were handed the reins of the Miracles by their resident songwriter Smokey Robinson long enough to take them to number eight with 'Mickey's Monkey'. This was one of the trio's few gimmick records. Brian: "Major Lance had a song out called 'The Monkey'. It was to join in on the dance craze."

It was 1964 that saw H-D-H make a - rather abrupt - shift from successful songwriters to pop phenomenon. This was in large part due to them beginning to write for a struggling Motown girl trio called The Supremes. What became a super-lucrative partnership actually started somewhat shakily. The writing trio had secured a top thirty hit for the threesome at the start of the year with 'When The Lovelight Stars Shining Through Your Eyes'. They then offered The Supremes a mid-paced piece of melancholy called 'Where Did Our Love Go', which had been turned down by The Marvelettes. "The Marvelettes.. refused to do the song - they hated it," recalls Dozier. "So we brought in The Supremes, being that they were low in the total poll as artists at the time and we figured that they couldn't give us any lip or any complaints. We more or less forced it on them. And they hated the song merely because they had gotten the word from The Marvelettes [about] this God-awful song that [we] had written and trying to stuff it down somebody's throat, so they were already in a dither about not wanting to do the song. They relented and went into the studio and did it but not without argument and bad feelings and stuff." Things became a little heated as the session developed, with Diane (then still to be renamed Diana) Ross particularly unimpressed by what she was hearing. Dozier: "Eventually Berry had to come down and take a listen because Diane was so distraught and pissed off about it. She told Berry that they always got the second-hand or the stuff that nobody else wanted. Berry listened to the song and said, 'Hey, I think the song is great. I don't think it's a huge, huge hit but it certainly can't hurt your career. I think it will be a top twenty for you all'. And lo and behold, the song was the song that made The Supremes. We sold about three million copies."

'Where Did Our Love Go' was the first of ten number ones that H-D-H would provide The Supremes in the space of four years and life would never be the same either for the girls of their writers. "All of a sudden they became these huge stars," chuckles Dozier. "I remember going to the airport to pick them up and they came down the steps of the airplane with these little tiny dogs and they were all bouffant-up. It was hilarious. But it was fun to see also and we were happy for them, as well as for ourselves."

Of course, whatever the quality of the songs they were given to sing, The Supremes' own charisma was a part of the reason for their success, something Brian is happy to acknowledge: "They had a great-looking look. It was very youthful. And the way they sing and they way they presented themselves and the way they presented the songs. It was just something that you just gravitate to. Especially Diane: the way she sounded and they way she looked with those eyes and whatnot. It was a special group."

With the songs H-D-H gave them (now with somewhat less resistance), The Supremes proceeded to become the darlings of America. 'Baby Love', 'Come See About Me', 'Stop! In the Name of Love', 'Back In My Arms Again', 'Nothing But Heartaches', 'I Hear A Symphony', 'My World Is Empty Without You', 'Love is Like An Itching In My Heart', 'You Can't Hurry Love', 'You Keep Me Hanging On', 'Love Is Here and Now You're Gone', 'The Happening', 'Reflections', 'In and Out of Love', 'Forever Came Today' - almost all of these titles are instantly familiar to the public and almost all of them were top ten US hits (usually chart-toppers). This success provided an element in the songwriting process that no amount of craft or technique could generate: "We were just feeling great about ourselves," says Dozier. "We had just come off the biggest hit the company had ever had - 'Where Did Our Love Go' - and we were inspired. Everything became not a work of drudgery but we became so hyped-up that we felt everything that we touched would be a significant song in the charts. It's very important to have that confidence." This confidence was not dented by the occasional failure of a Supremes song to hit the top spot, such as when 1965's 'Nothing But Heartache' could only manage a number 11 placing after five consecutive *Billboard* chart-toppers. Brian: "I was riding in a car going to lunch with a lawyer by the name of Ralph Seltzer. He said, 'Man I don't think you guys can do it again'. I said, 'Oh man - you kidding?' I was just so up and felt that I could do little wrong at that particular time that I could come up with any of those songs whenever I had to. I said, 'Watch - we'll come back with another number one'." Sure enough, the next Supremes single, 'I Hear A Symphony' became their sixth chart topper.

Some of the songs the trio provided for The Supremes made a virtue of simplicity. Dozier: "'Baby Love' was simple because we just took the same approach that we had on 'Where Did Our Love Go'. It was a fairly simple riff that we had. The chords slightly varied." Others like the ruminative and slightly surreal 'Reflections' (1967) assumed that The Supremes' audience was growing up with them. Brian recalls needing to make adjustments for such material: "That one was not hard to write but you had to re-program your program when you started doing certain kind of songs like that because it was different and presented another kind of move to get into." Eddie also rose to the occasion. It was he who came up with the title and theme, inspired by some shimmering special effects. "When I finished the track, it settled something when he started hearing those little electronic notes going in there," says Brian. "It gave him a kind of thing of 'Reflections'. That's the one tune I never gave him the idea on."

There was, though, one consistent thread through all Supremes records, as Eddie explains: "The first time we did 'Where Did Our Love Go', we lowered the key so that Diana Ross would sing softer than some of her earlier recordings. When we did things with Diana Ross, we would try to keep the key in her register. And basically we would try to write songs that were lyrically appealing as far as the female group and songs that would be lyrically fitting Diana's voice."

'You Keep Me Hanging On' was ultimately covered by umpteen artists, one of whom - Kim Wilde - had a US number one with it as late as 1987. Brian was most impressed by Vanilla Fudge's powerhouse 1968 interpretation: "They did a brilliant re-adaptation of 'You Keep Me Hanging On'. I thought they did a great job without doing the same kind of production. I was happy to hear it like that."

1966's 'You Can't Hurry Love' was inspired by the church music Dozier and Brian had heard so much of as children. Brian: "It came from an old spiritual song called 'You Can't Hurry God'. That particular song, we kind of figured it out early when we were doing it. It came with the idea: You Can't Hurry Love." Phil Collins would have a UK number 1 with the song in the early 1980s. Collins would later co-write the exhilarating 'Loco In Acapulco' with Lamont Dozier (UK number 7, 1987).

Though H-D-H thrived on pressure, they did come close to breaking point with the recording process surrounding 'I Hear A Symphony' (1965). Brian: "They said, 'Hey man, we gotta have this record in the next 24 hours' or something like that. I said, 'Dang!' 'Cos they really liked the record when they first heard it and they said, 'We gotta have this finished'. So I said, 'Okay, okay, we'll go ahead and finish it'. When I finished the track, I called my brother that night and said, 'We've got to have these lyrics'." Eddie recalls, "The only time that I did not take the time that I necessarily needed is when my brother woke me up at one o' clock in the morning telling me that he and Lamont had produced a track and that Diana Ross was leaving the next day and that I had to have a song written and dubbed by twelve o' clock that same day. That was the only time I was really pushed because I was actually writing the song while I was teaching it to her." With the vocal laid down, the finished master was back in the care of Brian, who recalls, "Berry was on his way out of town to England. I was already a vice president in charge of quality control. That meant that I had to take control of getting this record done, finished and okayed and mastered and get it all completed and put out. Berry called me the day after he left and said, 'You got that record ready?' I said, 'Well, I think so. Let me play you the master'. I played the master for him and he said, 'Brian - the voices are too far'. I said, 'Berry, I don't know if it's too far'. And he said, 'Okay man, you make the decision there. You go ahead and do it if you think it's right'. So I put the record out. The voice may have been out a little bit too far but it went to number one anyway. What the hell."

In fact, 1965 was probably annus mirablis for Holland-Dozier-Holland. Not only were they helping to make The Supremes the biggest female pop phenomenon of all time, they were also by now granting their Midas touch to male vocal quartet the Four Tops, solo act Margin Gaye (himself a fine songwriter) and veteran group the Isley Brothers while still continuing to turn out hit parade material for Martha and the Vandellas. In all, the team secured eleven US chart placing that year, of which four went all the way to the top.

With such a high level of productivity, more or less constant inspiration was essential. Luckily, in Dozier the team possessed a member whose brain was constantly whirring. "A lot of lyrics that I came up with would be at home," he says. "Ideas, titles for songs, I would definitely do at home because I would watch the news, the goings-on in the world, movies and listening to conversations between people on the street or in a restaurant. I was always looking for material. My neighbours used to say, 'There go that crazy boy with songs in his head all the time'. Which was a thing that I did. When you're a songwriter you're always very observant of the world around you." He admits, though, that this is his curse as well as his blessing: "I found it very hard to relax because I was always 'on', you might say, always looking for that next hit and when you grow up with that in you and having a competitive spirit, it just doesn't go away. Through the years it hasn't diminished at all, it's just gotten even more fierce. I'm writing more now than I wrote back then."

Brian says there was no pattern to inspiration striking for songs: "Under those creative auspices, you never know what's gonna come first. You might wake up in the morning and you got a title. Something might hit you and you might read something, the title come to you. Or you may wake up and you got a melody humming. It made no difference what came first." Eddie would drop in on melody-writing sessions and take notes about what was emerging and inform the other two of any requirements he could envisage himself having: "When they were doing the melody on the piano. I would tell them how many bars that I would need to write the lyric because I could listen to it and go through the bars real quickly to tell if it was too short to write to or if I needed a little more time to write to something." Asked whether he ever tried to contribute to melody, Eddie replies, "Very seldom."

Holland-Dozier-Holland had total control of the record-making process, from the original inspiration though the recording of the track to the mixing stage. For them, doing what many other great songwriters have done down the years in handing over a song to an artist or producer to do with as they pleased was out of the question. Brian: "I thought that that was one of the greatest things that a person could achieve, trying to get his product to be heard and understood is to go in there and produce it and do it like you think it should be done". Eddie: "[Brian] would get with the arranger and do chord sheets. He would actually go into the studio and out of his head would do the arrangements." Brian reveals that he would tell the musicians to play the songs in unusually high keys. "We cut it high to get a little bit more out of it - to get [the singers] to reach a little bit more for the song. Not that it has to be that way but we just felt that if they reach a little more, they get more drive to it."

So relatively musically unschooled were Dozier and Brian

(Eddie took no part in the production process) that, at least in the early days, they created bafflement amongst some of the Motown sessioners who played on their dates, as Dozier recalls: "I have a very unorthodox way of voicing my chord, not being a professional piano player and self-taught." He recalls one pianist taking exception to his approach: "We were in the studio and I was trying to show them how a particular song went. This was very in the early stages. I think when it was just Brian and I. I was playing a 'C' chord, which was very unorthodox, the way I had voiced it. They were saying, 'No, the way you got this voiced is more of a classical way of doing [it] and we're doing rock and roll/rhythm and blues here'. I said, 'Listen, when you change it - change that voice - you change my song. I don't want that like that, 'cos it gives it a whole different sound'. He said, 'Okay, well if you insist, but...' There's several ways of playing a 'C' chord and I was used to playing and hearing it a certain way and voiced a certain way 'cos I had a melody in mind that fit the song and it wouldn't sound the same if we changed the voicing of the chords." It was incidents like this that helped convince Dozier and Brian that it was imperative for them to see through the entire process of recording a song.

Dozier and Brian would use the same loose crew of musicians on almost everything they recorded at Motown: bassist James Jameson, drummer Benny Benjamin, pianists Earl Van Dyke and Johnny Griffin, and guitarists Uriel Jones, Robert White, Eddie Willis and Joe Messina. "We may change a drummer here and there," says Brian. "We very rarely changed the bass player. The piano player we used maybe two guys all the time. Guitar players we basically always used the same, and we may bring in a third one. But the crew 90% of the time would be the same throughout the Motown years."

"Brian and I would get in and more or less show the musicians what to play," says Dozier. "We would actually split up the room. We would show Benny Benjamin on the drums what was needed for this particular song and then I would work with the guitarist and with the piano player. Usually we worked with James Jameson as well: start him off with a bassline because when I started writing songs I always start for some reason with a bassline." However, Dozier is anxious to add, "It's one thing to show musicians how to play these things and give them the feeling of the song, but to execute it, the musicians themselves have to be very good. They have to listen, they have to be intuitive. And these guys were the best at taking what you had, understanding what you were trying to do and supporting your music. They were the greatest support system in the world. Also, they was very good musicians. They were probably the best that you could get. They had to be 'on' for some ten different songwriters and producers and each one of us had a style of its own and they had to learn all these different styles, from Smokey, Norman Whitfield and on and on and on. The guys made us all look good." The musicians were affectionately nicknamed the Funk Brothers.

The rule at Motown was that a production team was not generally allowed studio time until they had three songs ready. Dozier, though, notes, "If they felt very adamant about the songs, they could have two what they call giant songs and get away with going in with just two songs." Recording the backing tracks was a brisk business. Brian: "We would try to take about an hour for each song but we knew going in what we thought we wanted anyway. As you go along you may change it but we had a kind of a print-out in our mind of what we basically wanted." Achieving finished product could sometimes be similarly fast. Dozier: "If we went in on a Monday and recorded three songs, by the end of the week, those three songs would be completed sometimes. Depends on the process. If I had already did what I was supposed to do as far as starting the idea and the lyric, then I would pass it on to Eddie to finish and teach the song to the artist. You have to remember we were in a race with the rest of the producers for that particular release on the Four Tops or The Supremes or whoever it may be."

Brian Holland estimates that 70% of the time, he and Dozier would give his brother a title and/or a theme and the rest of the time would simply provide him with a blank cheque, lyric-wise.

"Basically, I wanted him to always stick with the melody," says
Brian. "I'd hum a melody to him on a tape and I'd say, 'You
wanna stick with that'. And he can come up with any kind of lyric
he wanna come up with but just stick to that melody and the
rhythm of the melody at all times... One or two songs he may
have struggled with. He'd say, 'Well, man I ain't got it right now'.
He had to wait. It took a few days for him to come up with it
sometimes. I never really pressed him. I tried to let him go ahead
and do his thing so he can get it right."

Even though his turnaround could be quick, such patience was
necessary for Eddie, who estimates that he would produce twenty
to thirty drafts before he was satisfied with a lyric. "In writing the
lyric, I had to use words that captured the feeling, the mood of the
music, the mood of the track and making sure that the artist sings
it can also capture the feeling," he says. Sometimes, this could
result in agonising: "Doing 'Baby Love', it took me one week to
decide to use 'Baby Love' because I thought it was very simple.
It was so simple that I didn't want to write it. I lived with the
track and I listened to it and I remember one thing that Berry
Gordy had said. His philosophy was: 'Go with the feeling'. So I
thought about that and I said, 'I don't like this "Baby Love" title
but the feeling is there." Not that he was averse to simplicity.
Eddie: "I tried to avoid sophisticated workings because it often
becomes very complicated and basically records are just designed
to have fun with. I wanted to keep it as simple and accessible to
whoever was listening to it because the one thing that I learned
being around Motown, we always felt that the business was very
competitive and when a person heard a record for the first or
second time, they should either like it or dislike it."

Another principle for H-D-H lyrics was that they should be
based around romantic love. Though their greatest success came
against the backdrop of the height of the 'Sixties civil rights
movement, H-D-H declined to go down the path pf some fellow
Motown writers like Ronald Dunbar whose 'Greetings (This Is
Uncle Sam)' - recorded by The Monitors - took issue with the
draft. "We may have thought about it but we never got into that,"

says Brian. "We always liked the love songs, 'cos love conquers all." Eddie adds, "I found out very, very early that females bought the most records during that time. So I would write songs deliberately to have female appeal, whether I wrote it on a female or a male artist."

There was one other principle of a H-D-H song, which applied to both tune and lyric. Brian: "We were very conscious of making melodies as happy as possible. Get a happy feeling. People tended not to want sad songs. They wanted something happy to listen to. But if we had to write a sad song, we'd do it." This would help explain why even an H-D-H tale of heartbreak like 'The Same Old Song' has a certain joyous quality to it.

Eddie's lyrics were submitted for his bother's and Dozier's approval before they were shown to the artist. Dozier: "There were times when we said, 'Well, you should have said this and that'. He was always running by the vocal with us to see if it worked for us. And then there were times when a few lyrics were out of place or it felt like there were too many lyrics or a certain phrase could have been said another kind of way and I would like him to interject it and put my idea into it. But mostly he would run the lyric by me knowing that I'm a lyricist as well. Brian and I would give our opinion of it. We all would shape it to make sure it was right when we got in the studio."

Brian admits that, though he and Dozier leaned on Eddie for words, he didn't appreciate his bother's lyric writing skills as much at the time as he should have: "I didn't have as much appreciation for his lyrics as I did years later. I started really listening to the lyrics and what he had done. He did a masterful job with those lyrics. Shoot, a couple of those songs, when you listen to them they were captivating, especially for women. When you listen to 'Baby Love' and 'Where Did Our Love Go' - kind of a woman's thing that could draw them in." He reserves most admiration for his brother's work on 'I'm Ready For Love', a US top ten for Martha and the Vandellas in 1966: "I listened to those lyrics one day very, very carefully and I said, 'Man, those lyrics are so strong'."

Incredibly, during this time Eddie continued to co-compose quite prolifically with other writers too, most notably with Norman Whitfield, with whom he created the Temptations classics 'Ain't Too Proud To Beg', 'Beauty Is Only Skin Deep' and (with the assistance of Cornelius Grant) '(I Know) I'm Losing You'. Despite the atmosphere of competition at Motown, this engendered no problems within the H-D-H team. "We thought it was fine," says Dozier. "We didn't feel any animosity towards him or Norman. Eddie would only help him with his lyrics or write lyrics for the Tempts when it didn't conflict with our schedule. He would only do that when we were taking a little break."

H-D-H were clearly an incredibly efficient mini-production line within the larger production line of the Motown label, yet Eddie shrugs off the idea that this must sometimes have constituted a grind: "There's nothing bad about it because we moved quite methodically so it was a bunch of people there working and at their craft and having fun with it." His brother says of the production line methods, "I think it was a good thing." However, he does add, "It was a bad thing a few years later because it was such a pressure thing and dramatic situation to be under the hammer all the time, because when a record start falling down - the life of a record at that time might have been five, six weeks at the most - you had to get back in there and not only to get back in there, you had to start thinking: 'What can I do differently to keep things going?' That was an awesome thing."

Dozier admits that sometimes records would go out in what he retrospectively considered an unfinished state, causing him a nagging dissatisfaction that was not even alleviated by its commercial success. "People would say to me, 'Well, what more do you want? The song went to number one and stayed number one for four or five weeks or more'. I'd say, 'Yeah but the song itself - you don't understand - the song I thought could have been a better piece of material'. Nothing is perfect but this particular song or that particular song, I thought if we'd had a few more days with it we could have made it into something else. But then again the point was made that maybe we could have messed it up too. Less is more sometimes. Sometimes you had to know when to stop and luckily we knew when to stop. Because of the deadlines we were forced to stop too."

Though the high productivity of the team was partly the result of the intense competition within Motown, it was a sufficiently friendly competition for members of different producing teams to drop in on the other's sessions and bash a tambourine or fulfil any other function they may have been offered. At the helm of this fury of creativity, of course, was Berry Gordy. Though Gordy was naturally something of a omniscient force, all concerned give him credit for never imposing himself on the creative process. Eddie: "Berry Gordy was an exceptional individual for the simple reason he really didn't interfere. He listened to the song, either he liked it or he didn't like it but he left it up to whoever was creating it to do whatever they felt and when the product came up he chose the best record."

The first hit H-D-H wrote for the Four Tops was the plaintive 'Baby I Need Your Loving', which scraped the US top ten in '64. "When I came up with the title for that, it was just a feeling," recalls Dozier. "I always tried to feel the track and the music. It sounded to me like it was crying out, a lament of sorts." 'I Can't Help Myself (Sugar Pie Honey Bunch)' was a US number five the following year. The parenthesised part of the title phrase originated in the Dozier family: "This was something that my grandfather used to say all the time when he used to welcome the people into my grandmother's house. People in the neighbourhood used to come to her to get their hair washed and beautified and he used to stand outside and welcome people - 'cos he was working in the garden. He had his own sayings: 'Hi sugar pie, hi honey bunch' and as a kid I used to remember those things. He was kind of flirting with the people who would come in to have themselves beautified."

The next H-D-H Four Tops single - after the writing team of Stevenson and Hunter had failed to crack the top twenty with 'Ask The Lonely' - was a shameless retread of 'I Can't Help Myself' whose very title seemed to be acknowledging the similarity: 'The Same Old Song'. Explains Eddie, "Back in those days, you had to be very, very careful coming off a hit song. If you took an artist too far from what he was doing we knew it often brought about not so much success." The apparently knowing title was accidental but Brian admits that some people were under the impression that the record employed the same backing track as the previous song with a new vocal. "It was on the same order as 'I Can't Help Myself' but it was a different track," he says.

Almost as if to compensate, H-D-H soon began making Four Tops records with a sound and style almost unrecognisable to those first singles. Part of the reason for this was the raw material with which they had to work in the shape of lead singer Levi Stubbs' epic voice. "He has a very, very strong baritone voice and you have to write something that's a little more biting," says Eddie. Pointing out the difference in writing for The Supremes and the Tops, Brian says, "We would write specially for The Supremes to come up with a love, pleading thing. The Four Tops sing a more harder, pushing kind of thing, a belting kind of tune. It would be a big difference between the two. The Supremes would never have been able to pull off, I think, 'Reach Out I'll Be There'."

That latter tune matched the achievement of 'It's The Same Old Song' in topping the US charts (it also hit number one in the UK) but the two songs could not have been more different. 'Reach Out I'll Be There' featured ornate instrumentation including flute and oboe, an exotic percussive track and an overall sense of grandeur. "We just wanted to keep striving for something different to make people listen to Holland-Dozier-Holland," says Brian. "'Reach Out I'll Be There', it was a masterpiece. It was a gem of a song. We had a quality control meeting. The guy said in the meeting, 'Man, what's wrong with that record's: that's too different. That record can't sell'. Berry said, 'Well that's what I like about it - let's put this out'."

Those who detected a certain classical element to the Tops' new direction were, according to Dozier, not wide of the mark: "Basically we went into what we knew and that was the gospel-classical thing. Gospel music and classical music have a kinship of sorts and we found that out. Brian and I both were reared on classical music and gospel music and that mixture we kept. That's another reason why we got along so well, because we understood what we felt. Those two types of music was what we stuck to with 'Baby Love' and 'Come See About Me', another gospel thing and feeling. And then it would change into 'Stop! In The Name Of Love' - we had signs of classical music. Or go to 'Reach Out I'll Be There', that has Russian type of classical. These things that had the overture type of classical approach to them because that was just in us."

Though the Tops were nothing like the commercial phenomenon that the Supremes constituted - they would not have another US or UK number one after 'Reach Out I'll Be There' - it is on their records that probably H-D-H's greatest aesthetic achievements can be found. 'Standing In The Shadows Of Love' (1967; number 6 in both the US and UK) was cut from the same epically anguished cloth as 'Reach Out I'll Be There'. This can also be said of that same year's 'Bernadette' (number 4 US, number 8 UK). The latter was a track that broke the team's rule of never falling back on the easy songwriter recourse of using a girl's name in a title. This was because the name had a resonance with all three men. "We needed a name and I just yelled out 'Bernadette!' and it felt good in the context of the track," says Dozier. "There was a girl that I went to school with in Harris Elementary. She was a beautiful Italian girl. She was eleven, twelve years old - my age - and I was crazy about her." Eddie: "Brian asked me to write the song called 'Bernadette'. I say, 'You crazy? Bernadette? What kind of a title is this for a song?' I looked at him and I could tell it was something he wanted to do because there was somebody he was involved with at that time. I say, 'Okay. I can deal with it'. I'd met her." Perhaps Eddie went along with the idea because a middle name of a wife of his was Bernadette. For his part, Brian says, "That was a real person. My girlfriend in high school. I wrote it about her. But then I found out later that each one of 'em had a girl named Bernadette and each one of the girls thought it was about them." Of his own

Bernadette, Brian says, "She's a judge now. She was very pleased." Dozier's own Bernadette is possibly still ignorant to this day of her (partial) footnote in pop history. After they had parted ways, Dozier only saw her once more, when the two were in their twenties. "It was the most horrendous thing I ever see in my life," he recalls. "She was pregnant, had one baby in her arm and two in a baby buggy. I said, 'Good God'. She had changed. She still had a beautiful face. I was just driving. I never stopped to say 'Hi' or anything. I just watched her as I drove down the street."

The Four Tops records were the proof that not all Motown records, as some alleged, sounded similar. The same could be said of 'Love Makes Me Do Foolish Things', one of H-D-H's lesser-known songs for Martha and the Vandellas. This 1965 single was a loving re-creation of the vocal group sounds with which the three had grown up. "You might say it was a dedication to the doo-wop material, groups like The Spaniels and The Flamingos," says Dozier. Other tunes the team devised for the Vandellas were more orthodox but no less easy on the ear: 'Nowhere To Run' and 'Jimmy Mack'.

Dozier reveals that it was only by chance that the Four Tops did not record 'This Old Heart Of Mine (Is Weak For You)', which the Isley brothers took to number 12 in the US charts in '66 (In the UK, it initially only struggled as high as number 47; on its re-entry two years later it went to number 3): "The Four Tops were on the road and then there's a song laying around - 'This Old Heart Of Mine', that was actually a Four Tops song - and then you've got a group that's waiting to come up to bat, looking for a hit, like the Isley Brothers, so we gave it to them. That the Four Tops were not around, it became their blessing." However, he also points out that this kind of switch became increasingly less possible as the years went on: "By this time we knew we were writing songs for The Supremes or the Four Tops or Marvin Gaye. We started stylising the songs for the artist."

Of H-D-H records whose lack of success surprised them, Eddie cites 'Without The One You Love (Life Is Not Worthwhile)', a 1964 Four Tops disc, although he admits, "Little bit too close to maybe 'Baby I Need Your Loving'. But one song we felt very, very strong about, all three of us, is called 'Wake Me Shake Me'. We thought it would have done a lot better than it did." Of the latter Four Tops single - actually titled 'Shake Me, Wake Me (When It's Over)' - Brian says, "I thought that was gonna be a huge record. I'da lost my shirt on that."

The team at least had the consolation of the fact that some of their songs were hits two or three times over for different artists. For instance, Junior Walker and The All Stars took 'How Sweet It Is To Be Loved By You' into the US top ten in 1966 only a year after Marvin Gaye had achieved the same feat. Walker did have a H-D-H hit written especially for him, no mean achievement considering he was a saxophone virtuoso with no confidence in his singing abilities. The team came up with '(I'm A) Road Runner' (US number 20, 1966), a record whose extraordinary saxophone runs are not the stuff of a standard instrumental break but parts incorporated naturally into the song structure. This stemmed from its origins as an instrumental. Dozier: "The track modulated and on the parts that he couldn't blow his sax well, when the key would change, the sax part didn't feel right, so we would just let him blow in the parts that it felt good - it was funky or had a nice feel to it - and in the other parts we put in something for him to sing. But he was really very adamant about saying, 'Listen, I can't sing, I can't do this and these songs that you write are just so intricate'. I said, 'This is not intricate - you can do this'. So he blew his horns on the other parts and then Eddie and I finally convinced him that he could sing." Brian adds, "It had a different kind of flavour because of the modulation. It was a modulation in there that caused his horn to go and sound and just bring it out and make it sound like a 3-D movie or something. It just went something quite different. We consciously did that."

In contrast to Walker's lack of confidence was the poise of Marvin Gaye. Gaye, of course, would ultimately go on to write songs as good as the efforts of H-D-H themselves, and it may have been this knowledge of his own potential that led him to decline to be dictated to in the studio in the manner in which H-D-H-produced acts would usually have to put up with. "Marvin Gaye, he did do it his way," says Brian. "'Can I Get A Witness' for one, he really kind of went into his own thing. He did it the way he wanted to do it." Said 1963 single was Gaye's first chart placing under H-D-H's auspices. They also gave him US top forty success with 'You're A Wonderful One', 'Baby Don't You Do It', 'Little Darling I Need You' and 'Your Unchanging Love'. However, the only real smash H-D-H had with Gaye - who used several different writing teams - was the aforementioned 'How Sweet It Is To Be Loved By You'. This blissful hymn of praise to a lover was a US number 6 in 1965. As well as the Junior Walker version, it also attracted a cover by singer-songwriter James Taylor, who made it a US top five all over again in 1975. "He did a wonderful rendition of it that has become my favourite rendition," says Dozier. "I think when you hear it now, it's associated with him more than Marvin Gaye."

In a way, this cover by Taylor was the culmination of the crossover revolution for which H-D-H were in large part responsible. Although there had been isolated examples of crossover like Little Richard, Chuck Berry and Otis Redding, the success of Motown meant that the chart segregation that the existence of the R&B - formerly race - chart constituted was being made obsolete. The notion of audience barriers evaporated a little more every time a white girl rushed to the record store to obtain the latest Supremes or Four Tops single. Although Eddie more or less shrugs off the idea of a cultural revolution ("We were just doing our job and enjoying it and was fortunate enough to be successful"), Brian and Dozier were certainly conscious of it.

Brian: "I would always hear the marketing and promotion guys coming and saying, 'This record crossed over, man'. 'Where Did Our Love Go', for one. 'This record has crossed over. We ain't never had anything like this before'. I would hear bits and pieces but it was hard for me to put it all together." Did it surprise him? Brian: "I was thankful but not surprised. When you feel a song, it's a universal kind of thing. When you feel a song and it has a great melody, you know that people will sing along. Everybody sings along with songs that they like. If they hear it and like it, they gonna say, 'I don't care if you're white, black, indifferent or yellow, brown'."

"I remember having a conversation with Berry Gordy about that when I first joined the company," says Dozier. "He was saying that this was an R&B company and in my mind I was saying, 'Well why does it have to be an R&B company? Why does music have to be specifically for a group of people? Why couldn't music be for everybody?' When I would have meetings I would always express this feeling and then eventually those feelings would be, you might say, incorporated in a thought and we became The Sound Of Young America. Not for just one group of people, but for all people. The sound of music, period, around the world. It became just this teamwork effort to break the colour lines and once we found that we could actually do that or had the power to do that and have music for music's sake, for all people, we just ate it up and really pointed in that direction. Everybody just sort of followed suit. I would say they followed Holland-Dozier-Holland in that respect."

Despite the high quality and innovation of Motown singles, it is generally agreed that in the 'Sixties their albums tended to be low quality, bulked out by secondary songs and unimaginative covers. H-D-H readily admit that albums were things with which they barely concerned themselves. "We just wanted to keep producing and putting out those singles," says Brian. "That's all they really cared about: get those singles out and keep 'em coming, keep 'em coming. They were satisfied with that until they found out the albums made more money."

Almost unbelievably, Eddie reveals that Holland-Dozier-Holland - who, it should be noted, are now responsible for more than 100 million radio and television airplays in America alone - could have been far more successful had they not been writing for Motown. "Because many songs that we would write, we never recorded because we felt they didn't fit what was going on at

Motown at that time or it didn't fit what we were trying to do with the artist," he says. "The fact of the matter is, if Holland, Dozier and Holland had the liberty - see, we were signed exclusively as writers - if we had the liberty even though we were signed to Berry Gordy's publishing company to create songs that Motown couldn't use for other people we would have been far more successful... If we could have took the songs, wrote 'em for the publishing company and the publishing company got them to other artists, we'd have been twice as successful. There's no question."

Anyone inferring that that quote indicates a dissatisfaction with the Motown company would be making a correct assumption, although it was the remuneration rather than the exclusivity that most vexed Holland-Dozier-Holland. In a later court disposition, H-D-H would claim that, though they were under contract until 1967, they had never been able to take a copy of the contract away to study. Come '67 and the end of their contract, the trio were in a good bargaining position and Gordy, apparently mindful of this, offered them each an annual $100,000 advance against royalties in order to retain their services. However, that sum could not inure the three to the suspicion crated in their minds by the fact that Gordy would only make verbal agreements about giving them the rise in royalty rates they desired and not a written contract. At first, the writing team simply downed tools. In 1968, however, they decided there was no option but to take the drastic step of departing the label with which their names had become synonymous.

"That was a very, very, very hard thing to do because Berry was our mentor in a lot of respects and also it's a shame that business has to always come into play," says Dozier. "We felt that if we couldn't get what we thought we were worth that we should just move on and start our own company. We just thought that we deserved more than what we were getting because we were getting very little of what we were selling and as a force that we were at Motown - a very big, important part of that whole machine - it was just more than us knowing or feeling that we deserved it. People would tell us, 'Hey man, you guys should have a lot more than what you got here. You need somebody to negotiate a better contract for you'. After a while, this starts taking a toll. We weren't thinking about the money part of it, the music always came first, but as you start getting successful and you start living a better life then you start requiring more. We never asked. We thought that it would just be given to us, what we were worth. But it doesn't work that way. We had to learn about the business and when we did find out the business - that we should have been receiving a lot more than what we were being compensated for - then it became a nasty situation, one that was intolerable and we had to leave."

"I never really wanted to leave Motown," says Brian. "Motown will always be in my heart. It was just a business thing. It had nothing to do with not getting enough royalties. It had something to do with the promises was made." Eddie gives the impression that he wasn't so concerned about the remuneration as the other two. This is presumably something to do with the fact that, through his collaborations outside of the H-D-H team, he may have been making more money than they were. Eddie: "It's a personal conflict that my brother had with Berry Gordy and me being the oldest I just reacted to it because I saw my brother was somewhat wounded by something."

What Dozier describes as a nasty situation proceeded to become far nastier. Motown launched a legal action against H-D-H, claming that they were in breach of their agreements with Jobete, Motown's publishing company. In addition to asking for $4m in damages, Motown successfully requested a restraining order that prevented them from taking their services to other record labels. H-D-H counter-sued for $22m, claming fraud and deceit, and attempted to have Motown put into receivership. The disagreements were ultimately settled out of court and left H-D-H free to set up their own label but neither Motown or Holland-Dozier-Holland would ever be quite the same forces again.

H-D-H's label Invictus was formed in 1967. Legally, the only one of the three allowed to work was Eddie, as Brian explains: "My brother, he was not under a production contract but he was under a writer's contract. He could go ahead and do things and get other artists and come in and do things. That was my brother's label." However, the H-D-H team was still operating, even if it was unable to take credit for its products. "We had just made this deal with Capitol Records that they would distribute our label Invictus, so we had to find another way to get the material out" says Dozier. "We were still writing because a lot of people expected that and a lot of people knew that we were still writing when they heard songs like 'Band Of Gold' by Freda Payne and 'Give Me Just A Little More Time' by Chairmen Of The Board. Everybody knew it was Holland-Dozier-Holland." Those aforesaid records were amongst the first Invictus releases. Their composition was credited to two ostensible new writers: Edith Wayne and Ronald Dunbar. "They were just employees at the company," admits Dozier. "I think Ronald Dunbar worked in the A&R department, so did Edith Wayne." Both of these records went to number three in the States and it seemed that the scene was set for H-D-H to turn the Invictus label into the chart sensation that they had done so much to help Motown become.

To some extent that did happen. Invictus achieved significant chart success over the following few years. H-D-H also set up two other labels, Hot Wax and Music Merchant. Yet few of those labels' records are as embedded in the public's minds as the team's Motown classics and, probably due to the man-hours they now had to devote to running their company, they were in no way as productive as they had been under Gordy's roof. Dozier certainly doesn't attribute this to any difficulty in having to start from scratch with new musicians. Though they didn't have access to the first-string Detroit musicians - who were under exclusive contract with Motown - he points out, "There were several other great musicians in town and it was just a matter of sitting down with them, doing the same thing as we always did. It wasn't much of a beat missed at all. When we got in the studio, we did what we were used to doing." Perhaps, then, H-D-H were psychologically put off their stroke by the legal shenanigans that necessitated skulduggery when writing and producing their work or perhaps that furious creativity engendered by Gordy's production line may have been the one ingredient that they could not replace when they became their own bosses.

In 1973, the very year after the injunction obtained against H-D-H by Motown was finally lifted, Lamont Dozier brought the H-D-H partnership to a close and signed to ABC as a solo artist. Dozier had come to the conclusion that the H-D-H production line that had worked so well for so long was now becoming too much like a committee for comfort. "We always collaborate or ran certain ideas around each other," he says. "That can be tedious at times. There was certain directions that I wanted to go in that I knew they might agree or they might not agree." Dozier was also weary with having to run his own business affairs and with problems within the H-D-H label's organisation: "The main issue was I felt that the arrangement that we had at Invictus was not what it should be. Unfortunately it was almost the same situation that I was feeling at Motown. Although we had some problems with the way we ran the company - it wasn't totally their fault - I just felt like it was enough difficulty coming out of a lawsuit with Berry Gordy and then going back into a situation with them that was haphazard."

Asked whether he felt at the time that Dozier was breaking up a partnership that worked, Brian flatly states, "I sure did. Absolutely." Dozier: "We ended on a sour note because naturally they didn't want me to leave because of the situation but I felt that we had a good run from '62 to '72 and it was time for me to move on. I had some dreams and things that I wanted it fulfil and it all was in California and New York, places of that sort. Unfortunately we had a row about it and it ended up in court but it was thrown out of court. The judge thought it was frivolous and we just parted ways."

One of Dozier's dreams - to be a successful performing artist in his own right - came true almost immediately. His debut album - appropriately titled *Out Here On My Own* - yielded two top thirty hit singles in the shape of 'Trying To Hold Onto My Woman' and 'Fish Ain't Bitin''. With obvious pride, he notes, "At the end of the year I got the award from *Billboard* magazine: Best New Pop Singer Of 1973, which was a milestone for me." Writing without his collaborators of the last decade had its pros and cons: "It was sort of hard to get used to being on my own but I always wrote lyric and melody so in that sense it wasn't a big change for me. I always completed songs on my own anyway. It's just that I didn't have somebody looking over my shoulder or listening - somebody I could bounce the song off of. I was my own judge and jury."

In May 1983, Motown celebrated its 25 years of success with a televised show at which just about everyone who had scored success with the label performed. The show occasioned a lot of fence-mending between Motown and the numerous employees and artists with whom it had fallen out due to Gordy's financial practices. It also occasioned a reconciliation between Dozier and the Holland brothers. "While we were there celebrating the Motown 25 thing, Berry suggested it would be nice if we did get together a 25th anniversary album for The Tops," says Dozier. The hope amongst the three was that this might lead to a permanent reactivation of the H-D-H brand but though the album - *Back Where I Belong* - was made, it became clear, at least to Dozier, that the business and creative ruptures couldn't be healed as easily as the personal one: "It went fairly well but what Berry wanted and what the Hollands wanted and what I wanted was so varied that we couldn't get together on it so it just disappeared. The whole idea of coming back together just fizzled out after that Four Tops album."

The Holland brothers' songwriting has not been as prolific as Dozier's solo work. They dedicated part of the 1980s to writing songs for films, commercials and television. The 1990s saw them making production deals. They remain busy, running the Holland Group organisation. Dozier, when interviewed, was putting the finishing touches to plans to stage his musical *Angel*, which he describes as "A fairytale about classical music versus rock and roll."

The three are on good terms and have discussed writing a book about their career. Writing songs together is another matter,

though not ruled out. "I don't know at this point," Brian replies
when asked about its likelihood. "I can't answer that. I wish I
could. I would love to. Sure. Absolutely. It was a very, very magical
chemistry there and I would love to rejoin it and see what
happens." Dozier says, "I never say never but they're doing their
thing and they have several artist on their label. I've got my own
situation as well, different things that I'm doing." Eddie's comment
is, "We talk and we meet and break bread, whatever. We just
have different interests."

Asked to name the best and worst H-D-H songs, Brian says,
"I couldn't even answer that 'cos I love em all. I really do. I love
all those songs. The worst obviously is gonna be the worse that
sold." But doesn't he think the public can sometimes be wrong?
"Sure I do. But hell, [it's] the public who buys 'em so I just go
along with that and go on to the next thing." Eddie is less
convinced about the infallible wisdom of the record buyer and,
though also declining to name a worst song ("Usually we felt
pretty strong about it") comes up with a list of favourites that
enjoyed a mixture of chart fortunes: " 'Bernadette', 'Forever
Came Today', 'Love Is Here Now You're Gone' and 'Shake Me
Wake Me'. The biggest sellers were not necessarily the ones I
like the most."

Dozier says, "I think probably the worst song was 'Gone Gone
Get Away'" (though it's not a H-D-H composition). "One of the
best songs would be 'How Sweet It Is' by Marvin Gaye or James
Taylor. There's a certain feeling that I had. I think it sort of wraps
up my feeling. A certain chord progression. And what it's saying
too. I think it sums up Holland-Dozier-Holland. It's like a fusion
of pop, R&B and a little bit of jazz, and a little bit of country."

All three are optimistic about the future of the craft of
songwriting. The Holland brothers express admiration for Kenny
"Babyface" Edmonds, who as co-written songs for Boys II Men,
Whitney Houston and Madonna, while Dozier enthuses about a
song he has heard recently, 'I Hope You Dance', a country hit for
Lee Ann Womack written by Tia Sillers and Mark D Sanders.

Brian expresses misgivings about the influence of technology.
"It's not like the old days: sequencers and things. Those sequencers

and those electronics and those gadgetries, you don't get into really feeling the song, get into the song emotionally like you used to." However, he adds, "I don't think songwriting will ever be on the way down. I just think there's a lull period that comes about but I think it'll break out again."

Though he likes some of it, Brian doesn't consider rap tracks to be songs as such. Perhaps because of his role as lyricist, his brother expresses a lot more admiration for the form. Eddie: "In some way, I think the people who do rap are better lyricists than a lot of the songwriters because rap people have an extreme ability to rhyme in a certain kind of way and some of the words that they use to rhyme I think they're as complicated and more sophisticated than a lot of songs. It does work without melody."

"I think it's fine," says Dozier of contemporary songwriting. "There's always gonna be music that is competitive, that is copied, and then there's that great piece of music that comes out of nowhere, it seems." He dismisses the notion of any malign influence by computers: "The real songwriters that come form the heart with their music will always be around. These guys can pick up a guitar or sit at the piano and just play what they feel. That's going to always be there because it's real and it conveys the human feeling and the spirit of what music is all about."

That human feeling is, for many, the bedrock of the artistic contribution of Holland-Dozier-Holland. However, Eddie Holland feels that while the team's commercial success may have been down to the propensity of their songs to impact on an emotional level, the musical nous of his two colleagues should not be overlooked. He draws attention to, "..the chord structure they used and the patterns of rhythm that they used working in conjunction with those chords." Modestly disclaiming much credit for the importance of H-D-H in pop history, he affirms, "Holland-Dozier changed the face of music and I think Holland-Dozier's probably two of the most unique creative people ever. There's always going to be a number one record, there's always going to be a number two record, whatever. But the difference is some product sounds more unique than others."

5

GRAHAM GOULDMAN

"In 10cc interviews, I used to say that I wrote this and that and they'd go, like: Wow."

Graham Gouldman is sitting in his west London office surrounded by evidence that indeed he did have a professional life prior to 'Donna', that first 10cc hit in 1972. On his walls, amongst other accolades, are an Ivor Novello award for 'Look Through Any Window' (a number 2 for The Hollies in 1965) and an airplay citation for the Yardbirds classic 'For Your Love' from the same year. Yet, to be fair, the lack of knowledge on the part of some journalists about the young Gouldman's freelance songwriting is understandable. When 10cc took off, it was as though Gouldman reinvented himself, shrugging off almost a decade of being unable for the life of him to achieve success either as a solo artist or a band member despite an apparently effortless capacity for securing hits for others.

Gouldman, born on May 10th 1946, was a self-taught musician. "[I was] eleven years old when I got my first guitar that a cousin of mine brought me back from Spain," he says. "My parents actually sent me to the Manchester School of Music. I lasted for about two or three weeks because all the guy taught me, blast him, was the scales. I didn't want to learn the scales. I wanted to learn the intro to 'Move It'."

Gouldman played in early-'Sixties Manchester bands called The High Spots, The Crevattes and The Planets. "Crap," he recalls of them. "We were just doing covers of Cliff Richard songs, basically." The Whirlwinds was the first of his bands to get a recording deal. "We did a Buddy Holly song, 'Look At Me'. The B-side ['Baby Not Like Me'] was written by Lol [Creme, a childhood friend, later his colleague in 10cc] because I didn't have a song at the time." 'Look At Me', however, was the sum total of The Whirlwinds' recording career: "I didn't like the stuff that the Whirlwinds were doing. It was kind of like a cabaret band. We used to finish with 'Alexander's Rag Time Band' and it was starting to get on my nerves. And that's when I said 'I've had it' and split off, taking Bernard Basso, who played bass, with me and a guy called Stephen Jacobson, who is [the novelist] Howard Jacobson's brother. And I had seen Kevin [Godley] play with another band and I thought he was a pretty cool drummer, so I asked him to join. And that was The Mockingbirds."

Gouldman's songwriting came about through necessity in 1964 when The Mockingbirds, then signed to Columbia, were looking for material. "Basically we wanted to make a record and we went round Denmark Street, or our manager did, and nobody was interested in giving an unknown Manchester band any songs and because of The Beatles I felt, 'Oh sod it - if they can do it, I'm going to have a go as well'. We recorded two songs for EMI, one of which was 'For Your Love'." 'For Your Love' was a superb composition, a message of devotion lent a haunting quality by its minor chords and stop-start structure. Gouldman: "Well, EMI turned down 'For Your Love'. They didn't like it."

Being a Manchester band helped The Mockingbirds secure a fairly prestigious gig as warm-up group on the BBC television chart programme *Top Of The Pops*, then filmed in that city. It caused the young Gouldman to find himself in a surreal situation. Following Columbia's rejection of 'For Your Love', The Yardbirds had shown greater suss and made it their first top 20 hit: "It was a very odd feeling to be the support band for a band that was

doing one of my songs." The Yardbirds' rendering of the number
added an exotic tinge with harpsichord and a bowed bass. Had
Gouldman been surprised by 'For Your Love''s rejection? "Yeah.
I thought we did a very good version of it." He is happy to accept,
though, that The Yardbirds' version was even better.

Despite the record's brilliance, Yardbirds guitarist Eric Clapton
was reputedly so disgusted with its commercialism that he quit
the band. "I think it was probably the last straw for him," says
Gouldman. "It's ridiculous really. First of all, I never considered it
a commercial or a pop record. The fact that it entered the pop
charts doesn't make it a pop record. It was so different. I think
he was a strange guy during that period."

The Mockingbirds' debut didn't fare so well chart-wise. "Very
poppy kind of thing," Gouldman remembers of 'That's How It's
Gonna Stay'. "It wasn't very good. Instead of using a cow bell on
the record, we used a milk bottle and someone came up with the
idea that we would call it 'That's How It's Gonna Stay - the Milk
Bottle Song'. So in the adverts in the *NME*, it showed pictures of
the band in a milk bottle. Like: 'Hey, we've come up with a brilliant
concept'."

The Yardbirds recorded two more of Gouldman's songs. Unlike
'For Your Love', 'Heart Full Of Soul' and 'Evil Hearted You'
(both 1965) weren't Mockingbirds rejects but written specifically
for the band. They featured the breathtaking fretwork of Clapton's
replacement Jeff Beck, although those assuming that it was Beck
who wrote their riffs are mistaken: the unforgettable droning lick
on 'Heart Full Of Soul' was on Gouldman's demo. "The riff is the
main thing for me," he says. "All the songs I wrote during that
period, I had the riff first. Always. To me, the first four chords of
'For Your Love' are a riff."

The Hollies' 'Look Through Any Window' is credited as a co-
write between Gouldman and Charles Silverman, then business
partner of Gouldman's manager Harvey Lisberg. "I was travelling
on a train with him," explains Gouldman. "He came up with the
title and that was his input into that song. Most of the melody for
that was written on the train." 'Bus Stop', the second single

Gouldman wrote for The Hollies, displays the massive influence his father had on his songwriting back then: "I used to stand at a bus stop every day going to work and I mentioned it to my dad. I came home one day and he'd written these lines: 'Bus stop, wet day/ She's there, I say/ Please share my umbrella'. I took those lines, went into my bedroom and just wrote the whole song, except for the bridge. He always used to help with words.

"Dad was a writer, although he was never a professional writer. For him to stick his neck out and give up regular work to become a writer would have been too risky. My parents were always very encouraging for me to get on because I think he kind of thought that he missed the chance and he wasn't going to see me miss a chance." Gouldman admits, "One could say that he should have been credited, but he'd always [jokingly] say 'Put your name on top of mine, directly over it rather than side by side'."

The Hollies recorded another Gouldman song, the driving social commentary 'Schoolgirl', in 1967 but it remained in the vaults for thirty years, finally appearing on EMI's *The Hollies At Abbey Road, 1966-1970* compilation in the late Nineties. "It was recorded by a few people," says the composer. "It came out with The Mindbenders, a production that I did, but it was never a hit. The Mindbenders' [version] was banned because the cover - it was one of the first picture bags - had a pregnant schoolgirl on the front."

The emergence of Hollies members Hicks/Clarke/Nash as one of the era's great song writing teams brought to an end Gouldman's involvement with The Hollies but by then he was working for another Manchester act, one whose teenybopper image was in sharp contrast to the musical credibility of The Yardbirds and The Hollies. Gouldman didn't consider Herman's Hermits a step down, however: "I love pop music and they could make good pop records. I always got on with the boys and I was always happy whenever they recorded any of my songs." Gouldman played uncredited parts on some of the Hermits records, along with John Paul Jones, who usually arranged them.

'No Milk Today', his first British hit with the Hermits, had been rejected by the Hollies: "The Mindbenders did a version of it, I believe, that didn't turn out very well. But Harvey Lisberg managed Herman's Hermits, so it went to them, thank God." It was another song heavily influenced by Gouldman's father: "He went round to a friend's house and he wasn't in and there was a milk bottle on the doorstep and he just started thinking 'Well, what does the milk bottle represent?' It doesn't represent that you've drank all the milk and you want some more. To him it meant that life had changed and someone had gone and there was no need to have any milk anymore because the person who you loved had gone away. When he first mentioned it to me I didn't like it. I thought the title was so odd."

'East West', released by the Hermits in late 1966, deals with the boredom and loneliness of life on the road. "I spent a lot of time travelling," he recalls. "that song came out of that. There was a very good version of that done by Morrissey on a B-side, I think the best version of it. He brings a certain extra lonesomeness to it." Gouldman's 'Listen People' was a massive hit for the Hermits in America, also in 1966, but wasn't released in Britain.

Despite the Hermits' lack of musical skills, they recorded a song which must stand as one of Gouldman's best and certainly most neglected, 'It's Nice To Be Out In The Morning', a thoughtful musing on the bleakness of proletarian life hidden away on the soundtrack of the film *Mrs Brown You've Got A Lovely Daughter*. "It's very Mancunian," says Gouldman. "My dad helped me a lot with that. Manchester United [are in there]: 'Bobby Charlton, Best and Law/It's a most fantastic day/When they play.' Also very typical of my dad are those lines in it: 'But a place is people more than things/It's the mums and dad and kids who love and give it life'. It's got a Northern-ness about it. Cheadle Hume is not a name that crops up in songs a lot."

Amongst other artists, Gouldman also wrote for Wayne Fontana for whom his 'Pamela Pamela' was a number 11 in 1966. "Kev and Lol were working on a project at college. It was a [film about a] character called Pamela. I offered to write the music. They never used it so I wrote a completely different set of lyrics.

I think Harvey gave them some derisory amount of money for the use of the title or the inspiration."

During this period, Gouldman was almost always writing in minor keys. "To me, a minor key was more soulful," he says. "It was more Jewish in a way. A lot of the music in the synagogue is in a minor key. And I'm part Russian as well. I have all these theories about why I always favoured the minor key but to me it's much more expressive. I like the darkness of it." Another Gouldman trademark was shifts in tempo. "Just to be different", he admits. "Maybe I did it once too often. In 'You Stole My Love' [by The Mockingbirds] there's a drastic change. The change in 'For Your Love' is a surprise but it's a good surprise."

What kind of speed did he write songs at then? "Fast. If I was really in the right mood, a lot of the words and all of the music came out. I knew almost as I was writing what the next bit was going to be. It was as if the song already existed in my head."

Mockingbirds records, meanwhile, were getting nowhere. After their debut, they released 'I Can Feel We're Parting' ("I thought that was a better song. It was kind of my going through my Bacharach period"); 'You Stole My Love' ("Giorgio Gomelsky, who managed The Yardbirds, produced the song with Paul Samwell-Smith and Julie Driscoll sang on it, the choruses"); the non-Gouldman 'One By One' and 'How To Find A Lover' - stiffs one and all. "Part of the problem," Gouldman admits, "was I was the singer as well and I don't think my voice was very good in those days. I really, really wanted The Mockingbirds to have a hit but let me put it this way, I'd rather The Hollies recorded something. It was more guaranteed." And the band's perspective? "There was never any bitterness, not that I was aware of. It was more 'Good on yer' rather than 'You bastard, why didn't we have that song?' 'You Stole My Love' I thought was a pretty good song. The stuff that we recorded that I did write for us I thought was very good."

Any suspicions the band might have had about Gouldman giving his best songs to others must have been mitigated by the fact that a single released under his own name in 1966, 'Stop! Stop! Stop!'

(not the Hollies number), was also a flop. Explains Gouldman, "I was given a track by a publisher called Mike Collier and they'd done this track and nobody liked the song. So Mike said, 'I've got this track, I've spent money on it, do you fancy putting a song on top of this track?'" Another non-Mockingbirds Gouldman project that year was a single released under the name High Society called 'People Passing By'. "That was a song recorded with a couple of friends of mine: a guy called Pete Cowap and a girl called Friday Brown. In those days you could do one-off masters yourself and just take them down to the record company that afternoon."

Despite his success, not all Gouldman's songwriting ambitions were realised. "I always wanted to get a song placed with Dusty Springfield. I wrote 'Listen People' with her in mind. I wanted to get a song with The Animals. And Cliff Richard. I did get a track recorded by The Shadows. I never had a title for it but the Shadows called it 'Naughty Nippon Nights' 'cos it had a Japanesey sort of feel. They were one of the greatest influences of my life."

The Mockingbirds split in late 1966 and Gouldman devoted himself for a while to composing full-time. He became artistically re-acquainted with Jeff Beck in 1967 on 'Tallyman', another of Gouldman's Manchester flavoured, father-influenced songs. "I didn't even know what a tallyman was then," he says. "It's someone who comes around like a rent collector. I was surprised that [Beck] did it, I must say. The verse was a bit 'major' for him."

That year, Gouldman made another record with Pete Cowap, this time under the name The Manchester Mob: 'Bony Moronie At The Hop'. "That was me, Pete Cowap and John Paul Jones and Clem Cattini on drums. It was a combination of the songs 'Bony Moronie' and 'At The Hop'. It was just a bit of a laugh really. In those days studio time was so cheap. We'd do it in three hours, if that."

In 1968, Gouldman joined his future 10cc bandmate Eric Stewart in the Mindbenders as guitarist, a move prompted by a feeling of depression on his part due to a dwindling number of hits. "It wasn't a very creative period. I'd lost my way a little bit. I was just looking for something else to do, something that might spark me off." Gouldman penned that band's final single, 'Uncle Joe, The Ice Cream Man' (August 1968), memory of which makes its author wince: "It was a poppy kind of 'Penny Lane' but not a billionth as good. It was terrible. Eric told me later Mick Jagger came into the studio and said 'What are you recording that crap for?'"

The same year saw the release of *The Graham Gouldman Thing*, a US-only solo album ostensibly produced by Herman's Hermits' Peter Noone but actually a Gouldman-John Paul Jones production collaboration. Featuring reworkings of four of his hits for others as well as new songs, it was a very baroque affair: "I love strings, always did. And woodwind as well. John's arrangements were beautiful." The album's highlight, 'My Father', a track in which a man confesses to idolising his dad, is not as straightforward as it seems: "I wrote that with my dad. I was writing about him and he was writing about *his* dad. Looking back on it, it could have been awkward but it wasn't." Was he disappointed by the album's bad-promotion-induced poor sales? "Not really, because it was kind of a sideline. I was happy to be a songwriter. I'd accepted the fact that it was never gonna happen."

Gouldman moved over to New York in 1969 to work for Kasenetz-Katz, the production team credited with the invention of bubblegum music through their Ohio Express and 1910 Fruitgum Co. records. (See the Joey Levine chapter.) "It turned out to be a bit of a factory," Gouldman says. However, he feels he wrote some good material while over there: "Bubblegum but slightly more sophisticated. There was a track called 'Sausalito' [released as an Ohio Express single] I thought was really good. It was kind of poppy. Not a million miles from good Herman's Hermits."

Back in England following his Kasenetz-Katz stint, Gouldman wrote 'Susan's Tuba' as a pastiche of the bubblegum sound. In true bubblegum tradition it ended up bearing another person's name, that of Freddie Garrity: "It was a hit in France. I don't know how it got to be a Freddie and The Dreamers record. I think Freddie put his voice on our track." By this time, Gouldman had formed a sort of British Kasenetz-Katz with Lol Creme, Kevin Godley and Eric Stewart at Stockport's Strawberry Studios, in which he had invested. When the four had a hit with 'Donna', it was effectively the end of Gouldman's days as a solo songwriter. 10cc would go on to rack up 11 top 20 UK hits (including three number ones) and a couple of Stateside top tenners, many of them co-written by Gouldman. Gouldman had finally achieved what he'd thought was "never gonna happen": a career in the music business in which he wasn't hidden behind the scenes.

Today, with 10cc no longer a functioning group, he is back working as a behind-the-scenes composer. He works with various artists with whom he is either paired by his publisher or whom he gets his publisher to approach if he and his various collaborators (he rarely writes solo nowadays) come up with something they think would suit a particular artist's style. "I really like to work with artists directly," he says, "'cos that way you have the artist on site, so to speak, so you can write something and if there's just one part of it they don't care for you can change it there and then." There is another reason for close involvement with artists: "No matter how good you are, if you want to get in today's market you've got to be very sussed and if you're not sussed you've got to work with the people that are. What happens is, they'll take your nice tunes that they can't do and put them with their production and wrap it up in a way that makes it modern and it doesn't matter that one guy was twenty and the other guy was fifty-odd."

Asked about the milestones in his non-10cc writing career, he says, "I always thought 'Bus Stop' was one of the best things I ever wrote because it was so instantaneous. As I was writing it, I knew what was coming next, I just kind of chased it. I didn't really do very much. It just came out and I followed it. And the worst song... Gee, I don't like to sound conceited but that's a real difficult one to answer. I was surprised that 'Evil Hearted You' [was a hit]. I had the Yardbirds in mind but I wasn't optimistic that they would record it and I was surprised that they did. Funnily enough, I find it a rather ugly song. There's just something ugly abut it. But I don't like to bring it down because it did okay. The thing is this, once you embark on writing a song, it must have a certain something to make you want to finish it. It must have its own legs because I start and discard more than I write. So the fact that something grabs me and makes me want to finish it, whether I'm writing it on my own or co-writing it, means that it has something. And every song is a little part of you. Even something like 'Susan's Tuba'. It was crap but it was ironic crap. It was a joke. That was probably a shit song but it was written as a shit song."

When it comes to the state of songwriting today, Gouldman opines, "I'm sure there's the same healthy amount of talent but I don't think it's being allowed to come out because the emphasis has shifted from songwriting more to production. The whole record is production-based. People are buying dance music rather than music to listen to. I'm sure they do listen to it but it's not in the same way and it doesn't seem as life-altering as music was for me. I mean, there was eating, sleeping and listening to music. I think if they were exposed to the good stuff it would be but unfortunately because it's all about figures now with record companies and not enough investment in talent... Also there are not enough entrepreneurs around. There are no mavericks anymore, no madmen. We need some madness."

He adds, "I'm sure there's good new talent coming up. I'm desperately trying to think of someone who I think's a great songwriter at the moment, someone contemporary, but I can't think of anybody. It does say quite a lot but also my taste is... I think Eminem is fantastic but it's a different type of work. I hope that they don't [give up] and I think that there are some people that will nurture them. I think there might be a bit of a backlash against the modern music. I think people always want really good songs."

6
BOBBY HART

The story of the Monkees is one of the strangest in pop history. They were the so-called Pre-Fab Four: a group manufactured in the mid-'Sixties to be an American equivalent of The Beatles. Manufactured in the strictest sense: although individual members had musical talent, they played almost no instruments and wrote almost no songs on their records, at least in the beginning. This may not sound the recipe for a runaway commercial success but before too long the 'band' were approaching The Beatles in terms of units shifted. This is a tribute to the skills of the men who composed most of their early material: Bobby Hart and the late Tommy Boyce, who brought to the project the same common touch which has led their theme tune to *Days Of Our Lives* being the most long-lived opening music in American TV history.

Bobby Hart, born on February 18th 1939, was raised as Robert Harshman in Phoenix, Arizona. He describes his background as "working class. My dad worked his way up from a janitor in a professional building to an x-ray technician, which is what he did for more than forty years." The family was fairly musical: "We were very involved in the Pentecostal-style church, which involved a lot of music. My dad played the banjo and my mom loved to sing, so I picked up the banjo from him and then got a guitar that was strung the same way as the banjo. Four strings, called the tenor guitar... I took piano lessons from maybe ten years old. For three or four years classical piano and then when I was in high school I went back and paid for my own lessons and took more modern piano." Hart also recalls, "I took violin lessons for years when I was real young, as a kind of a mistake. The salesman came by and said, 'Your son tells me he'd like to take musical instruction' and said, 'What would you like to learn?' I said, 'Guitar' and he said, 'Well, why don't you start off with something more simple - like the violin?' None of us were sophisticated enough to realise that all he taught was violin." However, Hart did eventually take up guitar properly in his early teens.

When it came to his musical tastes as a youngster, Hart admits, "I really hated what was passing for pop music up until when rockabilly came in. I listened to country music all the time I was growing up until Elvis Presley, and then I started discovering what was called R&B music at that time, or race music. I'd have to drive across town to the black section of Phoenix to find a record store to pick this stuff up. Elvis was the first to turn my head. I remember going over and getting songs by groups like The Moonglows and The Penguins. I really loved the southern black gospel music as well, which I would find in these stores: Professor Alex Bradford and Sister Rosetta Thorpe, those kind of acts."

Despite his early musical abilities, Hart's professional ambitions, from his early teenage years, lay elsewhere, if still music-related: "I thought I was going to be a disc jockey. That was what I had set my sights on. I remember the kind of a breakthrough was when I first heard the Gene Vincent song 'Be Bop A Lula'. I remember being up in the mountains [on] vacation. No-one else was around and I was singing that song and I realised, 'Hey, I could sing this kind of stuff.' That was a little bit of awakening of being an artist but still I thought I was going to be a disc jockey. I signed up for military service on the reserve plan which meant you only had to go for six months active duty and then meetings once a week to get it over with. As soon as that six months was over, I moved to Los Angeles to go to disc jockey school. I arrived here on New Years Day 1958 and found an apartment right off Hollywood Boulevard near this school."

Though Hart arrived with a couple of hundred dollars he had saved, he needed a job to support himself through the Don Martin School of Radio, at which point his father's printing hobby came to his assistance in securing employment in print shops. However, both printing and the disc jockey school began to dwindle in his priorities: "I got a job printing record labels and I would walk from my apartment down Vine Street. There was a little recording studio and it had a theatre-type marquee outside and they had put up there: 'Come in and see what your voice sounds like: ten dollars'. So on Saturday I got my nerve up and I went in and I laid down a little piano track, put down some background voices for myself and I sang, 'You Are My Sunshine' or something. From then on I was pretty hooked and I would spend all my Saturdays in there and more money than I was making doing demos."

Hart's status as regular Saturday fixture of the studio got him noticed by the kind of industry figures and their associates who frequented the establishment. "People would start coming in and saying, 'Hey that sounds pretty good, I wanna publish that song'. In a few weeks somebody said, 'Let me turn you on to this producer/manager who is having pretty good luck placing artists." Said producer/manager was one Jesse Hodges, whose importance in Hart's life cannot be underestimated for, as Hart reveals, "He's the reason I started writing, because on our first meeting he said, 'You sound pretty good kid, but what we need is artists who have their own material. So go home and write some songs and come back and see me'. So just because he told me to do so, I went home and wrote some songs. I had done maybe two or three things earlier on but in a very non-professional kind of way. I was quite religious as a kid and probably the earlier ones were more spiritual kind of compositions." A s for his new songs, Hart says, "They were rockabilly, basically." With the assistance of a drummer he met in the Vine Street studio, Hart made demos of his new compositions, which he then took back to Hodges, who recorded them and managed to secured him a deal with Radio

Records. "The two songs were called 'Stop Talking, Start Loving', which Jesse co-wrote, and the other song was called 'Love What You're Doing To Me'."

These songs (which have also been released on a subsequent Bear Family compilation of rockabilly rarities) were actually released under the artist's full name simply because Robert Luke Harshman was written on the contract. Radio Records arranged a comprehensive tour of West Coast radio stations to promote their new signing: "I quit my record label job and set off to do that and of course came back in a couple of weeks with no job and no record hit." Fortunately, Hart's printing skills meant he was always able to get another printing job while he continued trying to break open the door to stardom that that debut record had prised open ever so slightly.

Around this time, a character named Tommy Boyce entered Hart's life. Boyce was born on September 29th 1939 in Charlottesville, Virginia but relocated with his family to Highland Park, California at the age of twelve. Both of his parents were singers and it was his father who taught Boyce how to play guitar. "Tommy was also hanging out at Jesse's office," recalls Hart. "He was just fresh out of high school. He wanted to be an artist as well. He was a guitar player. He came out of the country music as well. He'd tried to make it as a singer in country music when he was in high school and he played pretty good rhythm guitar, acoustic." Boyce would become Hart's close friend and main collaborator in the 'Sixties, although when they first met Boyce was much more closer to Curtis Lee, a young singer whose lifestyle the bachelor Boyce could more readily identify: despite his youth, Hart by this time was married with two children.

It was Boyce who started making a name for himself first after he wrote (with John Marascalco and the artist) 'Be My Guest', a 1959 number 8 hit for Fats Domino. "I remember running into he and Curtis on Hollywood Boulevard," says Hart. "I remember Curtis announcing that Tommy had a hit with Fats Domino, which was a big break for all of us because it was someone that we actually knew had made the charts." Shortly after this, Boyce and Hart made a more profound connection: "Curtis got his family to finance another recording session - he'd gotten away from Jesse. He was putting together a session on his own. He had hired Jimmy Haskell, who had worked with Ricky Nelson, to arrange it. Curt and Tommy stopped over to the apartment one night and Curtis saw a song I was working on called 'Doctor Heartache'. Curt flipped over it. He decided to do that song and one of Tommy's songs at the session. We were to give the publishing rights to Jimmy Haskell because he was doing it as a favour - all he got out of it was the publishing. Basically, that was the first time I think that Tommy looked at me with a little bit of respect that I could write a good song." When Curtis Lee was subsequently signed by a manager who took him to the East Coast to develop him as a record act, the professional respect between Boyce and Hart grew into a personal closeness: "Tommy didn't have his buddy to hang out with and that's when he started to hang out with my wife and myself at the weekends."

Boyce had actually played on 'Girl In The Window', a self-composed record Hart had issued in 1960 under the aegis of a manager called Lee Silver. (A Hart record released after his debut on Guyden Records had previously flopped.) Though the success of this record was limited to regional radio play, it did mark a milestone in Hart's life: a change of name. Silver approached the man still called Harshman shortly before the record's release with some surprising news: "He told me, 'By the way, your name was too long to go on the label so I've shortened your name to Bobby Hart'."

Meanwhile, 'Doctor Heartache' made some headway: "My manager after that, Lee Silver took that and got a record by this artist by the name of Tommy Sands - he was married to Nancy Sinatra. That record went to 98 or something like that on the charts. That was actually technically my first chart record."

The friendship between Hart and Boyce was interrupted when Boyce was asked to travel to New York to write more songs for Curtis Lee. Hart, still having to make ends meet through printing work, found himself in a strange position when Boyce and Lee started writing hits like 'Under The Moon Of Love' and 'Pretty Little Angel Eyes' for Lee Curtis: "I was stuck in this little print shop printing the labels for their hits and feeling pretty left out."

The local success of 'Girl In The Window' at least provided Hart with an avenue to making a living from music. One night in 1962, travelling home from one of the weekend high school hops at which he was asked to sing his record, he and fellow hop act Barry Richards were appalled when they started discussing how much money they were earning for this activity. "I said, 'You know some people actually get paid for doing what we're doing every weekend'. He said, 'What do you mean?' I said, 'Nightclubs. I can play the Hammond b-3 organ and I can play the foot pedal so we don't have to get a bass player. What can you play?' He said, 'I'll play the tambourine'. He played the telephone better than anything - he was a great salesman. He got the Yellow Pages, got on the phone and got us a gig. We put a little twist band together. They booked us for a week and kept us for three or four months. We called ourselves 'Barry Richards and Bobby Hart'. Our flyer said 'Direct From Vegas', but it was direct from the print shop instead. First time I actually made my living from music. That was '62."

During this period, Nino Tempo, a musical colleague of Hart's, recommended him to record producer and arranger Don Costa who was partners with Teddy Randazzo in a publishing company in New York called South Mountain Music. Hart: "They were looking for young, upcoming writers. Donny signed me sight unseen and started sending me fifty dollars a week advance. They signed me as an artist and as a songwriter. That fifty came in very handy in those days."

Eventually, Costa agreed for Hart to travel over to the East Coast to record a session. Though the session - which involved a large string section and a professional producer - did not yield a record release, it led to Hart settling in New York and to starting work properly as a professional songwriter. It also led to him re-establishing his relationship with Boyce.

"They had these little cubicles set up in a big warehouse-type building on Tin Pan Alley there," says Hart. "A piano in each one. They'd have like ten of then and you could go in there and you could write all day long. They were paying me an advance each week for doing that. By then I'd split up with my wife and the payments were just making my child support payments. I remember budgeting myself 25 cents a day for food."

As well as being a partner in the publishing company, Teddy Randazzo was an artist who played Vegas lounges. In addition to his songwriting, Hart worked as a backing singer for Randazzo on his Vegas trips, working twelve weeks on, twelve off, an arrangement that lasted for more than two years. Hart remembers this period as a very exciting time, the energy of New York combining with the opportunities afforded by Tin Pan Alley to heady effect: "At that time the whole music business was pretty much located in two buildings across the street from each other: 1616 and 1619 Broadway, the Brill Building. You would get in the elevator and get assignments from publishers and so on. Everything just moved so quickly there."

This fact was proven by an incident, during one of the New York stays between Hart's Vegas visits: "At one point the advance money ran out from Don Costa's company. Tommy had been in New York a while before and knew a lot of other people. One day we ran into Wes Farrell in the elevator of 1615 Broadway and he said, 'I need something for Chubby Checker. I'm going to Philadelphia tonight and I need a song to play him. So Tommy and I went back to my little flophouse room and wrote a song which became a Chubby Checker single." Said record was 'Lazy Elsie Molly' and climbed to number 40 in 1964, Hart's first significant hit.

"So then we started writing with Wes Farrell," says Hart. "Wes was running another publishing company, Picturetone Music. During the daytime he was a professional manager. We'd meet him after business hours and we would write in the publishing office there, 1650 Broadway. We wrote this song called 'Come A Little Bit Closer' which he got recorded by Jay and the Americans. Right after the Chubby Checker thing." 'Come A Little Bit Closer' got to the dizzying heights of number three. Meanwhile, Randazzo proved a valuable contact, having just produced a hit record for Little Anthony and the Imperials. In late 1964 and early 1965, Hart co-wrote two top ten hits for said group with Randazzo and Bobby Weinstein: 'Goin' Out Of My Head' and 'Hurt So Bad'.

Around this time, Boyce and Hart decided to be each other's main writing partner. There was no assigned role - i.e., lyric or melody - for either of the two in their composing partnership: "No, because of the way we got together where we had both written by ourselves. We both did both and we both contributed to both." However, an idiosyncrasy of Boyce's became a rule for the pair: never to start writing a song without a title: "I've written with a lot of people before and since and everybody has their own style but that was a hard and fast rule for Tommy."

Their success as composers didn't mean that the two had abandoned their respective personal ambitions to be performers. However there were practical obstacles to the two becoming a recording duo: "Our musical tastes were different as far as performing. He was kind of bubblegum commercial-oriented and I was more R&B. I had more of a black sound going on."

Though they were now proven hit-makers, Tin Pan Alley was a ruthless environment where nobody was guaranteed work. "it would just be whoever was coming up that week," Hart remembers. "We would try to come up with something in their genre and you wouldn't always make it. Just because you wrote the last one didn't mean you were going to get the next one. They were being submitted material by a lot of teams."

There was a new threat to freelance songwriters in the shape of the fashion for self-composing that had been unleashed by the example of The Beatles. This threat, however, was something that Boyce & Hart managed to sidestep when they came to the attention of one Don Kirshner, possibly then the hugest name in publishing circles: "While I was on one of the tours in Vegas, Tommy got a call from Don Kirshner and he said. 'Come A Little Bit Closer' is one of my favourite records and I'd like to sign you, send you back to the West Coast, where we're opening our West

Coast offices." Boyce moved back West at the end of '64. He
called up his partner and advised him to give notice because he
could ensure he got the same deal he had secured. By the time
Hart had fulfilled his commitment to Randazzo and joined Boyce
in LA, some of Boyce's songs had already charted, including
'Peaches 'N' Cream' by the Ikettes and 'Action' by Freddy
Cannon. The latter was the theme song to the Dick Clark-
presented show *Where The Action Is*. Boyce had also written
some other theme songs. By moving into this area, Boyce & Hart
were able to avoid the drought that afflicted some writers, post-
Lennon & McCartney: "Things were really cooking out on the
West Coast. At that point, the music business basically was shifting
out West. That was supplanted in our case by the fact that we
were signed by a publishing company that was affiliated with a
motion picture company and a television company: Screen Gems
Television and Columbia Pictures. So we had all these other media
outlets that were offered to us. We were writing for whatever
artists were coming up and also being offered movie projects and
television projects."

The pair were commissioned to write the theme to a new
soap opera called *Days Of Our Lives*, one of their first pieces of
work in that area. "We met with Ted and Betty Corday," Hart
remembers. "They had created several other successful soaps,
going back to radio days, and they were starting this new one.
They said, 'We've just seen *Fiddler On The Roof* and we love
this song 'Sunrise, Sunset', can you come up with something like
that for a theme?' So we went home and wrote what we thought
was 'Sunrise, Sunset' backwards or whatever and they hated it.
So we tried again and they rejected it as well. To us, this was
another one of the many television shows that were being offered
and Tommy was saying, 'Hey, forget about these people, they
don't know what they want, let's go on to something else'. I said,
'Well, I got an idea. Here's what we'll do: we'll go in this little
cheap demo recording studio where they have a Hammond organ
and I'll play straight onto tape something that sounds to me like
soap opera music', (because I grew up on my mom's radio soap

operas).”

This time, the Cordays were pleased. The theme the pair composed was recorded with a full orchestra and continues to be used on the show today, making it the most enduring theme to any American TV drama in history. The pair, incidentally, share royalties with one Charles Albertine but Hart insists the latter had no hand in the composition. “That was a political decision that happened in 1976, I think, when the new copyright law came in,” he says. “Charlie Albertine did write a lot of other television music and somehow for some reason they put our name onto a couple of his things and put his name as a 12½ per cent partner on *Days Of Our Lives* theme. We’ve never gotten to the bottom of it. When Tommy was alive he never really wanted to tip the boat. He said, ‘Albertine’s widow is probably living on that money and we should just be thankful that we’re getting what we’re getting’ so I honoured his wishes after he died.”

The next major job given to the pair by Screen Gems was just as important and enduring as the *Days Of Our Lives* gig, although aimed at a very different audience. If the soap opera was aimed at middle-aged housewives, *The Monkees* was aimed at their children: kids who loved The Beatles and the pop scene in general. Hart: “We once again got called over to the Colpix pictures lot to meet with Burt Schneider and Bob Rafelson who were the producers who were dreaming this project up. Burt explained to us what he wanted to do which was basically an American Beatles on television. We convinced him that we knew exactly what was needed for the music end of it. This was about a year or so before the show went on the air. We were led to believe that we’d also produce the records.”

Boyce even harboured ambitions about he and his partner being cast as members of this Beatle-like band. “I think early on the decision was that they were going to keep us available for making music and not mix us up with acting,” says Hart. “We never actually formally went in and auditioned. We did sit in on a number of other auditions by other people. Tommy saw that as a vehicle for us. I never took it that seriously for some reason. I could see that it wasn't gonna happen. I think he held out hope that it might have happened but to me it didn't seem like it was too feasible."

Hart says he and Boyce were not daunted by being asked to write songs along the lines of the most successful recording artists of all time: "Tommy and I had spent a couple of years tailoring songs to artists. When they'd say, 'We need something for the Righteous Brothers', we knew immediately how to write in the Righteous Brothers' bag and it certainly wasn't hard to get into The Beatles. That was all over the radio airwaves and we loved it of course, like the rest of the world."

Their assignment remit was no more specific than the "American Beatles on television" line they had been given at that first meeting. "That's all they told us. It was just that one meeting. We kind of got it and it was up to us to formulate exactly how close to the Beatles and how fresh [to make it]. We couldn't do a straight rip-off of course, but we wanted it to be Beatle-esque. Their characters were also going to be fashioned that way. The show itself was visually very much like *Hard Day's Night* and *Help!*"

A practice in American television is to produce a pilot edition of a program. If this is deemed to be a success, then the show is commissioned. Boyce & Hart were asked to write three songs for the pilot. One of those three compositions was, naturally, a theme tune. The one they came up with, ironically, was more Dave Clark Five than Beatles: "We fashioned it on 'Catch Us If You Can'. Had that same drum thing... We would visualise a lot of instrumentation in the arrangement while we were writing. When we were writing the Monkees theme, we knew that that drum thing was a part of the song. We knew where it would come and we knew where the stops were and so on." The song was written remarkably quickly: "Tommy and I lived together at that point, shared a house, and we were walking down to the park. We tried to write out in the open air whenever we could. It had that walking cadence, which they incorporated visually once they shot the show. We had most of the melody by the time we got there and were building the lyrics." The other two songs were required for specific scenes. The pair provided the ballad 'I Wanna Be Free' "..for a love scene on the beach with Davy. And they needed a dance scene, so we wrote a song called 'Dance On'. It was kind of a throwaway. If I'd of known how many years later it would still be available on an album I probably would have taken a bit more time with that one!"

In contrast to the made-to-order nature of '(Theme From) The Monkees' (its proper title) and 'Let's Dance On' (ditto), Hart reveals that 'I Wanna Be Free', the third song, was "..one of the few songs that Tommy and I wrote that wasn't an assignment. We were always just writing for an act or for a deadline for a television show or something. I came upstairs one night at home and Tommy was strumming a guitar and he was starting something, 'I wanna be free..' And he said, 'Where does it go?' That's what he had. And I just kind of built it right into the next two or three lines: "Like a bluebird flying by me.." and we finished it together. We had that song already in our pockets so that was easy." The composition was later the subject of an unlikely cover by Andy Williams.

Of course, it is now part of rock folklore that The Monkees did not play on their early records. The 'real' Monkees - at least on all the Boyce & Hart-produced sessions - were, in fact, Hart and some friends of his: "It was at this point that I was playing local clubs with what was left of Teddy Randazzo's band. Teddy stopped touring. That's the Candy Store Prophets. Jerry McGhee on guitar, Larry Taylor on bass, Billy Lewis on drums and myself on keyboards and vocals. We actually added two more guitars. Other demo musicians that we had worked with. One is a guy named Wayne Erwin because he knew how to play that psychedelic style that was just coming, Hendrix screeching guitar-stuff." The other was one Louie Shelton: "Louie was just a great all-around player. Whenever we were ready to do demos, we'd track him down - he'd be in Vegas or he'd be on the road somewhere. So we made sure Louie was there. So we had three guitar players."

Although The Monkees would sing over the tracks their

producers laid down, in the pilot episode they didn't even do that: "We had the three songs for the pilot show already demoed and when they shot the pilot they let the Monkees lip-synch to Tommy and me singing the songs, so the pilot show was sold to the sponsors and to the network with them lip-synching to our sound."

Though their songs helped get the show off the ground, Boyce & Hart were subsequently disappointed to be told that they would not, after all, be producing the music for the records that would be generated by the show. "When the show was finally sold and NBC was on board and some big sponsors like Yardley and Kellogg's and they had RCA records on board, at that point Donny Kirshner got involved. Of course, he was our big boss but he was in New York, wasn't involved in this at all until the project was sold. So then he flew out and he said, 'Look you guys, you have a track record as writers but not as producers. We got to bring in some name producers'." Why were two composers so desperate to produce? "We saw the potential of what this could be and we knew the money was going to be in the records and not in the television show. We just felt like we had been given the job originally by the producers of the show and we had the vision and we had been formulating it in our minds. We felt like we knew what to do better than anybody else." Even with no experience of producing? "We had - because songwriters do that for the demos. That's how you learn to produce. At least in the old days that was a great [method] for learning how to produce records. Even though you were using small scale studios and there were low budget dates, still we were going out and finding these great musicians that were just coming up that nobody else knew about and using them on our demos."

Kirshner's attempt to find a producer for The Monkees was not successful, with Mickie Most, Snuffy Garrett and Goffin & King all being recruited in this capacity and all producing results deemed unacceptable. "Finally," recalls Hart, "we're almost to the time where the show's gonna go on the air. We're like a month, six weeks ahead. And they had no album. Tommy was the front man, the spokesman and the really outgoing gregarious guy. He was always puling Donny's shirttails saying, 'Look, we created this whole thing, we know what the sound is. We can do this'. Our proposal to Donny was we would go in and rehearse in a cheap little dance hall studio somewhere and we'd worked up our arrangement of what we think the song should sound like and you just come down. It'll cost you nothing - come down and listen. So he did. He came down and listened to two or three songs and he was very impressed. He said, 'Okay, you guys got the job again'."

The Monkees by now were singing on the recordings. Boyce & Hart decided to use sighing-voiced drummer Micky Dolenz and mop-topped heart-throb Davy Jones for most of the lead vocals. Hart: "We saw Micky and Davy as the leads. We thought Michael [Nesmith] sounded too country and of course he was off in another studio across town doing his own tracks which we weren't really aware of until later on, so he was doing his own music. We didn't think that Peter [Tork] had much of a voice. We tried to work him in on one or two songs but it was really rough so we always just requested either Micky or Davy and we wrote songs with them in mind, one or the other. And got on great with each of them."

Dolenz and Jones can be said to have contributed to the writing of a Boyce & Hart song on that first album. The closer 'Gonna Buy Me A Dog' features the pair telling some cringe-makingly corny jokes to each other in between verses. "We had written that song the previous year. We wrote it for an act that we had produced called Gamagoochi. He had had a minor local hit. We cut it with him as a follow-up to another novelty song he had had but just with the straight lyrics, not with the jokes." Usually, the composers would not allow more than one Monkee in the studio at once because so much time was wasted clowning around: "We would prepare the tracks and all the background voices, have completely finished and in the evening when the show had wrapped we'd get one of the guys over to sing the lead. This particular time was the exception when we had Micky and Davy together that night and once again they started goofing off and cutting up and it happened to work 'cos it was a novelty song anyway. They just spontaneously did those [jokes]."

Apart from '(Theme From) The Monkees', the most important song on The Monkees' eponymous debut long player was 'Last Train To Clarksville', the song that broke the band by going to number one in late 1966, a success which, contrary to many memories, actually predated the success of the TV show, which took a while to be a ratings hit. Of 'Clarksville''s origin, Hart says, "I was flipping the dials on the radio and just as I was pulling in my driveway. 'Paperback Writer' came on, the first time I'd ever heard it. New release by The Beatles. I just heard the fade out of it: 'Paperback wri-i-iter..' and I thought, just from hearing it for a split second, they were saying 'Take the last train...' something. Of course, the next day it was all over the airwaves, had nothing to do with trains or last anything. So I said to Tommy, 'I think it's a good title: 'Take the last train to..' something. At that point we were well through producing the first album but we needed another song. So we sat down and we started tossing out ideas for last train to.. where? He said, 'Every summer you go up to northern Arizona. What were some little towns called up there?' So I named Cottonwood and Clarksdale... He said, 'Clarksdale - what's that? Let's try that: 'Last Train To Clarksdale'.' He said, 'How about Clarks*ville*?' I said, 'Okay, sounds better'. That's where it came from."

When the pair took the studio band in to rehearse it, the song still lacked the winding guitar riff for which it is now famous: "We said, 'Okay we need a 'Paperback Writer'-type lick for the intro'. Louie said, 'How about this one?' and just played it. Either he had rehearsed it or he just had it'." The record is also known for its unusual, elongated shivering hi-hat. Remembers Hart, "This stuff was all cut on four tracks so you're pretty much mixing as you go. You had to get it live in the studio and you had to capture it properly on tape. Dave Hassinger, who was the engineer on '..Clarksville', manually rode up the part that had the hi-hat. He rode it almost from midway up to the top of the threshold on every fourth beat of the hi-hat."

Though the record's Transatlantic chart success vindicated the decision to use '..Clarksville' as The Monkees entrée, the song's lack of pop immediacy still makes it seem a strange decision, particularly as the anthemic '(Theme From) The Monkees' would seem to have been perfectly suited for that role. "That's what I was pushing for," admits Hart. "I thought that would be the easiest sell because of the most exposure and so on. We turned in the album and we had a listening party in the studio with executives and promotion people from RCA Records and Don Kirshner and basically we'd narrowed it down to the '(Theme From) The Monkees', 'Take A Giant Step' - a Carole King/Gerry Goffin song - 'Last Train To Clarksville' and a Steve Venet/Tommy Boyce song, 'Tomorrow's Gonna Be Another Day'. I didn't say much 'cos we were playing the songs for all these executives. I think I may have voiced my opinion to Donny Kirshner privately but anyway at the end of the thing the executives said, 'Give us any one of those records and we'll make a top ten'. That made me feel a little better. I didn't really believe it at that point. I think Donny was the one who ultimately said, '..'Clarksville' first'. I think it was probably the most Beatle-esque of the four."

It was almost certainly the success of that debut which started the domino effect that made The Monkees, briefly, the most lucrative industry in America. Kids could not get enough of The Monkees' records, TV programme and merchandise. Hart got a taste of the Monkees' popularity when the Candy Store Prophets acted as support act on a Monkees tour (a somewhat surreal situation - the 'real' Monkees supporting the Monkees who overdubbed voices onto their work). "It was wild," says Hart of the experience. "It was pandemonium. A sea of screaming girls. It was fun. It was also dangerous at times. I remember getting trapped in a stairwell once and almost pushed against the railing and not knowing if I'm gonna get out of there alive. Having them rocking limousines almost to the point of getting turned over. But it was a good experience. At the end of that first tour, which was twelve cities or something like that, we played the Cow Palace in San Francisco and Tommy flew up. He had not seen what I had been seeing for several weeks. When he saw what went on at the Cow Palace that night, he burst into the dressing room afterwards and said, 'Forget these guys - you and I should be up there'. He cooked it up with our attorney at that point to get us a record deal and of course we were hot enough we could pretty much have named any label at that point."

Though The Monkees were massively popular amongst their fans, they were despised by the counter culture, considered the epitome of The Man muscling in on a phenomenon that was supposed to be the antithesis of the old, exploitative free market order. Boyce and Hart were unconcerned: "We didn't really take it that seriously. The unit sales were outpacing anything that had been seen up to that point. We shot from making $125 a week advance from Screen Gems to making hundreds of thousands. Our whole lives changed so we were not really that concerned if some of the people didn't appreciate it. We realised how many people were appreciating it."

Boyce & Hart, naturally, didn't have any part in the way the programme was made and, apart from writing songs to fit the characters of The Monkees, Hart admits that their songwriting took little account of the premise of the series or its situations: "We were just making records. We just cut the first Monkee album and handed it in and they used it however they could." This helps explain the central dichotomy of the series: The Monkees, in the programme, were a band who were perpetually out of work - yet the songs they were playing in the musical interludes were some of the classiest pop of the era. Logically, Boyce & Hart should have been making bad, or at least rough-and-ready music. "We didn't care," shrugs Hart. "It wasn't a serious drama or you had to be literal. This was just pure entertainment - guys running around as a vehicle to sing these well-crafted pop songs. It was MTV before MTV. It was half-hour long music videos." He also adds, "We never made more than a couple of dimes to rub together off the television show. That's why we wanted to make the best records possible - that's where all the money was."

Despite the success they had engendered, Boyce & Hart were

to be disappointed by Kirshner again over their production role: "We had already cut the second album and Donny Kirshner said, 'You didn't know this but I've had producers on the East Coast and other producers doing Monkee records and basically you're going to be get two cuts on the second album."

They could at least take consolation that '(I'm Not Your) Steppin' Stone', one of their songs from what would transpire to be the second Monkees album *More Of The Monkees*, would chart in late '66, even though it was technically the flipside of the Neil Diamond-written 'I'm A Believer': "We had written that in 1965 for Paul Revere and the Raiders," Hart explains. "We just saw it as a Raiders/Stones kind of thing that they might do... They had turned it down. So that's another song we had laying around. They subsequently ended up recording it after it was a hit by The Monkees. I still think The Monkees' version is the best. That's Tommy and me doing all the backgrounds and doing all the "Not me girl!" and all the shouts. Everything except the lead." The song was also the subject of an unlikely cover by the post-Johnny Rotten line-up of the Sex Pistols in 1980. "I was never much into punk," says Hart. "It was just interesting that they would do it at all. I can't say it's my favourite. I was surprised. In fact, I didn't even knew about it for maybe a year or two. It wasn't a hit in this country. Somebody made me aware of it and got me a copy sometime after the fact."

One of the Boyce/Hart songs pushed off that second album (the caustic 'She' was their other offering on the record) was a surprisingly progressive affair called 'Through The Looking Glass', written with Red Baldwin. Hart says that he and Boyce were in no way inhibited by the demographic at which the show was aimed: "And once again I think we had The Beatles to thank because they were continuing to expand and that gave us permission to do whatever we wanted as well. Our demographic was 3-18 year olds but that didn't stop us. We had the mandate from the beginning, 'This is the American Beatles'. So we felt able to be as free as we wanted to and experiment."

The disdain felt for The Monkees mentioned previously

eventually led the group - led by Michael Nesmith - to rise up against their employers and demand the right to play on their own records (all except Jones were musicians and songwriters).Many feel that the resulting, third, Monkees album *Headquarters* is their masterpiece and a vindication of their stand but Hart is scathing about the mutiny. "We just thought it was stupid and we still think it's stupid," he says. "Michael Nesmith still doesn't get it. He's still saying the same old thing. Even Davy Jones, the other hold-out, is saying, 'In retrospect we really short-circuited our careers. We could have gone on at least a couple more years if we had kept in place the unbelievable opportunity we had with the best and most successful staff writers and producers available to us'." Hart attributes the mutiny to, "..Nesmith's ego and over Peter Tork's unhappiness that he wasn't able to participate. I understand that more than I understand Nesmith because Peter Tork wanted to be a part of it creatively but he wasn't allowed to. Peter was really shut out. Mike was allowed to go in the studio and spend all the money he wanted with the top studio musicians, make all records he wanted to make. He got at least two cuts on the first album and he would have had cuts on every album. His songs would not have been the singles but he would have been buoyed along by the singles that would have been written by the pop craftsmen. Nesmith still said very recently, 'I like "...Clarksville" but pretty much all the rest of the music was crap'. It was like almost a slap in the face to the millions upon millions who bought those records."

Nevertheless, Boyce & Hart continued to contribute songs to each succeeding Monkees album. They also, in the shape of the soaring 'Valleri', gave them another hit single. It was a song with a slightly tortuous history. Originally featured in the show, it remained unissued on record until 1968 "The idea was that [The Monkees] were going to produce so those cuts that we had finished did not come out in the form that they were in and 'Valleri' was one of those cuts. It was just a great record, I think even better than the one that eventually went top ten, but later on after they had peaked and their careers were starting to wane a bit, Lester

Sill said, 'We gotta salvage "Valleri". It's a smash and they need a hit. But we can't put out that one because you guys are listed on the Musicians Union contract as the producers and you can't be listed as the producers. You've got to go back in and try to recreate the record and not take production credit this time'. That's what we did. We cut it as closely as possible to the first version."

Hart admits that things panned out well for he and Boyce, for it gave them the time to pursue properly the solo career that Boyce had instigated following that dizzying taste of Monkee-mania: "We both got into the business to be singers. We always wanted that. What kept us from being partners as singers was our diverse musical tastes. I was the last hold-out. They had to convince me that didn't matter. I should just go along and ride the bubblegum crest and tailor something for the audience we already had, 'cos we were already in all the teen magazines as the producers of The Monkees and so on. People knew us. That was our audience so we should tailor some records for that audience. I kind of went along at that point. They allowed me to do my token R&B imitations on a few cuts - that was it."

Tommy Boyce and Bobby Hart had three top forty hits: 'Out And About', 'I Wonder What She's Doing Tonite' and 'Alice Long (You're Still My Favorite Girlfriend)'. "We finally hit our stride with 'I Wonder What She's Doing Tonite' and should have been smart enough just to stick with that but we kept experimenting and doing all other kinds of things. Our two biggest hits were right in that vein: 'I Wonder..' and 'Alice Long'. Both featured Tommy's rhythm guitar and uptempo fun pop music."

Nevertheless, Hart says, "Our careers were actually building quite nicely. We hired this really high-powered manager and renegotiated our deal with Screen Gems, which included our own record label and included a sitcom development deal for Tommy and I. That's when they put us to guest star in all the shows that they had running at the time: *Bewitched, I Dream Of Jeannie, Flying Nun*. And they were giving us acting lessons and developing our own show. This manager also got us a deal to headline the main room of the Flamingo at Vegas. Of course, we didn't have the name to draw so we had to hire a better known name so we hired Zsa Zsa Gabor. We had her singing a little bit. She's not much of a singer but she was a name. She'd come out and she'd do a couple of numbers with us where we dressed up in tails and she was in a hippy outfit. Reversal of roles and stuff. And then the comedian who opened the show, Sandy Baron, would come out and take questions from the audience for her. It was a good show, we got good reviews. It cost us quite a bit to mount and the plan was to recoup it by touring that show for a while."

It was not to be. A brush with the seamier side of the music industry devastated Boyce and caused him to quit music. Hart: "The manager basically embezzled money at the end of '69 and he took advances on our Vegas money and gambled it away at the tables and left town. It was kind of a mess. Tommy really looked on him on a personal level like he was our Colonel Tom Parker kind of a guy and they had this relationship. Tommy felt so betrayed at that point that he just walked away from the business even though we had all ready to go. We were supposed to tour Europe with Zsa Zsa. He was devastated and said, 'That's it, I'm out of the business'. We had to give a lot of money back to Screen Gems because we were not going to fulfil some of the things we'd contracted to do, including the sitcom."

Boyce's retirement from the music business in December 1969 was something Hart admits he was shocked by. "But then I - it didn't take me long - hooked up with another partner named Danny Janssen". Hart and Janssen worked on a variety of different projects, one of which was The Monkees-like music related TV programme The Partridge Family: "We did a lot of songs for The Partridge Family. None of the hits actually but we had songs on almost every album. Tommy and I had been offered to produce The Partridge Family and that was another thing we had to give up. They gave it to Wes Farrell. Danny and I began a relationship in the Seventies for Wes where we gave him the publishing on all our songs in return for him keeping us working as producers continually."

Hart's change of partner didn't necessitate a change in

composing technique. "It was the same thing. He had written songs totally on his own. He had had four or five big hits with Bobby Sherman that he had written by himself and so it was the same kind of collaboration. We both did melody, both did lyric." The pair also collaborated on songs for a children's puppet and live action series called *Sigmund And The Sea Monster* and the animated series about a female rock group *Josie And The Pussycats*. "*Josie And The Pussycats* was a project Danny Jansen was already working on when he called me up and said, 'Let's try to do some stuff together' so I got in on the tail-end of that. He'd done several projects for Hanna Barbera: *Scooby Doo* and others. So I did write two songs for *Josie And The Pussycats*." Their involvement in this area led to success in a more adult field. "He said, 'I'm doing all these cartoons and there's not much money in it but I've come up with some great studio singers who sing all these cartoon things. One in particular is Austin Roberts. I think that he can have hits and why don't we try to write a session for him and go in on spec and record him and try to sell him?' That was our first project after the cartoon. We took it to Wes and he put him on his Chelsea Records and it was a top ten record. It was called 'Something's Wrong With Me'."

This in turn led to a hit with Helen Reddy. Hart's and Jansen's follow-up for Roberts was the emotional 'Keep On Singing'. "It was about a singer's relationship with a father," says Hart. "Danny had lost his father and I think it was partly autobiographical from his point of view although I didn't see it that way at the time. I was just trying to write a story song and make it as interesting as possible." By coincidence, Reddy's own father had recently passed away: "Helen was on the road, heard the song on the radio and mentioned to her husband: 'Keep an eye on this record'. She said, 'If this doesn't go top ten or number one or something, I want to cut it', and she did."

Another person Hart collaborated with during this period was the film scorer Dominic Fronterei, with whom he was paired by Lester Sill. "I said, 'Okay, I'll meet with him'. He said, 'I do all these movies and I write theme songs for them but I want to do more commercial theme songs and have record success with some of this stuff'." Fronterei gave Hart a tape of a melody. Hart's first experience of trying to fit a lyric to an already written tune was a painful experience: "It was just like a mathematical puzzle to me to try to put a syllable to every note and make it sound conversational and make it sound melodic and make it tell a story. I've done a lot of it since. Over twenty or thirty years, I think I've learned how to do it a little bit but it's always hard."

Hart has worked extensively in the area of film music. "I was Dominic Fanteri's lyricist for two or three years. People would call me up basically. Usually, for the motion picture things they would come through the composer and so there would usually be melodies and I would just be asked to furnish lyrics. I've done that for a number of movie composers, one particularly, Alan Reeves, who is pretty busy. He does three or four films a year and he'll call me for a lyric every now and then."

Meanwhile, Hart's partnership with Janssen eventually led to a form of burn-out for both of them. "We were overworked as producers and didn't have time to really keep up with the quality. That first couple of years, we wrote a song a week. Fifty songs a year plus producing that many sides and more so it was hard to maintain the quality and keep that output up. Also around '75, Danny started losing energy. He had made some good investments in real estate and he was not getting around to write that often. The partnership had run its course basically. It was just at that point when the Dolenz, Jones, Boyce & Hart project came along."

The pairing of two Monkees and their original producers Hart mentions came about when a tour manager friend of Hart's came back from the Far East with news of possible work. "He said, 'There's a big promoter in Thailand who would really love to book The Monkees. What's happening, are they around?' So I called Micky and he said, 'Well nobody's around. Davy's kind of around. I haven't seen Peter for years. Michael isn't interested in touring'. So [the tour manager] took that information back and then came back next time with, 'They'd be interested - what about you and Tommy and Micky and Davy? They'd be interested in booking the four of you'. So I called up Micky and Davy and we had lunch and discussed it. We said, well maybe, we could give it a shot, see what happens, if the money's good."

Then something strange occurred. The Monkees, who had disbanded to a chorus of ridicule in 1971 - at which point Jones and Dolenz had been the only surviving members - suddenly found that they were no longer has-beens. "Once we said yes, then these other promoters started coming out of the woodwork and started promoting in the States," recalls Hart. "The first place we got booked was an amusement park, St Louis. That first gig, 23,000 kids showed up so that was kind of when we knew there was a market still there." Of the success of the tour - which was billed as "The Golden Great Hits Of The Monkees Show - The Guys Who Wrote 'Em And The Guys Who Sang 'Em" - Hart admits, "We were surprised because at that point we still didn't know. It was still a really looked down on rip-off kind of a project and it was never hip to admit you were a Monkee fan even ten years later. This was our first indication that there were these Monkee fans out there. Even though it wasn't hip to admit it, they'd come out to concerts. We ended up touring that whole summer of '75, into '76 and waiting for this South East Asia tour to materialise, which ended up being about the last thing we did together."

Hart says he wasn't surprised that Tommy Boyce was prepared to come out of retirement and take part: "By then he had tried two or three other careers and was needing money. He went through some real changes. When he quit the business he changed his name to David Tucker and moved to the beach and got a business card printed up: 'David Tucker - Poet'. Then he had put together a group called Christopher Cloud that he was lead singer of. Nothing was really happening so he was up for something by then. The point was it was such an easy gig. We knew the songs, didn't have to learn anything. It was just, go out there and do it and have fun. It was Boyce & Hart songs too [though] we didn't have as many." Hart also admits that the reason he and Boyce were given equal billing was a legal one: "We weren't allowed to go out as 'The Monkees'."

So successful was the project that it engendered an album, *Dolenz, Jones, Boyce and Hart*, released in 1976. For Hart, it felt like being in the studio in 1965 for those first Monkees sessions: "We brought together some of the same musicians. It was Tommy's and my first time to really enjoy writing like we had been doing in the 'Sixties together. We encouraged Micky and Davy to write for the project as well, which they did." For their part, the pair tried to write in the old Monkees style for the album.

"It could have gone on," Hart insists of the project. "The record deal was the blow, probably. We got a good record deal with Al Corey, who was at Capitol and he was really into the project and then just about the same week that the album came out he went to RSO so there was nobody there to nurture that project and it kind of fell apart."

Hart would have been happy to continue his rekindled composing partnership with Boyce but immediately after the Dolenz, Jones, Boyce and Hart project, Boyce moved to England. "He had kind of a dysfunctional father," Hart explains. "His father was always his biggest supporter but his biggest fly in the ointment emotionally. It was kind of draining. I think he moved to get away from him frankly. He felt like starting over. He did that many times in his career: he just wanted to start with a clean slate, not tell anybody who he was and just be somebody totally different." In England, Hart says Boyce "..changed his name again - this was about his fifth name change - to Tommy Fortune - and didn't tell anybody about his past success or anything. Tried to make it as a songwriter over there. He was playing some little coffee house, just him and his guitar. Finally, somebody said, 'Don't you know you have a top ten record right now?' Somebody who recognised who he was." UK 'Fifties revivalists Showaddywaddy took Boyce's early hit 'Under The Moon of Love' to number one in their home country in 1976 (and would have another UK top five with his 'Pretty Little Angel Eyes' a couple of years later). "So then he said, 'Oh I can't fight it' and he walked into Rondor Music Publishing and told them who he was and got a writing deal. But he kept his name Tommy Fortune."

Hart himself continued to find gainful employment: "After Dolenz, Jones, Boyce and Hart I wrote mainly with a guy named Barry Richards and Austin Roberts. Wrote for a lot of European acts." At that point, the same friend who had secured the interest in The Monkees which led to the "Golden Greats.." tour introduced Hart to some people at MCA Records. "A professional manager over there said, 'There's a couple of writers, if you'd be interested in co-writing? You can keep your half of the publishing'. So he hooked me up with a guy named Dick Eastman and he and I pretty much ended up being exclusive songwriters for most of the Eighties. Not with a lot of success but we did write pretty prolific and we ended up with five or six New Edition songs. One of them charted, the others were just album cuts." New Edition were a bunch of preternaturally stage-slick black kids rather in the manner of the Jackson 5. Recalls Hart, "They had had some pretty good success on a little tiny label down South and they had been bought out of that label or somehow gotten out of it by new management. This was going to be their major label debut. The manager looked me up because he knew my background [with] young music and asked if we would write. The first song we wrote was kind of Jackson 5-ish, 'My Secret'. Then we got to know them. We wrote with them actually on a couple of songs because the management was trying to encourage them to write." Hart did end up writing for a real Jackson, albeit one generally considered an ersatz one. After being contacted by BMG in Germany for material, he ended up producing one side for LaToya Jackson with moderate success.

Perhaps inevitably, the biggest money spinner Hart wrote during this period was a Monkees song: "We heard that they were putting out a repackage of The Monkees in '86 and that they were going to include a couple of originals, so we did something real quick and mailed it to Clive Davis at Arista Records. He woke me up early next morning and said, 'We were only going to do two but we wanna do this song too'. So [they] included the third song on the *Then And Now* album, which was a platinum album. It's called 'Anytime, Anyplace, Anywhere'."

1983 saw Hart and Austin Roberts being nominated for an academy award for 'Over You', which they composed for the film *Tender Mercies*. Hart: "The main character had an ex-wife who was a country singer so whenever they would cut to her singing in a nightclub or something, she'd be singing this song. That's what it was needed for." Of the Oscar ceremony, Hart says, "That was fun. Even though we didn't win, it was fun to sit the in the middle of all those stars." For the record, 'Over You' lost out to 'Can You Feel It' from *Flashdance*.

By this time, Hart had been in the music industry for more than two decades, ones in which huge changes had occurred in popular music. He says he never found it difficult to acclimatize to changed circumstances: "I never find anything hard to adapt to. Once they told me to go home and write songs and I did, I always approached it as just whatever anybody asked me to do. Tommy and I were like short order cooks in the 'Sixties. Dick Clark would call us up and say, 'I have a pilot and I need a theme song and I need it recorded by tomorrow afternoon'. We'd spend the night writing it and we'd run in and record it next morning. It was just try to fill the needs, whatever they are, and we always approached pop songwriting exactly like that. And on into the Eighties. There's certain types of music I never cared for and didn't want to participate in that much but I have done heavy metal projects, I've done just about [everything]. I did an album, co-produced and wrote lyrics and some of the melodies for a group called Red Satyr which came out mid-Nineties."

Of modern technology, he opines, "Everything's good if it's used in the right way. In the Eighties, when it was all synthesizer-driven and drum machines came in and all, is about that time when I put in my own studio in the house. You have to keep up with the times, learn how to programme the synthesizers and the sequencer and the drum machines." However, he does concede, "It's just a whole different way of working. It's just so tedious. We're doing master quality demos of this musical we're working on and thank God I have a young partner who's in his early thirties and just sits down there and does this stuff. You have so many choices and you're one note at a time and one guy's doing almost everything. It was much more fun in the old days when you went in with a studio full of musicians and three hours later you came out with four finished songs."

Tragically, Tommy Boyce - who wrote a highly regarded book about songwriting called *How To Write A Hit Song And Sell It* - took his own life on November 23, 1994. Hart observes, "People think that he took his life because he was depressed and it wasn't that so much as the fact that he had had a brain aneurism burst the year before and he was kind of being nursed back to health but they told him that that was a genetic defect that would definitely happen again and he probably wouldn't be as lucky the next time or one time. That he maybe could end up a vegetable. So he took it in his own hands not to let that happen."

Since he started writing nearly four decades ago, how does Hart feel the craft of songwriting has changed? "It's all different now. The writing is now all done by the producers and the artist - not all of course, there are exceptions but by and large producers and artists control the recording business from the artistic standpoint and it's got to suffer a little because when it was specialised and you had people like us who did nothing but learn the craft of writing and then passed it on to somebody else to sing, that specialisation made for a little more excellence, I believe. There are people who can do it all too, but also a lot of acts that probably could have bigger hits if they had just people who made their living just writing songs. The major publishers, they sign the artists, they sign the producers these days, they don't just sign people who only write."

Asked what he considers the best and worst songs he's written, Hart replies, "The worst songs you'll never hear. I think 'Let's Dance On' was pretty much of a throwaway to appear on an album that's sold so many millions. As far as the best, I'm most partial to 'Hurts So Bad' because it was top ten three times by three different artists. I like the Monkees things, especially, '..Clarksville' and 'Stepping Stone'. I'm still proud of 'I Wonder What She's Doing Tonite' - that stands up pretty well for me.

Which is kind if how I judge it. It's how they still sound after thirty years, if they're still entertaining or not. 'Days Of Our Lives' still sounds good, still sounds like a piece of soap opera music after thirty five years."

Despite his ongoing success in many different composing fields, Hart will almost certainly be remembered for a TV show that ran for a mere two seasons in the mid-'Sixties: "I've been nominated for a golden globe or for a Academy Award, for a Grammy, [but] I know that anybody who sees me or knows anything about my background will always see me as the guy who produced The Monkees. That's how I'll always be known." However, he asserts, "I don't think that I ever lost an opportunity because of my stereotype." He also adds, "I feel vindicated now that this many years later so many hip rock acts came out of the closet and say how they were influenced by The Monkees. They say things like they were as influential on them as The Beatles. It's not unhip anymore to be a Monkee fan after all these years."

7

JOEY LEVINE

Joey Levine accidentally invented a new form of music.

When 'Yummy, Yummy, Yummy', the song he co-wrote with partner Artie Resnick, became a Transatlantic smash in 1968 for the Ohio Express, it set the template for bubblegum, a form of pop aimed at a younger demographic than any pop before and which unashamedly operated on a level that its target audience could understand and identify with: bright tunes, nursery rhyme-like choruses and lyrics oriented around issues close to children's hearts such as sweets and games. Incongruously, the music itself featured flawless instrumentation, the consequence of a philosophy which assumed that kids weren't going to agonise about who played on a record and which therefore made it logical to use quick - and skilled - session musicians. Though Jerry Kasenetz and Jeff Katz, proprietors of the Super K Production Company which bought the song and marketed the record, are also key figures in the story, it is a story which almost certainly would not have taken place without Levine's creative contribution.

Joey Levine was born in The Bronx, New York on May 29th 1947, though grew up in Long island from the age of four. He came from a musical family. "My mother was a big band singer and my father led some big bands in the army and was an arranger and a pianist," he says. Not surprisingly, Levine himself got the music bug at a young age, initially playing piano, then moving onto guitar. He agrees with the accepted wisdom that composing is easier on piano than guitar but says his own keyboard skills are "..not good. Just enough to write. It's not like I'd sit down at a party and start to play 'Moon River'."

Levine's ambitions to be a songwriter developed early too: "I always loved music and I was one of those guys that would know all the writing credits on a song and would know all the label information. Kind of like a buff, like some guys would be in baseball and know all the players and their stats." He wrote his first songs "..probably around twelve, thirteen. I had even played them for some people in the business who had told me that musically I was alright but lyrically I was needing some experience. I had started to show songs at an early age, around Tin Pan Alley."

Levine went through the graduation rites of just about every musician of his generation: learning his chops in garage bands brought into existence by the galvanising effect of the success of The Beatles: "I was playing in bands when I was around fifteen. We were doing rock, we were doing pop. I had one band that did a lot of Beatle covers. I was in a number of bands who used to just work out and play cover songs that were popular at the time. You'd have a band or a different name of a band every couple of months and a couple of different guys you'd always rehearse with and get a playlist together with." However, Levine showed a creativity that marked him out from the bog standard musician destined for a 'real' job once their musical dabblings and their formal education were over: "On certain jobs, I'd start to make up my own songs. I'd just make 'em up as I went along. Like the guy in *The Beach* that visits you, comes up to you on an island and makes songs up on the spot. A lot of times people would even request songs that I'd written and I thought, 'What song was that? How did that go?'"

Levine's talent and, perhaps more importantly, his initiative got his foot on the bottom rung of the career ladder at an earlier age than most would-be songwriters. His haunting of publishers' offices ensured that his precocious talent was known of within the industry while he was still literally a schoolboy. As was the norm for the time, he would be paired with other writers. "A lot of publishers would recognise something in me and would team me up with people," he recalls. "It would just be: try to combine two talents and see what became of it. See if any magic happened. I used to take off from school as soon as I could to go down to different writers that publishers would put me with. It was a lot of fun... I wrote with Pete Anders and Vinny Ponci quite a bit when I was really young. They may have recorded one or two of my things with groups they were producing." By the age of sixteen, Levine had written with such celebrated - and soon to be celebrated - names as Chip Taylor, Carol Bayer, Estelle Levitt and Doc Pomus. "I was teamed together with guys who were having hit songs," he explains. "Publishers would sometimes say I was incomplete in myself of writing songs. I lacked lyrical experience or they thought somebody could add things so they put me together with different writers who they felt were successful. I can't say I wrote anything popular with them." Levine can't recall these collaborators - all inevitably far older than him - expressing resentment at being made to write with a mere kid: "I think they were open to whatever worked and they were professional songwriters. They came every day. They had their office, their cubicle, whatever, and they wrote. Their day was made up of writing so I think everybody was just willing to try to catch lightning in whatever way they could." However, he does add, "Sometimes we'd open up the page to write and it'd be, 'So whataya got?' So they'd kind of look to me. I think that even if they had an idea of where they wanted to go, it was like, 'Well, that's a good idea I have on my own - maybe I'll write that with someone else'. A lot of times, I would lead the way because they felt like it was for me to prove what I had rather for them to prove what they had."

He recalls that Doc Pomus - co-writer of such legendary songs as 'A Teenager In Love' and 'Marie's The Name (His Latest Flame)' - had idiosyncratic working techniques: "Doc, would throw out a title. 'I got a great title: "One Man Woman". Let's write something like that. Let's write an R&B song'. So I'd sit and write and Doc would kind of just talk on the phone and stuff and then he'd scribble some lines and hand them to me."

Though Levine was pleased to be working with 'name' writers, he was not so overawed that it affected his sense of realism. "Certain people, even if they'd be big, it wouldn't click," he states, matter-of-factly. "Personalities or writing styles, it wouldn't click. It's kind of like a feeling-out process and in the feeling out, do you want to continue writing with that person? Sometimes, even if the guy had a name and had had a hit or two, if I didn't feel it myself, the flow would be like, 'Well I don't really want to get back together'. And it wasn't just one way: it's like, 'Ah, kid's not really got it for me..' What worked felt good and what didn't work, it was like: next."

Levine's grafting was having an incremental rather than spectacular effect. "I had placed some songs with some artists," he recalls. "There was a singer, Ronnie Dove, that had a couple of hits and I had a song out with Joanie Summers and I had a song out by a guy named John DiAndrea and Gene Pitney, people like that. I didn't really make much money on them. I'd have records by artists who a lot of time were artists who hadn't made a name for themselves yet or artists that maybe were not as popular, because when the British Invasion came in a lot of these artists that were looking for material weren't happening as much anymore." Asked what were his favourite artists at the time, Levine says, "I loved the Beatles and I loved a lot of the English groups. The Searchers. I'd grown up a lot with the Four Seasons - not that I really loved their style but those were the groups that were happening at the time. I liked Presley but at that point he was a little older, his sound [was] that corny country Vegas stuff. I tried to write a lot of things in a Beatle mode - and a lot of that stuff ended up not getting recorded. A little melodic and songs that I felt were more expressive lyrically and a little further out but there was not artists that covered those things."

During this time, Levine harboured desires to be a performer but not particularly intense ones. "I had always thought of being an artist myself but I never thought I had quite a style that I thought I wanted to go out as an artist with," he explains. "Some of the songs I would write which I really liked, it didn't fit my singing style. The songs that I could sing I thought weren't songs that I wanted to put my own name on." He eventually decided that he could bear to be linked with a composition of his called 'Down And Out', which he released as a single in 1965 under the name Joey Vine. He was seventeen. "A lot of people really liked the demos at publishing houses and a lot of times they would either buy the demos to put out as records or I would get cover records," he recalls. "'Down And Out' is the first thing I put out on Hercules Records, which is a company that Al Galico had, who was a big music publisher."

In the absence of proper chart hits, Levine was making money from music in a rather roundabout and nebulous way: "I would write songs each week at home, come into the city and live off advances for my songs," he explains. "I'd go in with maybe five or six songs and maybe I could get advances on three of four of them. $150, $200 there. Pick up some money and pick up different relationships with different publishers."

In 1967, 'Try It', a song Levine had written with Mark Bellack, the drummer of a band he was fronting, achieved almost enough notoriety to become a *bona fide* hit. Placed with a band called The Standells - then little known but now semi-legendary through their iconic status amongst those who revere the American mid-'Sixties garage band scene immortalized by such compilations as Lenny Kaye's *Nuggets* - the song's sexual innuendoes were just a little too racy for the time. "There was a disc jockey in California, B. Mitchell Reed, who liked the record," Levine remembers. "Apparently the legal department thought it was a little risqué so he bleeped out certain things in the song and the bleeping actually added to the fascination with the song. 'By the way you look I can tell that you want some action' - stuff like that. It was just a risqué song. It was basically about, 'Let's just try having sex' - but at the time it was so obvious what you were talking about, it sounded objectionable." Bearing in mind Levine's tender years,

what did his mother and father think of the furore? "I don't think
my parents really batted an eye about it," he states. "They thought
it was kind of ridiculous. I didn't really think it was an obscene
song. It was just a teenage song." Unfortunately, the very raciness
that garnered the record attention and sales was probably what
prevented it from making a significant commercial breakthrough.
"It charted for a long time," says Levine. "It went to number one
in California, it was number one in Florida, maybe two other places.
It never seemed to pick up the national momentum at the same
time which I think if it would have it would have been a charted
record. I can't say that I saw a lot of money from it."

Levine's commercial breakthrough came when he hooked up
with lyricist Artie Resnick, although they didn't achieve immediate
success. Resnick had hits like The Drifters' 'Under The
Boardwalk' and The Young Rascals' 'Good Lovin'' to his name.
It was another publisher-suggested team-up, this time Irwin
Schuster acting as the matchmaker. "Artie had been writing with
Kenny Young," says Levine. "Kenny and Artie had been having
a lot of success but Kenny was more of a producer and he moved
to London so their partnership split up. Artie was in need of a
music person and I was in need of a lyricist. Irwin says, 'There's
this kid that comes up here and he's pretty good. Maybe you guys
should try a couple of songs' and it kind of just clicked because he
was such a clever lyricist. He kind of filled in the other side of it."
As with his other collaborations, there was a big difference in
age: "I think that Artie was probably around 12, 13, 14 years older
than I was." The two writers gelled artistically fairly quickly and
even got a good record with one of their songs when 'Patty Cake'
was accepted as the next single for The Capitols, who had just a
top ten hit with 'Cool Jerk'. "The first song that I really felt like I
was gonna have a hit," Levine remembers. "But the record
bombed."

Artie Resnick was also writing with his wife Kris and the
Resnicks and Levine would collaborate, either in pairs or as a
threesome. This led to the Third Rail project, which saw the three
record a folkie album called *ID Music* (1967). Levine: "It was

based on some records that Teddy Cooper had heard of ours. Ted Cooper produced a couple of hit records and Teddy was a friend of Artie's. Teddy was the executive producer on that. He liked the sound of my voice and suggested we do a project together." The resulting music was perhaps the most weighty of Levine's career: "We tried to do a project that was based on political and current kind of issues. I don't know if it was protest music as much as commentary on the time." To add to the air of gravitas, the well-known arranger (and songwriter) Al Gorgoni was commissioned to write string charts. "We had quite few musicians on there. There was a lot of strings. There was a kind of Beatle-esque approach to things." However, Levine adds, "All the songs tried to not be that serious." A single 'Run Run Run' - an anti-rat race themed song - received some airplay and became a moderate hit.

Though the lack of success of subsequent singles led to the record company not picking up the option for a second album, that semi-success with 'Run Run Run' was a good omen for the new Joey Levine-Artie Resnick songwriting team and in 1967 it truly seemed they had hit the jackpot when they were informed that one of their creations had been accepted for use by The Monkees, then probably second only to The Beatles in terms of record sales. Jeff Barry was acting as the producer for some sessions for the band that had been created as America's answer to the Fab Four and who effectively had free commercials for their records broadcast every week via their syndicated TV show. "Jeff was a good friend of Artie's," says Levine, "and he said, 'Doing stuff with this group and why don't you do it?' It was such a big gig, he was certainly not gonna give it away but he did include us and said, 'These are the kind of things we're looking for and you're welcome to do stuff'."

The composition which received a favourable reception from Barry was 'If I Could Play The Violin'. "It was basically this thing of, 'I'm not accepted by your parents but if I learned to play the violin maybe they would look more kindly on me'," Levine says of the song. "It was slated for a particular show and then there was a possibility of it reaching an album." Levine also collaborated with Barry for 'Gotta Give It Time' and 'Eve Of My Sorrow' for the Monkees project. 'If I Learned To Play The Violin' even got as far as a finished recording - Davy Jones was the Monkee who sang lead - before extraordinary developments in the Monkees camp scuppered its chances. Though Levine remembers the song falling from grace a little because the producers of the show began to insist on songs specific to scenes ("They started writing certain songs which they thought might be included in storylines: they'd send out the script and say, 'A song here about something like this'"), the palace revolution instigated by The Monkees after two albums is probably the main reason for the song never seeing the light of day. The Monkees, unhappy that they were not allowed to play on the recordings that bore their name, threatened to quit. The people behind the show acquiesced to their demands for self determination and Barry was replaced as producer.

Levine, personally, took the setback in his stride. "It was very optimistic to get something - they were so hot - but I always thought of it as a long shot," he reasons. "It was disappointing only 'cos you had your hopes up but it was a long shot that Jeff was really gonna say, 'Yeah, you're in'." After that false start, came the real breakthrough for Levine & Resnick. The Ohio Express were a band managed and produced by New Yorkers Jeff Katz and Jerry Kasenetz and had released a version of 'Try It' as their second single. "It seemed that through the 'Try It' record, the Ohio Express guys got in touch with me and I didn't really get back to them," says Levine. Resnick, noting that the group had achieved top forty success with their first single, 'Beg, Borrow And Steal', arranged a meeting with Kasenetz and Katz. The first song the pair played them at said meeting was a composition called 'Yummy, Yummy, Yummy'. "Actually we had written 'Yummy, Yummy..' for Jay and the Techniques who had just had a song, 'Apple Peaches Pumpkin Pie' and they turned it down," Levine points out. Kasenetz and Katz, however, thought the song perfect to their needs. "We went in the studio that week," says Levine. "They gave us a band that they'd been cutting records with and we cut the record and the record was out like a week later."

That the pair met with such a good reception from the proprietors of Super K was due to the fact that their song could be aimed at a particular and hitherto ignored demographic. "Kasenetz and Katz had said there was an area of music that wasn't being covered and that music had become kind of serious *and* folkie and there was a place for some younger music, a younger market," says Levine. "This sound started to develop out of this niche that they felt there was an audience for." The sound in question became known generically as bubblegum and became one of the biggest musical phenomena of the late-'Sixties music scene. Bubblegum's lyrics - as in the case of 'Yummy, Yummy, Yummy' - often centered around sweets and - also as in the case of 'Yummy, Yummy, Yummy' - were often not as innocent as they initially sounded. "It seems like a lot of our songs that Artie and I would write had sexual innuendoes," says Levine, "and it may have been based on the fact that 'Try It' kind of had that. Me being of an age of precociousness and everything, it was a subject that was on my mind yet didn't feel quite comfortable enough to write it in different ways so wrapped it up in this syrupy way."

Yet another part of the bubblegum template that 'Yummy..' helped set was the way that the producers could afford to not worry about integrity or truth when it came to the issue of the act to whom a record was credited. The Ohio Express' debut had actually been recorded by the Rare Breed and released under their name but subsequently reissued and attributed to the Express when the original record had flopped. Kasenetz and Katz realised that the kind of individual likely to buy 'Yummy, Yummy, Yummy' was so young that they could pull something similar. Firstly, the record was played not by the Ohio Express but by session musicians. Secondly, the person singing the track was not Doug Grassel, the Express' vocalist, but Levine himself. The sound of Levine's distinct nasally voice on the demo he produced had impressed both Kasenetz and Katz and Neil Bogart, head of Buddah Records, to whom the record was sold. Levine: "Neil Bogart heard it and said, 'You can't take that guy off of it. That guy's got a great sound. He makes the record...' So Jeff and Jerry convinced me and they threw me like a point on the record for singing it..'' Instead of asking Levine to record a proper vocal take, Super K simply grafted his demo performance onto the session musicians' efforts. "The background's flat and everything," Levine laments. "It was just a guide track put down for the group for them to replace." Levine also points out that he didn't even know for sure that his voice was going to be on the record until he heard it on the airwaves: "I knew there was a talk of it but I didn't know until I actually heard it on the radio going home to my parents' house one day. I was driving and before I got into the midtown tunnel they said, 'Pick hit of the week, 'Yummy Yummy Yummy' by the Ohio Express'. It was like - 'Wow! Just cut that record last week.' I didn't even know that the record company liked it or that it was going to be anything."

These almost farcical circumstances didn't hinder the record's success in any way. In mid-1968 'Yummy, Yummy, Yummy' climbed to number four in the US charts. It also reached number 5 in the UK, though the latter was - apart from the success of 'Simple Simon' by the 1910 Fruitgum Co., another act from the Super K stable - the only notable impression bubblegum made on the British consciousness. "It took off right away," Levine notes of 'Yummy''s chart performance. "I hadn't had any experience with having a big hit. Up at that point it was just kind of a dream to have a top ten record."

Levine would become the regular lead vocalist on Ohio Express records, something about which he felt ambivalent. "Kasenetz and Katz owned the Ohio Express and owned the name so they felt I guess, 'Well we can do anything we want to do'." Did he feel sorry for the real Ohio Express and, in particular, Grassel, who had to lip-synch on TV appearances to another person's voice? "Yes I did! It was like, 'Boy these guys kind of lost their gig. They go on the road, they gotta sing these songs' and I'm sure that they resented it quite a bit. Like, 'Hey, we were doing just fine'. I never even knew if they even liked those songs. 'Cos later on the Fruitgum Co., the lead singer, started to get involved in his albums and write his own material and it was so different than what he was doing [before]. 'Cos he hated what was being put out under his name and he wanted to turn it around so he started to write what he wanted, which was so counter to what he was doing in a single recording light that it was like he never had a chance to turn the corner unless he would have just changed his group name and his identity almost."

Inevitably, Levine was asked to supply the follow-up to 'Yummy, Yummy, Yummy'. He and Kris Resnick came up with 'Down At Lulu's', a pumping celebration of a fictional music venue. The record sold disappointingly, only climbing to number 33 in the US. Levine wasn't too surprised. "I didn't think it was as strong a song," he states. "'Yummy, Yummy..' just had something about it the second you heard it. It just attracted you. 'Down At Lulu's' seemed like just a regular song... Certain things you would just hear and you would just know immediately, 'Boy, something about that. Good or bad, there's something about it'."

Levine accepted the lesson learnt quite quickly. The third single presented to the Ohio Express was 'Chewy, Chewy'. "It was like, try to get back to a formula," Levine admits. "At that time in the record business, the follow-up record would almost sound identical to the [first] record."'Chewy Chewy' - another half-innocent, half-sly song with a melody as clinging as a piece of gum - featured a short, wordless vocal hook sung in falsetto. Levine acknowledges that this became a trademark of his songwriting in that period: "A lot of little background things, silly little background hooks that I don't know whether they were written in to begin with but as the session came about. It's a riff."

The B-side of 'Chewy Chewy' was 'Firebird', a piece of classy pop that proved great work can result from base motives: "Jeff and Jerry, who were pretty extreme business guys, had gotten a thing offered to them to put out records [to promote] products. So they came to us and said, 'Would you write some car songs because we'll get 'em out and if we get them released, we get money from the car companies?' I know Artie and I never saw any of that money but we released the song 'Firebird'."

Over the next couple of years, Levine, usually with one of the Resnicks, gave the Ohio Express such hits as 'Sweeter Than Sugar', 'Mercy' and 'Pinch Me (Baby Convince Me)', all adhering to that bubblegum formula but all, in their way, the output of a pop production line as thoughtful as Motown's. With Super K also racking up hits with the 1910 Fruitgum Co. and other assorted groups (said records almost all played by the same session band), it was a pop production line which, also like Motown, was a phenomenon. Like any phenomenon, it attracted a large array of bandwagon jumpers like The Cuff Links, Tommy Roe and The Archies. The genre definition has also retroactively been given to The Monkees and Tommy James and the Shondells simply because of the young demographic/session musicians factors. However, The Monkees and the Shondells actually predated the first bubblegum records.

Levine was intimately involved in every aspect of making the records, taking the burden of production on his young shoulders: "I'd be involved in all areas of the making of the record, from the arrangement to the mixes, I followed the whole production through." Levine feels that the intricate nature of his demonstration tapes made the move into formal production inevitable: "It's like, 'The guy has a good feeling for production'. A lot of the demos I would do with music publishers, they would always like the production sounds and the things that came out of them." Levine says of his production method: "They're rhythm- oriented. There's also that eighth kind of feel and that push. Bo Gentry's record of 'Mony Mony' [recorded by Tommy James and the Shondells] is a conscious effort to do what I was doing - that feel, that drive." Levine took as much enjoyment from orchestrating events in the studio as he did from the actual composition: "I loved the process of being involved and in the studio and participating and playing or jumping up and down or conducting."

As with any production line, the atmosphere at Super K could be rather intense. "You'd go into an office and you'd write," Levine remembers. "There'd be assignments and sometimes they'd have groups: 'You've gotta write for this group or this guy'. You'd write on certain days, you'd have your rhythm section on certain days, you'd overdub on certain days. Each creative group under their banner worked to schedules and recorded their songs. You'd be given your schedule: 'Here's when you have the studio'."

Levine recalls the main contribution of Kasenetz and Katz as being great cheerleaders: "Obviously, you were their meal ticket. They would cheer you on: 'You gotta do this, you gotta do that, we need this, we need that'. They would push you to write because a lot of times you didn't feel like coming in and writing that day. They'd hunt you down and say, 'Where are you?'" Apart from the deal with car manufacturers, Levine can't recall ever being told what to write by the pair: "They never gave you directions". Kasenetz and Katz did, whoever, cop plenty of co-writing credits. "Their names are always on the B-sides," Levine wryly notes. "They took the B-sides. They didn't write. At the time, it was like, 'Okay, there was the B-side' - but a B-side would make as much as an A-side."

Though Super K shifted far more singles than albums, Levine drew no distinction between songs destined for 45 release and those that ended up on long players: "All my songs, I would try. When you sit down and intentionally try to write a hit, that always become a hard thing. So when you wrote album cuts and just write things you want, it would be a more natural writing situation."

Despite, or because of, the incredible commercial success with the age group at which the records were aimed, bubblegum was sneered at by older audiences. In an age when the likes of The Beatles, Hendrix and Cream were trying to shed pop of its image as teenyboppers' music, bubblegum seemed an unwelcome throwback. At the time, Levine didn't let himself worry about his lack of credibility nor did he hanker for any greater artistic fulfilment. "Those records were just fun to make," he points out. "I wasn't doing artistic songs. Songs that I would write that I really liked that were artistic didn't seem to find their way anywhere. We didn't have an active publishing company at that point because Kasenetz and Katz were publishing and we were publishing our own stuff. It wasn't like we were showing a lot of outside songs. We were just writing for our acts and we didn't really get much into writing songs for other people. We were so busy with the little industry that we had created." Levine treated his more profound songs as a mere exercise: "I wrote some songs here and there and I would get my rocks off but a lot of them I didn't even put down."

Astonishingly, while Levine was busily working at the heart of an industry that generated millions upon millions of dollars, he was also still at school. It meant him having to divide up his day for optimum effect. "Whether it was high school or college, I'd go during the day and then I'd go down to the city for a couple of hours, work out some tunes and then split back," he explains. "In college, I tried to arrange my schedules so I'd start as early as I could and finish as early as I could, then go to the office and work... I had every intention of becoming a graduate and going on from there to probably another school and becoming a professional person, probably law or something. I was more serious about music than my schoolwork but my schoolwork was an issue. In high school I had gotten as good as grades as I could get and I split my time quite a bit in high school. I was glad to go to college. There was no question I was not going to go to college. Certainly the activity that I was experiencing in the music business tore my interests." Did his extra curricular activities make him a star at school? "I don't know if I was a star but I had a little notoriety. It didn't hurt. Friends of mine knew I was doing it. It wasn't like a big issue of the school was aware of it that I knew of. It was, I was doing what I was doing."

Now that Levine had achieved success, the chance to become a solo star was there for the taking. "I had offers from labels to sign, have advances and build up my career and everything," he says. "At all times, even though flattered, I just felt like 'I don't know if I want to become Johnny Cymbal or Tommy Roe and have this career'. I kind of liked it the way it was. I had anonymity.

I didn't have any stigma or any preconceived notion about myself. It was like, 'I can just do whatever I want and I can do it without fronting it'."

Another Super K act for which Levine wrote was Crazy Elephant - as per usual, an extravagant name chosen for a fictitious group. "They had found this guy Bob Spencer and they had asked me to write a song for Bob," Levine explains. "The funny thing was, that particular day they came in and they said, 'Jesus, you gotta write a song for this guy Bob Spencer' and Artie wasn't around." However Ritchie Cordell, another writer whose name became synonymous with bubblegum due to his work for the 1910 Fruitgum Co. and Tommy James and the Shondells, was in the building. "They put Ritchie in the room with me and basically put a pad in Ritchie's hand and said, 'Take down what he writes' and the song just kind of plopped out and that was it. Ritchie was involved in it but not as heavily as Artie would be involved in it. I wrote a lot of that song myself."

The song in question was 'Gimme Gimme Good Lovin'', a driving rocker with a harder edge than most of the Super K material. It climbed to number 12 in the US charts in 1969. It was the kind of material that proved the genuine talent that lay behind the bubblegum craze. A similarly 'credible' project was Levine's work for the Shadows Of Knight, an American garage group the type of whom was shot to posthumous semi-stardom by Lenny Kaye's 1972 compilation of such raw, exhilarating and unsuccessful acts (The Third Rail also featured on *Nuggets*). However, the permutation of the Shadows of Knight that Levine produced contained only leader Jim Sohns from the line-up that had had a US hit with 'Gloria'. Levine's production here was less dictatorial than on other Super K projects: "[I'd] give some thoughts and give some interest and feeling to the music but wouldn't become as involved in certain things they wanted to do as opposed to the stuff I wanted to do." The album featured 'Shake', a pounding Levine/Kris Resnick original held in high regard by bubblegum aficionados.

Bubblegum had become such a cultural presence - Neil Bogart, supremo at Buddah Records, on which most of Super K's productions were issued, even made the cover of *Time* magazine through it - that it was becoming self-referential. 'Captain Groovy and his Bubblegum Army' was a single released in 1969 (by which time Super K had graduated from being a production stable to a record label) while the same year saw the issue of 'Bubble Gum Music', a record credited to The Rock and Roll Double Bubble Trading Card Company of Philadelphia 19141, which, though nothing to do with Super K, checklisted several of their songs in an anthemic celebration. (Levine had no hand in writing either.) Ironically, the 'Captain Groovy' record, with its threatening ambience and lengthy guitar solos, sounded as far removed from bubblegum as could be.

Kasenetz and Katz decided to promote their own name a little more and embarked on a project known as The Kasenetz-Katz Singing Orchestral Circus. This involved a concert at Carnegie Hall featuring the Ohio Express and the 1910 Fruitgum Co. (the real bands as opposed to the sessioners who appeared on their records) plus other colourfully named but less successful acts from the Super K stable such as the St. Louis Invisible Marching Band, the Teri Nelson Group and J.C.W. Ratfinks. "I attended the rehearsals, I didn't go to the concert," Levine remembers. "I thought it was silly. All the bands playing together and everything. It was very unmusical, I thought. Wasn't really well thought-out or out together. It was kind of a bash." The project, though, did spawn a fine single in the shape of 'Quick Joey Small (Run Joey Run)', a Levine-Artie Resnick story of a prison break-out with Levine taking the lead vocal. The second album spawned by this project, The Kasenetz-Katz Super Circus, featured another version of 'Shake': though it employed the same backing track as on the Shadows of Knight's version, Joey Levine's voice replaced that of Jim Sohns.

Their incredible commercial success and imperviousness to disdain for their genre notwithstanding, Levine and Resnick were increasingly unhappy at Super K. "With Kasenetz and Katz, there'd been some parting of the ways with everybody," Levine asserts. "Kasenetz-Katz may have been able to go on a lot further. They just got a little greedy. We were all a little upset with the numbers we were getting and the figures and how we were being paid and we had gotten an offer from Mike Herb who was with a company and they suggested we form a label. Artie put it together and next thing you know we had a label." The formation of the pair's L&R Records and the extra work and responsibility involved meant that Levine was required to make a decision about his schooling. "My schoolwork was certainly suffering and my grades were going down," he says. "My parents had even said, 'You've slipped from being a fairly decent student to you're just barely getting by here'. I said, 'Listen, I gotta follow this through. It's the chance of a lifetime and I'm enjoying it and I can't just give it up to become just one of the guys at school. I've got something that's working here, let me follow it though'." Levine dropped out of his Liberal Arts degree course and concentrated full-time on music.

Around this time, Levine co-authored a song with Mark Bellack called 'I Enjoy Being A Boy (In Love With You)' for the Banana Splits. A group of life-size furry loveable monsters miming to well-crafted pop performed by slick session musicians, they were yet another result of the bubblegum craze Levine had helped start. 'I Enjoy Being A Boy..' was actually only made available on a mail order double EP which one had to send away 50c and two Kellogg's box tops to obtain. For such a rarity, the song had a big impact: many years later, it was a staple of the live set of, of all bands, R.E.M. "I read it in an article that they had been playing it and he [Michael Stipe] had credited me," says Levine. "Like, his first interest wasn't really The Beatles, it was basically bubblegum music." Perhaps Stipe had been impressed by the song's utterly surreal lyric which spoke of cucumber castles and cranberry seas.

Despite securing a major hit with 'Montego Bay' - a Jeff Barry/ Bobby Bloom composition which Bobby Bloom took into the top ten in 1970 - L&R Records turned out to be a rather short-lived enterprise. "The record label folded because even though we had had some nice activity of songs, there was accusations within the company and backbiting," Levine recalls. "It was like, 'These guys are out of control, they had all the success with this thing now all of a sudden they're using strings and orchestras and budgets are getting big'. All of a sudden, they pulled the plug on us."

The label may have been doomed in any event: relations between Levine and Artie Resnick were deteriorating due to Levine writing outside the partnership with Bo Gentry and others. Levine: "Artie became a little upset about it: 'We're partners, it's Levine-Resnick.' It was like, 'Gee, I was just growing and trying to write with other people and enjoy other things and be with some guys who were more my contemporary'. Not that Artie wasn't a contemporary guy, wasn't a great guy, it was just I wanted to try other things. It kind of moved us apart. At the time, I was a young kid and I didn't really understand the upset-ness. It was like, 'Gee, I just write music and I like to write with a lot of people'. I think there was resentment on both our sides... When they pulled the plug on us that kind of ended Artie and I because all of a sudden we didn't have that common space, that office space, so I started writing out of my apartment and he went back to New York."

When L&R Records folded, Levine went through a period of uncertainty about his career: "At that time, I didn't know what I was going to do, if I was going to continue in the music business or not. The advertising business kind of found me. I found myself doing it fairly easily and successfully."

Levine was approached by an advertising industry employee named Arnold Brown who had been impressed by his work under the Crazy Elephant banner. It led to Levine being commissioned to write the music for a Cocoa-Puffs commercial: "I did that commercial and then I got called to do a couple more: one was 'Sometimes you feel like a nut/ Sometimes you don't' which was a big commercial which even runs now - Honey Nut Cheerios. They still use the musical theme." Things rapidly snowballed from there: "All of a sudden I was this kid walking around the city with my guitar and writing advertising, from Dodge to BM Goodridge.

I learned the business and started to do it in my own form out of my apartment and little by little started to build up a following, a constant amount of work."

Levine found that writing jingles required basically the same principles as writing pop hits: "It's to write something memorable or interesting enough to grab people's attention. The only thing is, you're writing within a short format of time. It was kind of easy. I found it to be very prolific, a kind of easy thing to do. It just swept me up and took me along."

Almost as if to prove that he could still write chart records, in 1974 Levine helped propel 'Life Is A Rock (But The Radio Rolled Me)' into the US top ten. The track was a novelty song whose rapid fire lyric attempted to checklist just about every major song and chart act in rock history. It had started with Levine's old friend Mark Bellack: "I was doing jingles then and Mark Bellack came to me with this song that he had written with these guys - Dolph and DiFranco. I liked the song very much but I hated their production. I said, 'Let me go in and help you produce it. Change some words and do this and that'. The basis was there. It was basically formed. I just wrote some new sections and wrote some new lyric. It was like a time capsule of rock and roll." The record was ultimately released under the name Reunion, with Levine on lead vocals, and climbed to number 8 in the US charts.

However, this did not presage a return to full-time hit-making by Levine. Indeed a bad experience put him off the idea of attempting to make such a return forever. "I got together with some guys", he relates. "They had found a song called 'Dancing In The Moonlight' and we cut the song and we gave it to RCA. In the middle of RCA having it, there'd been a change of the powers-that-be. They sat with the record in their library and then it was cut by King Harvest. The record started to climb up the charts. I became very disenchanted. This record was going to be a big hit. It could be my record, which would mean production deals and an infusion of energy in my career and you guys are just gonna sit on it because you say that you missed the timing and now there's a record out and you won't chase it." It brought home to Levine how happy he had been in advertising and the reason for that happiness: "The record business is just so filled with bullshit. Between my experience with Kasenetz and Katz and my experience with that record and experience on other levels with just doing business... The business was so convoluted whereas the advertising business that I'd gotten into was so straightahead. It's like, you did your job, you got paid your money. There was no shenanigans, no accounting needed. It was just like a honest business compared to a business that just seemed like, 'Man, everything is such a struggle here, it's such a fight to just get what you deserve'." Though Levine still occasionally wrote songs, the energy and enthusiasm left over for such activities was low. "I had started so young writing songs and producing records, that even in an early age I'd already been doing it for eight or nine years," he observes. He adds, "In the new business, the respect I got and the interest I got was so exhilarating that it was almost like, 'Why would I want to go back in that other arena and knock my head against the wall and be judged by whoever when I've found a level of respect and economic satisfaction?'"

Levine now runs his own adverting jingle company, although does still find time to compose complete songs, such as his work in the 1990s on *The Dragon Tales Show*, a children's programme on PBS. Asked which of his songs are his favourites, he says, "Once I've finished songs I've never looked back on 'em: 'Do I like it, do I love it, do I enjoy it?' There are songs I've written that never came out that are probably my favourite songs that I wrote. All I can say is that usually the song I'm working at the current time becomes my favourite song - until it's out of my system."

Looking back on those heady bubblegum days, Levine says, "It became upsetting a little afterwards, that it was so frivolous, the music, and was so unimportant in terms of its longevity or its implications on society. When you'd do an album with one of our artists, it certainly wouldn't sell the way an Eric Clapton would sell or a Stevie Winwood would sell." Although he acknowledges, "But that was obvious to us. We were manufacturing a certain thing. We weren't an artist who was creating his own sound and his own identity," he does add, "Today, I'd like to say I wrote, 'Strange Brew'. It would have been nice to say, I wrote 'Strange Brew' in terms of how people feel about it."

Nevertheless, when it comes to the perception of bubblegum, Levine has observed a swinging back of the pendulum. Bubblegum, much like the music of The Monkees, has acquired a credibility in recent times on the grounds that good music is good music and cynical and/or artificial origins don't make much difference to its enjoyment. "It seems to be quite a fascination," he says. "I've done a lot of interviews on it and people have re-established it and I see it being picked up as commercial and I get a lot more special packages that are put out with it."

At the end of the day, Levine is glad to have been a bubblegum merchant. "It was great. It was a great experience and it led me into career opportunities which were wonderful and put me in a situation of being a successful songwriter on whatever level I've been accepted on. It's always been a fun way to make a living and it's afforded me opportunities which I may not have achieved." He sums up, "Who knows what would have happened if I'd became lawyer?"

8

CHIP TAYLOR

It's doubtful that there were prouder parents in this world than the Voights of Yonkers, New York. In adulthood, their three sons - all close in age - would all achieve prominence and acclaim in their chosen professions. Eldest brother Barry would become one of the foremost geologists in the world while middle brother Jon become an Oscar-winning actor. The youngest, James Wesley Voight, would achieve as great or even greater immortality. As Chip Taylor, he wrote some of the most famous songs of the twentieth century, 'Wild Thing', 'Angel Of the Morning' and 'Try (Just A Little Bit Harder)' among them.

Chip Taylor was born on March 21st 1940 in Yonkers, approximately 45 minutes outside the city of New York. "My mom and dad both [came] from poor families so we lived in kind of a lower middle class place in Yonkers," he recalls. Taylor's father had once been a promising golfer: "He played in tournaments but he hurt his back when he was 20 or 21 years old at the Canadian Open and he wasn't able to play after that so he just taught golf." Conditions for young Wesley and his two brothers improved when he was around eleven or twelve: "He moved us to a nicer section of Westchester County. For the first time, the kids had separate bedrooms."

Taylor confirms the impression of a household seething with raw talent waiting for its chance: "When I was about seven years old or eight years old, my brother Barry would constantly be in the woods with my father's brother after school looking for rocks and things like that. He loved fishing as well. And Jon, every night he would do like little routines for us to make us laugh. We loved Sid Caesar and he would do those kind of routines for us every night. So he was like the stand-up comic in the family." As for Taylor himself: "I had my ear glued to the radio - hopefully to hear country music - and my dad would let me stay up late to do that. So at a very early age we had our sights set on the direction we wanted to go into."

Taylor says the family was not particularly musical but adds, "My father was like a frustrated everything. He used to love to listen to the crooners of the day, Bing Crosby and others of that ilk. He'd just kind of sing along with them - or sing without them! And he used to take us to movies after school. Dad was into the arts all the time. But there was no real professional artist in the family."

That Taylor's first musical passion was country is, of course, highly unusual for a New Yorker. "My dad used to let me listen to the radio late at night," he says. "As long as it didn't keep anybody else up, he would let me put myself to sleep: go in the little hall and just get close to the radio and listen to the stuff. This was in the late 'Forties. One night when I was listening, I heard a station from Wheeling, West Virginia and I said, '*What* is this?' I just loved it. I became a fanatical country fan, even though you couldn't hear it on any kind of radio station in New York. And then a new country show appeared every Saturday, playing the top ten country songs of the nation. I was very engrossed in that music."

Asked what specifically attracted him to this genre, Taylor says, "It was more the sound to me. Some of it was very simple stuff. Hank Williams, especially as Luke the Drifter with the talking recitations thing, and Lefty Frizzell were the first to make an impression on me. I loved Lefty's 'Long Black Veil'. I also really liked the cowboy stuff like Gene Autry. In the mid-'Fifties, I got

into Johnny Cash, Jerry Lee and the Sun Records things but also
the warm sounds of the Louvin Brothers and the Browns. Jim,
Ed, Maxine and Bonnie Brown just had this sound that gave me
chills. It was at this same time that I discovered the race records
from down South, like Hank Ballard and the Midnighters."

The first instrument Taylor took up was the violin, at the age,
he estimates, of seven. "I was so into music that I asked if I could
have a violin and my parents gave ma a violin," he recalls. "I
started practicing. I didn't know this until later on: my brothers
went to my parents about six months into my screeching with the
violin practicing, and they said, 'You've got to change his instrument
- we can't take it anymore!' So they bought me a ukulele for
Christmas and the violin kind of disappeared. A few years later I
turned to the guitar, which is a similar instrument." It was the
guitar that became Taylor's instrument of choice for writing: "Once
in a while, I compose on piano but nine-tenths of the time I'm
composing on guitar - or thin air." Other instruments he plays are
keyboards and harmonica. He adds, "I did play violin on my early
albums, just fooling around. It took me about four hours to play
one simple lick."

By the age of fourteen, Taylor had started writing his own
songs, including one called 'Faded Blue'. "This was the first song
I ever demoed," he says. "I had a whole bunch of other ones. It
was a country-ish song but with my New York influence it sounded
more rockabilly." The composition was written for his schoolboy
band, the Town And Country Brothers. The combination of country
and rockabilly impressed Henry Glover of King Records who
signed Taylor and his chums to a recording contract after hearing
it. Taylor was still only fifteen years old. His colleagues in the
Town and Country Brothers were Greg Guardiack on guitar and
a drummer named Ted Daryll who would later achieve fame as a
co-composer of 'She Cried', a top five hit for Jay and the
Americans in 1962. Taylor: "It was a trio and Henry loved the
sound of my demos but when it finally came time to record, the
head of the record company, Sid Nathan, had told Henry to spare
nothing because he was hoping I was gonna be their great white

hope. I was the only white artist signed to the New York division of King Records. [They] hired the best musicians - Panama Francis on drums and Nicky 'Guitar' Baker, of Mickey and Sylvia fame, on guitar - which really meant my band didn't play. They were cool sessionmen but they weren't the sound of my band. I just played acoustic guitar as I sang." Though Taylor was obviously excited to have a career as a recording artist while still at high school, he also acknowledges, "I didn't sound very good on the records and the songs weren't great either. We didn't record 'Faded Blue' at the time, which is the original one he liked. I thought it was one of my best. Instead, he recorded stuff that he felt might have been more commercial. At one time I would cringe when I would hear this stuff but I don't mind it so much now."

Said records were put out under the name Wes Voight and the Town and Country Brothers. "My manager and the people from the company were saying that my name was too hard to pronounce on the radio," reveals Taylor. "That was the days of Fabian and those clicky names. They said, 'Why don't you pick an easy one?'" Wesley Voight became Chip Taylor. The Taylor part was simply an invented name. The Chip bit derived from the fact that Taylor had visibly picked up some of his father's golfing skills: "I was a good golfer. That was the thing I was thinking of doing for a living. I was particularly good around the greens. I was this little twerpy kid who couldn't hit the ball so far but could pitch and put with the best of them, so my nickname became 'Chip'." The new name was possibly the only significant benefit Taylor derived from King: "Shortly after my name change, I left the company. I had my first hit on Warner Brothers the following year as Chip Taylor, so that kind of stuck. I became known even to my family as Chip straightaway."

After two years of making records but not hits, Taylor went off to study at Springhill University in Mobil, Alabama and to play golf. "I was trying to decide whether I was gonna get in music or whether I was gonna be a golf professional," he says. "I'd won several junior championships. But I decided when I got down there that I had to give music one more shot, so I went back to

New York." Returning home, Taylor kept the wolf from the door by playing golf tournaments and working for his father while planning his assault on the music industry. "I was just afraid that I wouldn't be able to succeed," he explains. "If I wasn't going to be able to make it, I'd have to take my second choice: being a golfer, which wasn't bad. What happened was, I started to play in some tournaments, and then I hurt my wrist, which was the real blessing. When I hurt my wrist, I decided I didn't want to just stay at the club and give lessons. So I said, 'Dad, I'm gonna spend two or three months seeing what I can do in the city'."

Taylor began making the trek into New York City every day in order to try to sell songs: "It was like going from one publishing company to the next, trying to get thirty dollars or forty dollars advance and if you could sell three or four you could make a hundred bucks or something like that for the week and that might be enough to get you through." Taylor got what he acknowledges is a very lucky break at an unusually early stage: "Chet Atkins - who was not only the great guitar player but who was also the head of A&R for RCA Victor in Nashville - heard one of my songs and wrote back to the publisher and said something like, 'I don't know who this kid is but I want to hear everything he writes. It's hard for me to believe he's from New York but he certainly can write a country song'. So he started recording my songs. He recorded 'Springtime' with the Brown Family, which were my heroes, then I had 'The Long Walk Home' with Floyd Cramer, an instrumental, then 'If You Were Mine, Mary' with Eddy Arnold and he influenced Bobby Bare's producer to record my song 'Just A Little Bit Later On Down The Line'."

Not too long after that, a measure of security was provided for Taylor when one of the recipients of Chet Atkins' letter became the professional manager of April Blackwood Music, a CBS publishing company. Says Taylor of the letter recipient, "He called me into his office one day and said, 'I'd like you to be a staff writer here. Which means we'll pay your salary - a lot more than you could have made by selling four or five songs a week - and there'll be an advance against royalties and you don't have to write five songs a week. You can write ten songs a year. I don't care what you write'. So all of a sudden, I was: 'Oh my God - this is great'."

Despite having had a minor hit on the Warner Brothers label in the shape of 'Here I Am', Taylor now devoted his energies to writing for others. "When I had the hit on Warner Brothers, it was just a singles deal," he recalls. "It wasn't a big enough hit to record an album and I wasn't making a living as a singer. But right in the middle of that, somebody recorded a song of mine, a jazz artist called Bill Henderson, and that made me feel, 'Well maybe I can write for other people'. It wasn't that it was the primary thought in my mind but it was a way to stay in the business, maybe. So in the back of my mind I still wanted to be an artist but the writing kind of took over. And I loved writing for other people. I loved people recording my songs. That was a big thrill."

Henderson notwithstanding, the first hits Taylor had were on the country charts, those Chet Atkins-assisted records mentioned above. Those who might be inclined to shrug at a record 'only' been a hit on the country charts would be labouring under a misapprehension: such is the vastness of America and the sales of country songs there that a number one country hit could be the equivalent of hitting number one on the pop charts in Britain. Nevertheless, it was certainly cut off from the national charts. "They had their own chart, their own everything and it was a totally different thing than the pop business," says Taylor. "You might find a country thing on the pop charts once in a while but not reversed. You'd never find a pop thing on the county charts."

Though country music often evinces a sophistication in lyric content it is also known for not being as melodically adventurous as rock or pop. Taylor - who has not only proven himself a writer of great melodies but has also written country songs throughout his career in parallel with his pop writing - acknowledges this but says that he doesn't find country limiting: "I think that some of the country melodies, although very, very simple, they take little different turns every so often. It's almost like when I liked Luke the Drifter: I liked him because of the message he was giving and because of the feeling that he would give from speaking. It's the same in country. I don't think you want to let melody interfere too much with that simple communication of spoken word. It doesn't bother me that sometimes there's a similarity in melody. My feeling was, if I just let a song develop without thinking too much, it usually turned out a little different. Most of my things were real simple and organic. The stuff I wrote for the Brown Family and some of those things that I did in the early days were simple almost like Irish folk things. Some of them don't have far-reaching melodies but they're little haunting things." Taylor also avers, "The inflections are so important in country music that just a little twist can make something sound very original. You listen to some of the wonderful Merle Haggard things like 'Today I Started Loving You Again'. Those kind of songs, although very simple in nature, have their own uniqueness in melody. Just a little shift here and there will make the words give you chills."

However, Taylor is the first to acknowledge that such subtleties leave the composer at the absolute mercy of the performer or producer, something that was brought bitterly home to him with an early song of his called 'On My Word'. Though Cliff Richard took the song to number twelve in the UK in mid-1965, for Taylor it wasn't the cause for celebration one might assume. "This song was one of the hard luck songs of my career," he laments. The song was written before Taylor signed up to April Blackwood. Publisher Aaron Schroeder, who also ran a small record label, informed Taylor he liked the song enough to put it out under Taylor's name. "About two weeks later we were offered a certain amount of money for half the publishing by Andy Williams' company," reveals Taylor. "Andy was coming out of a series of six number ones in a row and that was going to be his next single... He wanted to put the song out as a single but they wanted to publish it. Things like that happened all the time. They wanted to have half the publishing and they would offer a certain amount of money against the royalties. They were confident enough that it was going to be a huge hit that they'd give us ten thousand dollars right away so I'd have money in my pocket and stuff like that... The publisher said to me, 'Well, you have the choice, Chip: do you want your record out or do you want the next number one song for Andy Williams?' He was a cool guy, this publisher... He was one of these guys that played life the way you could play it. I thought about it for a day and I came back to him and I said, 'Nah, the hell with Andy Williams. Let's put it out myself'. Those are the kind of decisions you make. What the hell was I thinking about? It didn't sell a copy." A few years later, during which interim Cliff Richard had made it a hit on the other side of the Atlantic, Taylor received a call from Schroeder: "He says, 'Cross your fingers: Brook Benton (who was just coming off 'Rainy Night In Georgia' or whatever), he's doing a session in New York. He loves the song, they're gonna record it and they're flying the Nashville musicians into the city'." Taylor was excited on more than one count: "These are guys I know. They weren't like my best friends but I had a nice feeling with these people because I'd been down there a few times and had a little country success so there was a certain amount of respect that was floating around." Taylor went to watch the song being recorded: "When I got to the studio about a half-hour before the session was to start, all the musicians were there and there was a record player there and they were playing my song on the turntable. Then they took it off and they had made their notes and all of a sudden they started to play it. And I had never been so excited at a session, because the thing sounded so good. It was one of these songs that had this kind of little groove to it. Brook was singing it and he sounded so great. I was in the control room listening to this and then walking outside, talking to the musicians, telling 'em, 'Oh my God - I love this. it is so great'. And Brook was just killing it. It just looked like to me it was gonna be one of my favourite records of all time. There was no question in my mind that it was gonna be a hit."

Unfortunately, nemesis struck for the second time when the record's producer arrived: "I don't want to mention his name. He's a nice fella.. and he's produced some good records. But this wasn't one of his good days. He kind of had a flashy way of being and seemed to want to make everybody know that he had entered the room. He looked around and he listened and listened and all of a sudden he pushes the button down and he says, 'Alright boys - are we gonna just keep foolin' around here or are we gonna make us a hit? Now, stop what you're doin', give me a heavy backbeat on the two and four and let's make this a hit'. Well, he took this cool little groove and he turned it right into this ugly, regular, nonsense thing that had nothing to do with the feel of the song. It was just a horrible experience. I walked away, thinking, 'Oh my God, what a bad break this is. I was so upset, but It wasn't something I could interfere with. I just went out and said goodbye to the boys. I said, 'Thanks for trying, I appreciate it'. I was so sad that day."

Though an extreme example, Taylor observes that this kind of story was not uncommon for the time: "The rules that they played by were, you hired an arranger, and that arranger wrote charts for the hired musicians - including the drummer - and they played every beat and every note the way the arranger wrote it. There was no, 'Sit back and let loose and let go'. The young writers of the day were trying to change that. We were producing our demos in a more organic way, to capture the feel of the song. And some of the new producers were starting to copy that and get less formal in their approach. You were always glad that someone wanted to record your song but you just prayed they wouldn't lose the magic. You were liable to get some very strange kind of recordings of your songs back in those days, particularly in the pop arena." Things were different in the country field: "In Nashville, they would take your demo - if they liked your song, they probably liked your demo as well - and it felt good because that was part of it to them. It was how something felt that was important. They'd have a record player right there and they would play your demo and the musicians would write their charts from your demo. Maybe a different key change but they would hear what it was doing and then they would try to capture that. But in pop music, I never saw one session where they played the demo." The pop old guard, though, was not long for this world: "After a while, as we were taking over, we would just get so angry at those kind of things, we would do them ourselves or something. The Shadow Morton's and people like that. You got people who really understood what we were doing and could transfer it."

In early 1966, Taylor enjoyed more UK success when The Hollies took 'I Can't Let Go' to number two in their home country. The song was one Taylor wrote in collaboration with Al Gorgoni, a well-known arranger and producer with whom Taylor was close. The song was originally recorded by Evie Sands - an artist he and Gorgoni were producing - whose version was released by Red Bird. The day on which Taylor and Gorgoni got together to write the song did not start auspiciously: "We were both in bad moods and nothing really was coming out that was any good. Everything he did, I didn't like and anything I did he didn't like. As close as we were, we weren't that close that day and it was a trying time. A real good example of how difficult writing together can be, particularly if you're not formula writers." The two decided to get some distance between them for a while. "Then within a half-hour or 45 minutes, we were both trying to find out if each other was alright and by that point Al had started this little thing where he was singing: "You got me going/I need you.." and stuff. I don't know if he had the words but he had that little melody. So he had something that sounded like what the chorus ended up being. And I was chugging away with the verse: 'Feels so bad baby it hurts me/When I think of how you love and desert me/I'm the broken-hearted toy you play with..' and I kind of had that going with the little thing to start with: 'I try and I try/And I can't say goodbye..'" The two melodies were welded: "This is the first time I ever did anything like this. I was so happy to be with Al again and be okay with him and I really did like what he had and he really liked what I had. So we just said, 'Let's try to see if they fit together'. I think it turned out pretty good."

However, it was The Hollies rather than Evie Sands who made the track a hit, rendering the song's riff in their own keening guitar style and decorating it with their distinctive harmonies. They also cranked up the intensity of the song. "In the version that Evie did originally, even though it was fairly uptempo it wasn't as uptempo as The Hollies'," Taylor says. "But it still had that pounding thing where it just kept going." However, he does acknowledge, "Our version of 'I Can't Let Go', I think it was kind of cool but it just wasn't as good as the Hollies' version."

Though he was now gaining some power in the studio, the experience of hearing a version of a song of his whose production, and hence sound, he had not had a part in was something with which, naturally for a freelance songwriter, Taylor would become accustomed. It would seem that, whatever the surprises involved, often the experience was pleasurable: "There were certain people that brought their own thing that you liked. I loved The Hollies' [version], even though it was quite different than what I'd imagined it - because ours was more like an R&B version - it still was very cool. To get a record by people like that or Jimi Hendrix or Janis Joplin - these people brought their own thing to it. They might take your song and make it different but they would bring a rock and roll energy that was a true energy to it. I always liked that. It was when somebody took away that energy that you'd get hurt." The Hollies would also record the Chip Taylor songs 'Son Of A Rotten Gambler' and 'The Baby'.

'I Can't Let Go' was unusual for Taylor in its collaborative origins. Unlike almost all the other subjects of this book, he has opted to write on his own during most of his career. "I find it a difficult thing to write with other people," he explains. "Generally when you write with somebody else, you want to be quiet a little bit and listen to what they're doing. My writing is not so much that I'm trying to write a hit song. That's not what I go at when I'm writing. I just try to write something that inspires me and then I hope it's a hit song. But when you write with somebody else it's more like you're almost crafting. Even though my songs are so simple that they sound crafted and I guess in the aftermath, as I get going, there's a certain amount of crafting that goes on. But as you're writing with somebody else, more of that's taking place so I think sometimes it's hard to let both people be inspired, unless you're very close to the other person. If you're really loose with the other person then you can let nonsense, silly or stupid things come out and not be embarrassed. Half the things that come out of me when I'm trying to write a song are things that I edit out because they are nonsense. If you can't let yourself be loose like that with somebody it's kind of a stiff way to write. With Al, on the other hand, we're so close to each other that we could kind of get the best out of each other."

Taylor seems to slightly discount his early British hits when he says, "My first big success was 'Wild Thing'." However, there's no disputing his appendum: "And that changed everything."

'Wild Thing' started with a phone call from a producer named Jerry Granahan, with whom Taylor had never previously spoken. Granahan was recording a band called Jordan Christopher and the Wild Ones. "He said that he had a problem because all the songs that Jordan had written or the songs that they had for the session didn't sound like hits to him," Taylor recalls. "He wanted to try to go elsewhere for a song and somebody had said, 'Well, there's a guy named Chip Taylor who's writing some really interesting rock and roll things. He said to me, 'Do you have anything?' I said, 'Well, I don't know if I do or I don't but let me try to write something today for you'. I was so flattered that the guy called. I guess that was 'round two o' clock and my demo session was at five or something like that. So I just started trying to lose myself into some kind of a feeling. Maybe the reason it came out 'Wild Thing' was because of the group's name was Jordan Christopher and the Wild Ones so maybe that was just somewhere in my brain. I just started to drift off and chug away on my guitar and some magic stuff started to happen A lot of times that's happened to me. Some of my best things have come when somebody's asked me to do something." If the name of the group provided - albeit possibly subconsciously - the lyrical inspiration, the music derived from some of the Southern material Taylor loved: "It was drawn from Memphis kind of stuff with all the stops in it, like 'Blue Suede Shoes'. That's kind of where it comes from."

His description of the creation of 'Wild Thing' almost makes it sound as though Taylor was dragged along in the composition's slipstream: "The studio was a couple of blocks away from the place where I wrote it, which was my writing little place over at 1615 Broadway, which was April Blackwood Music. I had planned on doing a demo of a country song that day but then I wrote 'Wild Thing'. I called the engineer, Ron Johnson, and asked him to set my stool up and have the microphone in place and just as soon as I got there to just put it in record... I hadn't quite finished 'Wild Thing'. I wasn't exactly sure what I'd say in the pauses. I decided not to be too prepared and just sing what I knew and let other stuff come out of me. So I did that and it lasted like four-and-a-half minutes. We edited it down to three-and-a-half." 'Wild Thing', a song that would sell millions, was thus completed in less than three hours.

Though 'Wild Thing' doesn't mention sex explicitly, its lyric - in which a narrator tells his lover he wants her to "sock" it to him - was somewhat risqué for the mid-1960s. "It sounded like it might be a hit to me," Taylor says, "but I was worried because it was so sexual. I was a little embarrassed by it and afraid to be there when somebody heard it. After the demos came over from the company, I took all the demos that were there in the little cubicle space marked 'W' that the manager had for the various demos and I put 'em on top of the thing so he couldn't find them."

Of course, the song would become famous as a hit for British band The Troggs - and as a staple of Jimi Hendrix's live repertoire - rather than as a Jordan Christopher number. Explains Taylor, "I sent it over to Jerry. The session I think was two days later from the time I'd done it. He recorded it but it was another one of these things where on the session they had an arranger that was arranging horns and strings and drumbeats and stuff like that. So my cool groove that sounds just like The Troggs, or if you slowed it down, like the Jimi Hendrix records, all of a sudden became like [enunciates slowly] *dah-dah, uh-ah*. With horns and strings arrangements. It didn't have a great feel. I don't know if it ever came out. But I always remember and appreciate Jerry asking me for a song for his group. I think he caught a bad break here because the horns, strings and arranger were already booked for the other songs and so he recorded my song the same way. He would have been better off cutting it on a separate session."

Perhaps it was just as well. Fate doesn't recall whatever happened to Jordan Christopher and the Wild Ones but when the demo fell into the hands of Troggs producer Larry Page, both The Troggs and Taylor shot to prominence in their fields and neither ever looked back. "My publishing company had a deal with Dick James where everything that was written out of our office had to be sent to Dick James' music company in England," says Taylor. "So every month they would get a stack of new songs. From what I hear, Larry Page and Dick James were friends and when the stack came in, Larry had just signed The Troggs and they were ready to go in and do a session. They needed one more song and so they got this new stack of demos. I don't know if Larry heard it first or what he did was grab the whole stack and give it to the boys and tell them to go through it and see if they found anything. [It depends] on who you talk to as to what happened but I know when they stopped and they heard it, they said - Reg [Presley, Troggs singer] said to me - 'This is either gonna be the biggest bomb or the biggest hit ever'." Page, incidentally, has estimated that there had been five different versions of the songs released in the US before The Troggs recorded it.

The Troggs' record - a great murky primeval roar of a single with a salacious vocal from lead singer Reg Presley and an incongruously pretty ocarina solo - was actually close in sound to Taylor's basic demo. "It sounds very much like the Troggs' record," says Taylor of his template. "Almost identical to The Troggs record, including the ocarina solo." Except that the ocarina solo - which The Troggs faithfully replicated - wasn't an ocarina at all. Taylor: "We were playing the song back after I did the demo. As I was playing it back, my engineer, Ron, started doing this thing with his hands like you almost do with a blade of glass to make a whistling sound and I said to him, 'That's cool. Can you do this?' I hummed a little part to him and he overdubbed that and then we edited that together. If you hear the demo, it's exactly the form of The Troggs record and it sounds - aside from the fact that's it's just an acoustic guitar and me playing and me stomping on the floor and banging on something to give a little accent here and there - it sounds exactly like The Troggs. [The Troggs] thought it was a ocarina so they just tried to duplicate it."

The Troggs took the song to number two in their homeland and right to the top in the States in Summer 1966. Taylor was as delighted with the record's aesthetic brilliance as its statistical success: "I think I had a copy of it earlier but I remember when I first heard it on the radio. I'd just gotten married and I was swimming in a little swimming pool by the place where Joanie and I were living and I had the radio there because somebody had told me that they had heard it on the radio and it came on and I remember thinking, 'Oh my God! I love this record'."

A year later, Jimi Hendrix - then an unknown in the US - played the song in his show-stopping, guitar-immolating performance at the Monterey Pop Festival. Hendrix's distortion-drenched rendition of 'Wild Thing' would remain a staple of his live repertoire. "I saw a film of it shortly after," Taylor recalls of the Monterey rendition. "Somebody had a film and asked if I wanted to come to see it. It was another one of these things where, 'Oh my God - what have I done?' But I loved it. What an amazing performance."

'Wild Thing' is almost certainly the most famous song Taylor has ever written -and the least typical of his songs. However, Taylor dismisses the idea that this might cause him a sense of frustration: "Most of the people don't know who wrote that song. They think nobody wrote that song! I think if people do know I've written the song then probably they know I wrote 'Angel Of The Morning' as well. It doesn't bother me because I like 'Wild Thing'. I liked it when I wrote it and it was really an inspired song in its own way. It was based on stuff that I like."

Understandably, The Troggs asked Taylor if he had any more material they could record. The song with which he provided them, 'Any Way That You Want Me' was released in Britain at the end of the same year, eventually going top ten. It was a stark contrast to 'Wild Thing': a plaintive ballad with string parts. In recognition of Taylor's importance in their career, when the Troggs released a comeback album, *Athens Andover*, in 1992, it opened with a new Taylor song, 'Crazy Annie'.

It's perhaps of a measure of the art-first, commerce-second ethos Taylor mentions above that, regardless of the success of The Troggs record of 'Any Way That You Want Me', he continued to tinker with it, adding an interlude that first appeared on a subsequent version released by Evie Sands which he and Gorgoni produced. "I just felt it needed something else even though it was successful," he reasons. "I just felt like it was an unfinished work. Once you get into rock and roll you don't care what anybody else says! You let your spirit take you." Taylor's decision was vindicated not so much by the Sands single selling half a million copies but by the fact that it seems to have been accepted as the definitive version: "Since that time, everybody that records it uses the interlude."

Also in 1966, Taylor had success with 'I Can Make It With You'. "Somebody had asked me if I would write a song for Jackie DeShannon, so I wrote that with Jackie DeShannon in mind," he recalls. Though DeShannon recorded it, Texan trio Pozo-Seco Singers had the bigger hit, nudging the US top thirty with their rendition.

By this time, Taylor was content to be a hit-maker for other people rather than a recording artist in his own right, though this was just as much due to insecurity as the success he was enjoying. "I liked the idea of writing hits for other people," he says. "In the back of my mind, I think it was a safer place to be than to put yourself out there. I always had this burning desire to be a hit artist. But I hid it for a while and I was very comfortable being behind the scenes and I liked having the successes I was having, although I never kind of looked back at it too much. I just kept chugging away, doing things. I always liked the idea that people were doing my songs. It was a thrill for me to have Janis Joplin and Jimi Hendrix and The Hollies and all these people. But not singing myself was more a shy thing, I think. At one point, somebody at the publishing company came over and said to me, 'We've had an enquiry, Chip, if you'd be willing to go over to England because there seems to be some interest in you working with Mick Jagger'." To this day, Taylor is not sure what the work would have entailed, although suspects it may have had something to do with writing for Jagger's girlfriend Marianne Faithfull. "When I got that message, I was a little embarrassed, afraid that if I went over there and showed these people how little I knew..." he says. "That I only knew a few chords. It was one thing for me to write a song behind an office door, to go into a studio with nobody around and record it, it was another thing to play in front of somebody and show them what I was doing. I kind of just withdrew. It made me nervous so I never even responded to it."

1968 saw Taylor accidentally become a part of an historical landmark when his song 'Storybook Children' became a US hit for the very first interracial singing duo: Billy Vera and Judy Clay. "I was starting to do some work with Billy and thinking about recording a record with him but I wanted to get a song that everybody would like, everybody would say, 'It's a can't-miss' kind of thing," he recalls. "On the way down to the city one day, I remember driving by this field and - this is one of the first times I ever wrote a song based on the title - I looked over to a couple of kids walking hand-in-hand across the field. I was thinking about something I was going through at the time or something like that and I thought of the title 'Storybook Children'. When I got to the city, I asked Billy to play me a song called 'To Be With You' by Joe Cuba. I got to love this song from hearing Billy play it with his band. I thought that kind of feel and flavour would fit what I had in mind. [I] began writing 'Storybook Children' in private so I could let the inspiration flow and then asked Billy to come in and help me finish it up. I thought it was a really strong song."

The original idea was for Vera to record the song as a duet with the woman with whom he was then working. Taylor: "Then Jerry Wexler heard the song and loved it and suggested we do it with Judy Clay. So Jerry brought Judy Clay to the table. It originally was for an interracial duo, but not Billy and Judy." The fact that the record was by an interracial duo caused a mini-sensation upon its release, the implication of sex between blacks and whites being something of a taboo in the States at the time. The revolutionary nature of the record was something that had barely occurred to Taylor while it was being made: "Because I felt like I fit right in with African-Americans, nothing frightened me about any of that. It didn't bother me at all. It was just like, nothing. Falling in love with a black girl would be nothing that would be anything that unusual for me to think about. I never thought, 'We're breaking ground'. It seemed like we were always doing stuff organically so if you broke ground, you broke ground."

In an age of black militancy, of course, there could sometimes be just as much resistance from the black community about interracial sex as from whites. However, Taylor points out, "I think they were the first interracial duo to perform at the Apollo and I didn't see that show but Billy said it was very well accepted. But see, Billy was a soul singer. This is the thing that I always felt being around black people and black musicians: if you had soul, they didn't care. It's like, they liked the Everly Brothers. I always felt I accepted them, they accepted me."

Taylor would contribute more material for Vera and Clay, all in an R&B or soul vein. "It wasn't really a switch for me," he says. "'I Can't Let Go' and 'Welcome Home' and 'Angel Of The Morning', all of these things had some R&B flavourings to them. But when we were working with Judy and Billy, I just went right to the direct R&B, the southern kind of R&B. The simple R&B things were easy to write." Taylor's most successful offering for the pair was 'Country Girl - City Man', co-written with old friend Ted Daryll, a top 40 hit in early 1968. (It was also the subject of a cover by Ike and Tina Turner.) However, Taylor's personal favourite amongst the numbers he wrote for the pair is 'Reaching For The Moon', of which he says, "One night we were down in Muscle Shoals and I wasn't totally happy with what we were recording the next day. I started writing it about four in the morning and woke Billy up and said, 'Come on, help me finish this thing'. I think that's the one that broke them up finally. Jerry Wexler was getting some complaints about the interracial thing so there was a question of whether they would really try to break 'Reaching For The Moon' or not. Jerry, Billy and I all thought it was a hit but the record company finally backed away from promoting it."

1968 also saw a Taylor song achieve hit status on both sides of the Atlantic in very different versions. 'Angel Of The Morning' is an elegant composition which is probably Taylor's second most well-known song. The process involved in its writing is the quintessential example of what Taylor refers to as his "organic" method. "I spent an hour-and-a-half just playing nonsense things to myself and I loved the feeling of the chords against this slow kind of thing," he says. "I think I had heard somebody playing what sounded like 'Wild thing' really slow, almost like a ballad, so in a different key I was fooling around with that idea playing it in 'A', and using a suspension on the 'D' chord. I don't know much about music at all and I didn't know much about the guitar but every once in a while I would take my finger off or add a finger and something would happen and I would like it. I loved the feeling of the chord with that suspension and when that melody came out with those words, I just got a chill. A lot of people said, 'You must have thought of the title first' or something like that. That title just came as it came in the song."

The song's first couplet came fully formed: "'There'll be no strings to bind your hands/Not if my love can't bind your heart'. Set against that melody, that's magic. I didn't think of that. I didn't say from my brain, 'I'm gonna say this'. I didn't even know what the hell it meant. It just came out. I said, 'Oh my God -what is that? That's beautiful'. The rest of it just fired itself right through. A tremendous passion that goes with that kind of stuff. That's why it works and that's why people like it - because it's inspired."

As to why he thinks the word 'Angel' came into his head, Taylor offers: "Most of my writing comes from personal experience and taking it in a kind of fantasy trip. There's somebody usually I'm thinking about, some relationship I'm thinking about, and then just letting it drift to someplace that I may never have been before and then putting myself there. 'Cos I'm a good dreamer. That's what I do whether I write or I don't write. I drift off into these kind of things."

It is because of his organic approach that Taylor is bemused when the author asks him about composing technique. "The way you speak about it is exactly the way I wouldn't think about it," he says. "It's almost like, 'Is this a formula that works?' or something like that. The great thing about 'Angel Of The Morning' or 'Any Way That You Want Me' is that they're so inspired. I write melody and words at the same time and I hum nonsense things until something comes out. So I don't think about what I want to say, I let the emotion carry me. In those songs the emotion just totally took over and just carried me. So there's magic in those songs. I'm not talking about it from a brain point of view, like I was so smart to bring this magic. It's just organic stuff that goes into those songs. So you couldn't predict that. You couldn't say, 'Okay let's write one like this, that'll work like this'. Maybe you can get a little setting like that [but] if the magic doesn't come it doesn't make any difference what you do. You can get any kind of setting you want - if the magic doesn't come it's not worth anything."

The first version of 'Angel Of The Morning' was recorded by Evie Sands, with Taylor and Al Gorgoni producing. "I played the song for them," Taylor recalls. "In fact, I wasn't sure if they would like the song or not. I was actually prepared to do it with Billy Vera's sister if Evie didn't like it. In those days I was so shy I was afraid nobody would like anything I was doing. I played it for Al and Evie and they really loved the song. We recorded it with Evie and we released it." However, it seems fate had determined that Sands would never have a hit with a Taylor song: "The company that it was on, Cameo Parkway, went bankrupt the week the record shipped. There were 10,000 records shipped and they were all sold. There were no other records to be gotten. It was number one everyplace it was played. It was a real heartbreak for Al and I because it looked like we really had broken an artist and now it was in litigation. Nobody could get the record." Taylor's and Gorgoni's joint heartbreak was alleviated: "The April

Blackwood Company had some relationship with Chips Moman and Tommy Cogbill out of Memphis and they had been interested in my writing, 'cos I wrote kind of Memphis. They loved 'Angel Of The Morning' and they heard it and they said they wanted to record it with somebody." That somebody turned out to be Merrillee Rush and the Turnabouts who took it to number seven in the US in mid-1968. At almost exactly the same time, a version by black British chanteuse PP Arnold became a top 30 hit in the UK.

"The PP Arnold version was far from the version that I had written but those people that were working with PP at the time - she was with the Mick Jagger crew [Immediate Records] - they were good at what they did", Taylor says. "So whether it was exactly right, at least you knew it was gonna be rock and roll and soulful because that's what they were all about. I was a little taken aback when I first heard that record because it was so dissimilar, but I liked PP and I liked the edge that she gave to it, so I thought it was pretty cool. There's been a lot of different versions of that song and most of them I've liked."

Amongst the other versions are a 1977 record by Mary Mason which, intriguingly, turned 'Angel..' and 'Any Way That You Want Me' into a Chip Taylor medley. "I was so flattered," Taylor says, confirming that he could see the logic behind the idea: "I think those two songs have a certain kind of power and a certain kind of structure. They have a similarity to them."

'Angel..' raises an interesting point about Taylor's songs: "'Angel Of The Morning''s a very rangy song and a lot of my songs are very rangy because I tend to use a lot of different emotions as songs go on. It might carry me to different places and I sing kind of deep when I write them myself. Sometimes I stretch that a bit but I don't think about what I'm doing and then somebody says, 'You know, I don't know if anybody can sing the damn thing'. I was able to do these things as demos but [whether] you carry the power of those things or not... 'Angel Of The Morning' is much better off sung by a girl than a guy. The power of it lends itself better to a girl's voice."

Taylor struck up an occasional writing partnership with the highly successful writer and producer Jerry Ragavoy, composing 'I Can't Wait Until I See My Baby's Face', which achieved success for both Baby Washington and Pat Thomas. The pair wrote another song called 'Try (Just A Little Bit Harder)'. The song was intended for Garnet Mimms, who had recorded the Taylor composition 'Welcome Home' (also recorded by Dusty Springfield and Walter Jackson). "We wrote it as a ballad, and I'm not sure if Garnett recorded it or didn't record it," Taylor says. He was just as uncertain as to the fate of the next incarnation of the song due to a passion in his life that was becoming as important as songwriting: "I was a gambler. I was a horse player, so part of my life every day was involved in thinking about making bets. I would study for a couple of hours every day and make a bet every day, or two, and that was taking up a lot of my thinking. I remember Jerry calling me one day. He said, 'I'm doing a session with Lorraine Allison and I need an uptempo song for Lorraine. You think there's any way that we can change "Try (Just A Little Bit Harder)" into an uptempo song?' I think he called me in the morning or something and I needed to be out at the racetrack in the afternoon. I said, 'Well let me see if I can come up with something'. I remember I put it into the same 'E' 7th groove as 'On My Word'. I started fooling around with it on that basis and had something in about a half-hour. I went over to Jerry's office. I said, 'Jerry, what do you think of this?' and I started playing it for him. He was listening to it and writing it down. He says, 'Yeah, I like that, I like that'. Jerry transposed it and banged away on the piano a little bit as I played guitar. We spent maybe 25 minutes and that was it. Then I heard he recorded it with Lorraine and I really didn't pay that much attention to the record and stuff like that and so I didn't ever really think about it for quite a while."

Finally, the song achieved a prominence which Taylor, however distracted he was, could not help but notice: "A few years later, I was listening to the radio. I caught the tail-end of a song that sounded pretty cool, but I wasn't sure what it was. The D.J. said, 'That's the new Janis Joplin single'. I didn't even know it was mine. Jerry called me up that day. He said, 'You know, we got the new Janis Joplin single'. I said, 'Sounded familiar but I had no idea it was ours'." Joplin executed 'Try (Just A Little Bit Harder)' in her inimitable wracked and intimate style. Taylor: "What she did to it, particularly live, was exactly the same as the song was written except she put this cool interlude in it where she'd just rap to the audience and tell them a story for a while. I loved that. She was amazing."

Regardless of how many years and whatever tortuous routes it might take for a song to become a hit, Taylor's pace when it came to writing was a brisk one: "They come very fast to me," he says. "Either they come or they don't come and when they come, if it sounds inspired, then each comes fast. It's not that I won't rework a song but usually the essence of a song will come within a few minutes. I may sit there doing nonsense things for a while but once the song starts to come, the essence of it will be there within 15 minutes or something like that. And sometimes that song will be *finished* in 15, 20 minutes. 'Angel Of The Morning' was written in 20 minutes."

Riffs and instrumental refrains were often an integral part of the song: "A lot of times, I'd have in mind little arrangement ideas that I'd make sure when the lead sheet was written would contain that, so people would see that. I'd make it part of something that was important." That notwithstanding, Taylor says that his demos were usually very basic: "A lot of times it was just me playing the guitar, overdubbing something and if there was something that I thought was important to the song I would make sure that that was there. 'Any Way That You Want Me', the original demo was just a guitar-voice demo and a double voice and banging on something. The original 'Wild Thing' was the same thing. Some of them were a little bit more intricate. The ones that were more intricate as demos were the ones [where] I was making actual records. Like when I was recording Evie Sands, Al and I were making records and those records *became* demos because people covered them."

By the late 'Sixties, Taylor had overcome his insecurities

sufficiently to start recording as part of a trio with Al Gorgoni and Trade Martin. After Gorgoni, Martin and Taylor had put out some well-received music, Taylor was approached by Neil Bogart of the Buddah label and asked if he would like to record a solo album. Taylor accepted the offer and recorded *Gasoline,* released in 1971. "I was trying at that point to write stuff for myself, just stuff that I wanted to do as an artist," Taylor recalls. "Some of the songs ended up being quite personal. It wasn't necessarily something I was trying to do, but that's the way the stuff came out. And they were more folk-flavoured. Throughout the Seventies I only did one album that had a rock and roll edge, and that was the *Gasoline* album."

Gasoline featured Taylor's own rendition of 'Angel Of The Morning', which the record company decided to release as a single. "They thought they could break it," he reflects. "I really liked the staff at Buddah. They were a bunch of nice people. The song ended up getting up to 101 in *Cash Box* and not on the charts on *Billboard* and 118 in *Record World.* That's as high as it got and then it went down." The record's failure inspired a new song by Taylor, '101 In Cash Box', which featured on his 1973 album *Chip Taylor's Last Chance*: "The song is just a little funny look at music business stuff: guys who try to help me and break my record but aren't able to and how it goes up the charts and down - you get the guy on the phone one day, [the next] you're a has-been." Behind the good-humoured response lay a genuine desire to achieve significant success as a recording artist: "There was always some hope that that would happen, that something would break for me. I continue that right now."

A measure of how keen was Taylor's desire to be successful is the fact that a traumatic incident in 1980 caused him to effectively retire from music for a decade-and-a-half. Taylor had recently left Columbia Records after they had declined to release a song he felt had single potential. "I went to Capitol under the promise that they would support a release of mine in the country division," he says. "But when my single finally came out they in fact didn't support it... You have to understand the politics in the

States with record companies, particularly if you're an artist that's a country artist. At the point, I had a little bit of a country following and I needed the country support. The country divisions in major record companies ran autonomously and they didn't want to be dictated to them what they had to support and not support." Taylor's single, 'One Night Out With The Boys', was the number one requested record on several stations. "I thought for sure I had a hit," Taylor recalls. "One of the stations called me. He said, 'You're not gonna believe what happened. The Capitol promotion rep was just by. He said to please not play your record, they were not gonna get to that record for a while. They had several they needed to promote first'." Inevitably, Taylor raised questions about this approach: "There was a big meeting with the head of A&R at the company, who had signed me, the chairman of board of directors (both of whom I liked very much) and the head of promotion in Nashville who refused to promote me. When the dust cleared, I lost the battle. The chairman of the board told me, 'I'm sorry to tell you this Chip, but we're gonna lose this battle because the country division is having such a great year that I can't fight them'. We'll make it up to you next time'. I said. 'I totally understand. But I don't think there will be a next time'."

Taylor decided that the music business was no longer worth the candle. Unwilling to put himself through the hassles involved in being a recording artist and aware that in an age of self-composing performers, returning to his freelance writing role of the 'Sixties wasn't really an option, he became a professional gambler. Music barely impinged upon his life: "Bonnie Raitt recorded a song I wrote with Billy Vera called 'Papa Come Quick' and once in a while I'd write a couple of songs but it wasn't the day where everybody was looking for songs. And I was just perfectly content to be doing my gambling. I was getting enough money from my royalties to not worry too much. I needed to supplement it a little bit and I was able to do that and make a fairly good living."

Taylor's gambling activities centered around betting on horses and playing blackjack. "It's a job," he says. "It's a skill. You've gotta work very hard at it. Harder than you do almost at anything. It's a real involved science. You cannot win unless you treat it like a science. I had a partner that was the biggest money maker of all time and we shared information and I did well over a bunch of years." His blackjack playing skills rival those seen in the *Rain Man* movie: "I had very good card counting skills. I've got very good memory and could remember things. I always had a way to beat the casinos - until they started to ban me and make it uncomfortable for me to play."

Taylor's fifteen-year spurning of the music industry ended when his mother fell ill. "One week, instead of going to the race track, I spent it with my mom and that week I picked up the guitar and each day I wrote a song and played it for mom and she would talk to me about it. I just had a really great week with her." The direct and instant feedback reminded Taylor of a tour of Holland he had made in 1975 when a record of his had broken there: "The only time in my life I ever toured for more than a couple of weeks. When I played for my mom I remembered that spirit that I had in Holland and I said, 'What the hell am I doing here? This is what I should be doing'. All of a sudden, I made a big, big life change. It reminded me of the spirit I had when I played with my high school band. We used to play in bars. This was a re-birth for me, going back to that period of time where I just couldn't wait to play for people. Now that's all I want to do."

Having been away from music so long, it was far from certain that - notwithstanding the permanent presence of 'Wild Thing' and 'Angel Of The Morning' on Gold radio playlists - many would remember who Taylor was. Taylor: "The record company, little company I was doing business with at the time, suggested that I let people know what I'd done. Do an album of my hits." The result was the punningly titled *Hit Man*, on which Taylor tackled all of his major hit songs. Since then, he has barely looked back, not least in the way he has made up, with a vengeance, for his previous disdain for live performance. He releases albums on his own Track Wreck label, including the massively ambitious *Seven Days In May*, a suite based around a true incident from Taylor's personal life. There has been some discussion of turning the album into a stage play. "I'm probably selling more records now than I ever was," Taylor reveals. "Particularly in Europe. I have a little base in Holland and Scandinavia and England. I'm still not selling anything significant but at least I'm selling more than most folk artists are." Taylor is very happy to report that some of this success is due to fewer restrictions in the modern music industry: "It seems like there's more of a shot now, with the internet and with a lot of different forms of radio. Now's there's more of a shot for anybody who has talent to at least be able to get their stuff out there. Back in the days where I was fighting the record companies, it seemed like if you didn't play by their rules there was almost no way you could get heard. Now, at least I feel like selling my stuff across the stage and having my own little record company and on the internet and reasonably decent distribution, my fans can find ways to get [my] music."

He doesn't, however, feel the time he spent away from music from 1980 until 1995 constitute wasted years. "I never look back," he says. "I had a wonderful creative time with gambling."

Taylor's interest in reactivating his freelance writing - an avenue now theoretically open to him again in an era of manufactured acts with no or little composing talent - is negligible: "I don't treat it so much like a business like it was in years gone by. I don't have a branch of my company down in Nashville. Basically, every so often if I hear something for somebody, I'll send it down to them. I'm really much more into just doing my tours and staying with my fans." In light of this, it's ironic that when the author spoke to Taylor in early 2001, 'Angel Of The Morning' was in the process of becoming a hit yet again in the hands of reggae star Shaggy. "They call it 'Angel' and I own half of the song," says Taylor of Shaggy's somewhat re-written version. "He sent a copy over to me and asked if it was alright. I thought that his record was really cool. We agreed that we'd call it another title because he used some other elements in it as well and we worked out a deal where I own half of that copyright."

Meanwhile, the 2000s also saw Taylor obtaining a new lease

of life as a performer. His *Black & Blue America* album - released in 2001 - was his biggest-seller to date. He then hooked up with a fiddle player named Carrie Rodriguez. The two issued two duet albums which became the biggest-selling albums of Taylor's career, thanks in part to the recent birth of the Americana chart, a sort of alternative country chart that finally set Taylor free from the shackles of the country establishment that had once disgusted him so much as to bring about his retirement.

Though Taylor is flattered that younger artists value his songs, he sometimes finds that they are more *au fait* with his compositions than he: "After I just came back to making music, I was at the Bottom Line and Marshall Crenshaw said to me, 'Chip, I just did a show and they asked me to do something that I wish I'd written and I did your song "Julie".' I said, 'Pardon me?' 'Your song "Julie".' 'I think you got the wrong guy'. I totally forgot that I wrote a song called 'Julie' for Bobby Fuller Four. I had no idea. I couldn't remember it. That's what happens every once in a while."

Taylor sees cause for optimism in the state of songwriting today: "The kind of stuff that I listen to is mostly the roots-orientated stuff. I listen in the car to Lucinda Williams or Townes Van Zandt. If I listen to stations, it's gonna be stations that play that kind of music. Since Shaggy's record's become so big, every once in a while I turn on the pop stations and listen to that and I think it's fine, I think it's okay. I think there's a lot of good things, as in every age, including the rap stuff. There's good and bad in everything. I think where it becomes bad is where it sounds very clonish. At almost every turn in music, you'll get that. You'll find some groundbreaking things and then record companies have a habit of trying to capitalise on those and they record a lot of crappy things that ten years from now will just be on a junk pile - nobody'll care. There'll always be some cool things coming up. For a singer-songwriter, I think it's a better time now than it was ten or fifteen years ago. Even though you don't hear them as your main street pop things, there's a chance for these people to be heard and I think you're going to get a lot of great things. I think a bunch of artists in that area are coming up with some cool things. Maybe not in the mainstream, but if that's all you're listening to then you're missing a lot of great songs."

For himself, Taylor says his writing technique has barely changed over the years: "I just have what I have in terms of my musical ability and I just let stuff happen. It seems like when I come back to making music now - 'cos now I'm touring and I'm out recording all the time and doing things mainly for myself - that my stuff may lean more folkish or countryish. Some of the things don't. It depends where I'm heading a little bit, where I wake up and what side of the bed I'm on but no, I don't think there's much difference at all."

Except for one thing: "I'm writing more than I ever wrote these days."

9

TONY MACAULAY

"In songs like 'What Becomes Of The Broken Hearted', they do a blind minor-third shift. They just change key from 'A' to 'C' without any chord and they're very exciting because of it but if you watch kids singing along to it, the kids couldn't hear the key change. So if you're going to put any modulations in, the modulations have to be totally written into the song so that a child of five can follow the melody line. Only we'll know that there's a lot of clever stuff going on. The trick is, finish the song and walk to the pub and if we can sing the whole song without an reference to the chords then it works. And if you can't, then it's too clever by half."

In discussing his approach to songwriting, Tony Macaulay is revealing the scientific mind of a man who trained in civil engineering before entering the music business. It is almost certainly that meticulousness of approach that led him to be one of the most in-demand songwriters for a full decade from 1967-onwards, a position he only relinquished because of his desire to try his hand at other disciplines. His success in those other fields - he is now almost completely dedicated to writing thrillers - has meant that he composes rarely these days but the extent of his artistic as well as commercial genius as a pop songwriter is

revealed by a glance at just a few of the Gold radio staples bearing
his name: 'Build Me Up Buttercup', 'Sorry Suzanne', 'Love Grows
(Where My Rosemary Goes)', 'Kissin' In The Back Row Of
The Movies', 'Don't Give Up On Us'...

Macaulay was born on April 21st 1944 as Tony Instone. His
story is slightly unusual because he was not one of those countless
figures set on a musical career path by a momentous first hearing
of 'Heartbreak Hotel'. "I couldn't have been less interested in
any of it," he says of the original rock and roll explosion. "It just
went by me. My mother was a marvellous pianist who played
Rachmaninov right through to Rogers & Hammerstein and I grew
up with all that." Things changed when Macaulay enlisted at King's
College in Wimbledon, an establishment he describes as "a second
rate public school" whose "sole interest was making sure you
graduated with a first in buggery and bigotry". He explains, "I
was in my first year there and the whole class got put into detention
for taking a minute's silence during a chemistry class when we
heard Buddy Holly had been killed. I didn't know who the fuck
Buddy Holly was. I systematically borrowed records off people
and over the following year or two familiarised myself with
everything to do with Buddy Holly. My interest in pop music stems
entirely from my interest in Buddy Holly." However: "I never
wrote like Buddy Holly, strangely enough. Once I started writing,
I was much more influenced by Burt Bacharach, Holland-Dozier-
Holland. My earlier songs were a fusion of those two styles."

Macaulay started playing the guitar but was thrown out of his
own band at the age of sixteen for not being good enough. He
wrote his very first song, 'That Ain't You And Me', at the age of
eighteen while doing his civil engineering degree. "Piece of shit it
was, too. One of the very, very few things that didn't get recorded
by somebody at some time."

In time-honoured fashion, he tried hawking his songs around
London's Tin Pan Alley. Len Black at Essex Music, unimpressed
by his songs but impressed by his determination, offered him a job
as a plugger, which he started a month before his 21st birthday.
This necessitated changing his name, as his cousin Anna Instone

(who he actually only met once) worked for BBC radio and Essex were worried that charges of favouritism might be levelled. The name Macaulay was plucked out of a telephone directory. Amongst acts whose records the renamed Instone handled in his two years at Essex were The Who and the Rolling Stones.

"The day I joined the business, a guy who was virtually my father's age called John Macleod came into the office asking if there were any lead sheets to do. We went and had a drink together in the pub and it turned out that he was an arranger and a proper pianist." The two quickly realised that they could be mutually beneficial to each other. "John had never really made it as a songwriter," explains Macaulay. "He had all the experience, knew a lot of harmony, had a lot of arrangement skills. I had a tremendous amount of energy but not a great deal of information. The two of us together were pretty dynamite for a while because we covered the waterfront." As with all but one of Macaulay's songwriting partnerships, there was no clear division of labour: both supplied lyrics and melodies. Macleod also inspired Macaulay to broaden his musical horizons: "I quickly realized that playing a dozen chords on a guitar was only part of it. To really be a journeyman - or a bespoke - songwriter, you need to play the piano as well. So we started writing songs together and all the time he was playing I was watching where his fingers were going. I stayed in the office after everyone had left - I got locked in a couple of times, had to sleep on the floor - and taught myself the piano. I figured out the chords from the guitar and transposed them to the piano."

This dedication was not, initially, rewarded with any commercial success, despite the fact that the pair got their names on a couple of records. Macaulay: "We just couldn't get started. Later on, out of the dozen songs we were hawking around, eleven of them were top ten hits." In 1966, their talents were at least recognized enough for them to be signed up to a publishing deal by A. Schroeder. The deal, though, would eventually became a millstone around the pair's necks.

In early 1967, Macaulay bluffed his way into a job as house producer at Pye. "I had realised, having got to know all the other pluggers and all the other key people, that you never stood a chance in getting a song recorded unless you were the producer," he says. "You had to be on the inside looking out." His contract with Pye, although it didn't involve a percentage on the records he would produce, did mean a weekly wage of £28, "which was quite a bit of money in those days." Surprisingly, he didn't exploit his newfound power by getting acts to record his compositions: "By this time, I'd lost all faith in my own songs. I thought, 'I've got to go out and get the best songs I can get'. I systematically went through every publisher in the industry and got nowhere after six months. The deal was unless you had a hit in the first year you were dead. I was very depressed and John was saying, 'Why don't we do one of our songs?'"

Macaulay decided to act on Macleod's advice when one day required to audition a band. "I turned up and there was this multiracial group who I thought were fucking awful and they had a very pushy manager who said, 'Have you got a song?' Well the strange part was, we did. We had a song that was really only a chorus, and only eight bars at that, just repeated twice, but very strong melody line with a moving bass part." Said song was an infectious piece of soul-pop titled 'Baby Now That I've Found You'. "We worked [it] out very quickly and we took them into this studio," continues Macaulay. "It was a fucking disaster from the beginning. The bass player was playing total bollocks and the singer was hopeless. The line: 'Darling I just can't let you-too' - he couldn't get that to save his life. Gradually we started to solve the problem. John played piano. We got a session bass player. Even then, we couldn't get beyond the vocal problem." This latter obstacle was overcome by getting Macleod's recreational barbershop quartet to sing the line. The barbershop quartet then had to be given other parts on the record to sing to prevent the line sounding incongruous. "I heard it on the Monday morning," says Macaulay of the finished product. "I thought it was absolutely marvellous. I couldn't believe how good it sounded." The label shared the composers' enthusiasm and released the record under the name The Foundations. Despite considerable promotion, it sank without trace.

Fate intervened several months later when the newly formed Radio One, unwilling to play material that the pirates had, started looking for records that had undeservedly failed over the previous few months. Macaulay: "So the eighth record played on Radio One was 'Baby Now That I've Found You'. Went straight in the charts about 26 and within a couple of weeks was number one." The record also climbed to number 11 Stateside.

After the years of failure, now came a tidal wave of success. In late 1967, Macaulay and Macleod achieved the stunning feat of deposing themselves from atop the British singles charts when 'Let The Heartaches Begin', performed by Long John Baldry, nudged aside the Foundations hit. The record couldn't have been more different to 'Baby Now That I've Found You'. "Louis Benjamin, who was [Pye's] managing director, wanted to try and find an Englebert Humperdinck and in his naivety picked Long John Baldry." Baldry, at that point, was almost the beautiful loser of the R&B circuit: almost the only figure from the early 'Sixties British blues scene not to have become commercially successful. Many were stunned to see him singing such a string-drenched piece of melodrama as 'Let The Heartaches Begin'. "He was desperate for some commercial success," explains Macaulay. "People have said, 'How could you have given such a blues singer something so blatantly commercial?' But it was his idea, not ours. I wasn't absolutely certain that song was a hit. Louis Benjamin said, 'What have you got that would suit him?' That was the only strong ballad that we had. But Macleod came up with this sensational arrangement with these guitars moving in two parts." The intricately planned nature of the record was par for the course for Macaulay and Macleod: "Everything was worked out. John and I would spend as much time working the arrangements out as we did writing the song. We were very clear what all the riffs were going to be and what all the string lines were going to be. We discussed it as we wrote the song."

The pair's names were now hot. Producer Mickie Most decided that one of their compositions from the first Foundations album, 'I

Can Take Or Leave Your Loving', would be an appropriate song for Herman's Hermits and gave them a UK number 11 and US number 22 with it. Macaulay: "People started digging up all our songs and everything got recorded, good or bad."

Having to write singles and album tracks for all their acts (Pinkerton's Assorted Colours were another group with whom they were working at the time: they would eventually have a US top five hit in 1969 under the name The Flying Machine) meant the resuscitation of a songwriting team that had actually been more-or-less dormant. "Once we'd used up all the stuff we'd written years ago - which we did quite quickly - it was a big shock to suddenly sit down and write again," recalls Macaulay.

Yet another Pye act Macaulay and Macleod took on the writing and production duties of was the female trio Paper Dolls, with whom they had a UK number 11 with 'Something Here In My Heart (Keeps A-Tellin' Me No)'. "It was a big hit, they got a huge amount of publicity and become absolutely impossible," says Macaulay. "They changed their manager twice a day. I wrote 'Build Me Up Buttercup' and I was going to do it with them and they never turned up to the studio. The whole band's sitting there. I was livid. I went and did the song with The Foundations."

Macaulay's and Macleod's track record with The Foundations (now with a new lead singer) had been respectable rather than spectacular after that first single, them scoring number 18 and number 48 with their UK follow- ups. 'Build Me Up Buttercup', another slab of joyous pop-soul, was the first hit Macaulay didn't write with Macleod. Instead it was Mike D'Abo who copped the other half of the publishing: "He lived down the street from me and we were friends. I went round there one night and our girlfriends were chatting in the kitchen, so to kill the time 'til dinner was ready we wrote that."

D'Abo had the riff and some of the melody. "I just wanted to have a strong verse and get some interesting chords into it, have a little story," Macaulay recollects. "Songs like 'There Is Always Something There To Remind Me' - the chorus was just that one line. I actually call that a sniff-and-miss-it chorus. My choruses are 16-bar choruses, real substantial choruses. You don't want the whole thing filled up with padding for one good bit." As for the peculiar title phrase, Macaulay reveals, "'Build Me Up Buttercup' was the dummy lyric, like 'scrambled eggs' was the dummy lyric for 'Yesterday'. We were always going to change it right to the last minute. When it came to put the lead vocal on, we'd none of us thought of anything better. That was the first one I did the arrangement on my own." Macaulay, incidentally, suspects that 'Build Me Up Buttercup', which hit number 2 in Britain and number 3 Stateside, was the inspiration, melodically, for Abba's 'Waterloo'.

The first solo Macaulay composition to make the charts was 'Baby Make It Soon', which gave Marmalade a UK number 9 in mid-1969: "It was a funny little song that I knocked out one evening very, very quickly and without any thought. They made quite a sweet little record of it. I never thought it was a hit, particularly."

The fact that he'd managed to write a hit without a partner didn't tempt Macaulay to do it all on his own. "Once I was successful and used to having three or four major hits a year, the sheer volume of material you need to turn out to service all these acts, you can't possibly do it on your own," he says. He also reveals, "You're looking to collaborate with people who've not only got good ideas but who record acts themselves. So the song you turn out, if it isn't suitable for one of your own acts it may be suitable for one of theirs... As soon as a new writer established himself, I got to know him quite quickly and we started writing, so I was writing with everybody that was worth a goddamn at one point." During the course of 1969, Macaulay, partnering either Macleod or Geoff Stevens, wrote songs for Tom Jones, Scott Walker, Sandie Shaw, Tina Tott, the Committee, Jefferson, Flying Machine and The Hollies, as well as more material for The Foundations and Baldry.

"I spent hours sweating over the psychology of how the songs were put together," Macaulay says. "For example, if it was an unknown artist, we felt that if we started with a long, engaging verse, by the time they got to the chorus, the disc jockey would take it off and play another one, so if it was an unknown artist we'd start with a bit of a chorus just to tell them how good it was going to be. If it was a name artist, we could afford to start with a verse and then get that nice lift into the chorus so that you lulled them into the mood of the song, so when the chorus came it was a sort of big thrill." He unblushingly acknowledges the functionalism of their approach: the first band to come along and prove they were able to sing a song were given it. "When you're hot, you're hot and you're desperate to capitalize on the fact that you can get stuff played on the radio." How much material was he discarding? "Nothing, because everything was written down and if we got sixteen bars into it and it didn't sound like a hit, it was dumped there and then. If it sounded like a 'maybe', then it was an album track, or if it was really shitty, a B-side."

One of his best compositions in '69 was the gloriously contrite and soaring 'Sorry Suzanne', written with Stephens and recorded by The Hollies. It was an important disc for The Hollies, who had just lost Graham Nash and thus seen the rupturing of the band's internal writing team of Nash, Tony Hicks and Allan Clarke. Macaulay: "Tony Hicks asked to meet me and that was the only song I had and I hadn't decided what to do with it. I said, 'If you want to do something with it, you better do it damn quick because I've got a whole bunch of my own acts..' They did it straightaway and they made a very good record of it. I was thrilled with it. Suzanne was the name of a bar girl. I knocked a pint of beer over and said, 'Sorry Suzanne'."

Macaulay would co-write another single for The Hollies the following year in the shape of 'Gasoline Alley Bred', this time with Roger Cook and Roger Greenaway: "That was the only song I wrote with both Greenaway *and* Cook, because even though Cook's name appeared on a lot of them, he was never there. They just did a Lennon & McCartney and credited each other always. I started it with one and finished it with the other. A girlfriend came up with the title and the idea so I gave her a small percentage of mine."

By 1969, Macaulay had begun to realise that he needed to get away from both Pye and Schroeder. "I was getting 28 quid a week and expenses and I was not getting any publishing money because Schroeder was a complete crook." The fact of how much better he should have been doing was underlined by the kind of people attempting to headhunt him. He recalls, "One day I was in a pub where everybody [at Pye] drank and this black guy with a couple of bodyguards came up to me and said, 'Hi, my name's Berry Gordy Jnr. I'm looking for Tony Macaulay'." Macaulay, though, didn't quite apprehend what an honour was being bestowed on him by this visit from Motown's head honcho. "I remember distinctly thinking, 'If they'd sent Berry Gordy Snr., I might have been impressed'. I didn't realize that Berry Gordy was Berry Gordy Jnr. so I was quite offhand with him. You know: 'Listen sonny, next time your father comes in town get him to call me'." Musical history, and Macaulay's own life, might have been different if he'd accepted Gordy's approach, but Macaulay says, "Well, he didn't pay anybody either, did he? So I don't particularly regret that."

Of the labels attempting to woo him, Macaulay went with Bell, who offered him a $1m advance (payable over four years) and, crucially, damages to settle the deal with Pye. It would take far longer to escape the clutches of Schroeder: seven years and legal action all the way up to the House of Lords. Part of the deal with Bell involved Macaulay owning the masters to the songs he produced and wrote and only leasing them to the record company, that way hugely increasing the revenue normally accruing to a songwriter. "Trouble is," he says, "income tax was 83% at that point. You could get a Rolls Royce and a chauffeur because that was on the company but you couldn't do anything personally much because you were living on 17% of your income. I didn't get a great deal richer."

Macaulay's debut for Bell couldn't have been more stunning. "Within weeks of signing the deal I was writing with my neighbour Barry Mason, who's a lyricist," he says. "I don't usually work with lyricists. We were working on a ballad and I stopped halfway through writing this thing and I said, 'This is all very well but I've never going to have a hit with it'." About an hour later, the two had completed a somewhat more uptempo number, 'Love Grows (Where My Rosemary Goes)'. "I called my manager and played it over the phone to him. I was absolutely certain it was number one. Never had a doubt."

Having just joined Bell, Macaulay had no artist to record it with so instead booked a group called Greenfield Hammer and an orchestra and went in the studio. "Even did the vocal backing lines, everything," he reveals. "We just did two takes of it and time ran out." One of the backing singers at the session was Tony Burrows. Macaulay heard him playing a tape of his voice to a female backing singer. "I thought, 'That's quite an interesting voice'. I said to him, 'Can you sing through your nose? I've looking for a vocalist for that track and I want him to sound very Bronx/Brooklynese'. He went away and learnt it and we stuck his voice on and some handclaps and that was it."

The record was a pop classic, the kind of which make the listener happy to be alive as soon as it started playing. Not surprisingly, the record, under the name Edison Lighthouse, went to number one in the UK. In the US, it got as far as number 5. To this day, it can be heard with almost tedious regularity on Gold radio. Yet it was the end of Macaulay's association with the manufactured band. "I never made another single with them," he says. "I knew they were a one-hit wonder. Also, that record is one of my favourites of that period and I just thought, 'If I do something different, people'll say it's not recognizable as that group, if I do something the same they'll say it's formularised. I know I can't win so I've not going to spoil the euphoria of that hit'."

Despite him almost earning back his advance with that one record, relations between Macaulay and his new label soured remarkably quickly. "the difficultly was that I changed my style pretty radically after that. Started writing songs that were ultimately hits for Glen Campbell and the Fifth Dimension. Much more mature material. They didn't want me to do any of that. They wanted more 'Love Grows..'"

1970 saw Macaulay, with various partners, make the charts

with Andy Williams, The Hollies, Englebert Humperdinck, Picketywitch and Johnny Johnson and the Bandwagon. The latter's 'Blame It On The Pony Express' (a Macaulay/Greenaway/Cook writing credit) was one of the most interesting things Macaulay has written from a lyrical point of view. "It gets the whole history of the Pony Express into it," he says. "We got it out of a dictionary." Macaulay also wrote 'You're A Star', which was recorded by Carl Wayne and became the theme to British TV's talent-spotting *New Faces*. The Humperdinck hit was 'My Marie', written with Mason: "Anything I wrote with Barry he'd take straight along to [Humperdinck manager] Gordon Mills. It was a ballad and it was quite a nice song. I think we had him vaguely in mind when we wrote it." Does this mean he would usually tailor his style to that of the established acts with whom he had hits? "No, not really. The hits I had with outside artists were never intended for them."

In 1970, Macaulay took the Songwriter Of the Year title (for his work during '69) at the first Ivor Novello Awards. The ultimate accolade? "Oh Jesus Christ, I should say so. I was beside myself." Even better was to come. The following year he placed a song with none other than Elvis Presley: "Freddie Bienstock, who was his publisher, contacted various British writers who were successful." The song with which Macaulay came up (on his own) for The King was 'If I Get Home On Christmas Day'. This was one song that most certainly was written with the artist's style in mind. "That was an absolutely studied piece, a bespoke suit," says Macaulay. "I remember making phone calls asking 'Does it put Elvis off if the person [on the demo] sings like Elvis?' and they said, 'No quite the contrary - he only thinks it's for him if it sounds like it's been demoed for him'. So we intentionally made it sound like Elvis. In fact, the guy on the demo sounds more like Elvis than Elvis." Placing the song, of course, involved more than the thrill of hearing his words coming from the mouth of the ultimate rock icon: "It was on an album that sold 11 million." Macaulay, who would write two other songs for Presley, says of the singer, "I met him a couple of times. It was like meeting someone who looked like Elvis and sounded like Elvis but you couldn't believe it was Elvis because Elvis somehow occupied a place in one's imagination that didn't seem possible."

During his time with Bell, Macaulay's new adult style alienated the label so much - they repeatedly turned down songs that became hits - that he ended up achieving more chart action for other companies including, ironically, Pye. When his contract came up for renewal, he declined. "Even though Bell were due to pay me a £50,000 bonus to stay on, I said 'No, I didn't want to stay'. The day I quit was the day we recorded 'You Won't Find Another Fool Like Me' with the [New] Seekers."

Macaulay describes 'You Won't Find..' (released on Polydor) as "A piece of shit. It sounded like an old Connie Francis thing to me." However, the New Seekers, and the public, loved it: "It went to number one. It put my career right back."

The following year, Macaulay embarked on one of the projects which has given him the most pleasure when he helped resurrect the chart career of The Drifters. "When I was writing, I was either Levi Stubbs in my head or Ben E. King," he says. However, writing for a group who had first become famous (in a slightly different configuration) in the 'Fifties posed a slight problem: "I said to Roger [Greenaway], 'The girls aren't going to fancy these guys anymore... It's got to be humorous. Why don't we do a real 'Fifties concept - kissing in the back row of the movies?' And we got the chorus almost immediately. We had a great deal of fun doing it."

Amongst the UK hits Macaulay and Greenaway scored for The Drifters over the following three years were the afore-mentioned 'Kissin' In The Back Row Of The Movies', 'Down On The Beach Tonight' and 'You're More Than A Number In My Little Red Book', each record a deliberate pastiche of what The Drifters had originally stood for but no less exhilarating for it. "All those songs were written with tongue-in-cheek," says Macaulay. "'Let's make it always like there's a party going on on the record'. We'd say, 'Well we've done the beach, we've done the cinema, what else is there to do that people did in the 'Fifties?' In our mind's eye we never went later than 1959 and we used some of the production techniques and values. Back to back with that, I was doing some of my best work in America with ballads with some of the best lyrics I've ever written and it was a huge release to do that kind of thing."

Another 'Fifties icon whose career Macaulay helped resuscitate around this time was Duane Eddy, who reached number 9 in the UK in 1975 with a song inspired by one of Macaulay's lovers: "My girlfriend at the time said, 'Christ you spend as much time hugging me as you do that bloody guitar'." 'Play Me Like You Play Your Guitar' again featured a sound as authentically 'Fifties as possible. "I made him bring over the original twangy guitar," says Macaulay. "The record was an echo of 'Mr. Guitar Man'. We even did a quote from it. The whole thing was really just me re-living my childhood."

In 1976, Macaulay found himself going through a barren patch. Relocating to Los Angeles, he found things just as bleak there until he suddenly received a call from Larry Uttal, who had been his boss at Bell but was now working at an American label called Private Stock. "[He] said, 'Have you heard of David Soul?'" The man who played the blonde half of the *Starsky And Hutch* TV detective team was signed to Private Stock and had already done very well with his first album. After being sent that debut, Macaulay played Uttal a silky ballad called 'Don't Give Up On Us'. "He said, 'Fly out tomorrow and record it with him'."

Macaulay had come up with the song during a drive from LA to San Francisco: "I wrote the song about my first wife. It's all about getting pissed and being sorry about it: 'I really lost my head last night/You've got a right to stop believing'. So it was really a very personal little song. Nice lines in that. One of the best lyrics I've ever written." It was also a departure for Macaulay musically. "All my songs have quite a wide range - they're all a journey to the hook where you belt out those high notes. 'Don't Give Up On Us' is the only song I've written which lies within an octave and is all mid-voice."

Of the recording of the song, Macaulay recalls, "It was the most extraordinary session of my life. David was extremely pleasant. We laid the track with part of Steely Dan and Elvis Presley's rhythm section - I put together a wish-list band. I took the tracks back, got off the Red-Eye at six o' clock in the morning and went straight in the studio at nine with a sodding great orchestra. They were so desperate to get the record out that they wanted me to mix it there and then. I went to bed for two-and-a-half days. Got up, turned the radio on and the bloody thing was on the radio! I thought, 'Christ - that's a lousy edit'. I'd edited two mixes together - the piano disappears after twelve bars. Nobody seemed to notice."

The single topped both the UK and US charts in early 1977. Although the actor was a one-hit wonder in his native land, Macaulay had several more hits with Soul in Britain, the second of which - 'Silver Lady' - Macaulay cites as one of his favourites of the records with which he's been associated. "Tremendous energy and excitement in the track," he says.

His success with Soul and continued success with The Drifters earned Macaulay a second Ivor Novello Songwriter Of The Year award in 1978. "It was astonishing," he says. "I couldn't believe they could give it to anybody twice, let alone at the other end of a decade." However, in Macaulay's eyes it was a valediction rather than a platform for continued chart success: "I was getting so mixed up with theatre and other things that interested me, I felt very much like that was the bookend of it all. Bespoke songwriters - that was a dying breed anyway. When I went up to get that award a second time, I was very conscious that most of the people that were sitting there were in bands themselves. What did affect me a lot, when I first became successful I met Richard Rogers and Johnny Mercer, a lot of the great songwriters of that era. I was very shaken by how bitter they all seemed. They were all going on about how terrible pop music was now and how they hadn't had a hit for twenty years. I absolutely resolved that I was never, ever going to be like that. I'd had a charmed existence anyway, an incredible run that was going to produce income come-what-may. The important thing was to move on and do other things and start learning new skills." That process had already started, with some of his chart hits having been lifted from unfinished musicals he'd been working on. One example was 'Let's Have A Quiet Night In', David Soul's fourth UK hit. The same was true of songs he gave to Gladys Knight around this time.

Macaulay had had a false start in his prospective new career when a musical he wrote about Laurel & Hardy with renowned British sitcom writers Dick Clement and Ian La Frenais failed to make the stage. However, Louis Benjamin, Macaulay's old boss as Pye, gave him another chance at the medium when he became head of the Stan Moss theatre chain. Macaulay's suggestion was a musical version of the 1920s Broadway hit *The Front Page*. It reached the British stage in 1982 with a star-studded cast that included well-known British television and stage actors Dennis Waterman and Anton Rodgers, although not without some problems. "We had a huge setback," Macaulay recalls. "Four days before we were due to go into rehearsals, the director died. Peter Wood came in to direct it. He panicked and started making drastic changes to the show. He said, 'Fuck Dennis Waterman, just cut the bloody book - make it move quicker'." Despite mixed reviews, the show won awards (including another Ivor Novello for Macaulay) and ran in the West End for most of the year. "But the show was hugely expensive, so when Dennis Waterman's time was up they couldn't afford to run it anymore, they couldn't get anybody to replace him," says Macaulay. The show was, with some musical alterations by Macaulay, later a resounding hit in Chicago and played for a season in New York.

Although audience reaction to his stage shows could be bad as well as good, it afforded Macaulay a privilege he had never had as a writer of records: "Somebody said recently that I've sold 52 million records - but I've only ever seen one person buy one. You never get to see the audience enjoy what you do."

Czar Of The Movies was Macaulay's next stab at a musical and was directed by the legendary Bob Fosse. It was at Fosse's suggestion that Macaulay not only wrote the music but the show's script. "I thoroughly enjoyed writing the book," he says. "I really enjoyed hearing people speak my dialogue." This opened up yet another career path for Macaulay. A line in a newspaper gave him an idea for a novel about the Japanese staging a revenge for their defeat in 1945 by causing chaos in Wall Street fifty years to day after the Allies' victory. At the suggestion of his second wife (a journalist) he wrote an eight-page treatment and sent it to three agents, two of whom called back within 32 hours. He co-wrote the book - called Sayonara - with his wife, them publishing it under the name Elliot Marshall.

He wrote his next book *Affairs Of State* (*Enemy Of The State* in the UK) on his own and under his own name. "That sold over 200,000," he says. "Jack Higgins put a quote on the front: 'Incredible new discovery, best thing of its kind since *Day Of The Jackal*'. I did another one called *Brutal Truth*. Next one is called *Changing Damnation*, about the cloning of Christ. And I've just finished another one. I actually lecture about writing thrillers now, here and in America."

Does he enjoy writing novels more than pop songs? "It's a totally different set of thrills," he replies. "Writing pop music is very visceral. Just to stand in the middle of a good band or orchestra when they're playing or to hear it on the radio for the first time... It's like sex - instant. Writing a book is a very gradual process. It takes me fourteen-to-fifteen months to do it. It grows very slowly, even though the idea might come to you very quickly."

Although he considers himself to be mainly a novelist these days, Macaulay states that he is willing to work in any of the mediums in which he has found success. When this author spoke to him, he was back in the studio for the first time in years. "'Build Me Up Buttercup' was the key thing in [the movie *There's*] *Something About Mary*," he says. "That's created a whole new life for me. I've just done a new song for a major picture. It's the best thing I've done in a long while... As far as I've concerned, if anyone'll pay me to be creative at 55, I've just damn glad to be busy and working on all sorts of things."

10
CHINN & CHAPMAN

In the years 1973 to 1975, the two most important people in the British music industry were almost certainly Mike Chapman and Nicky Chinn. This pair of songwriters/producers were responsible for a tidal wave of hits: the Chinnichap sobriquet they devised for their publishing company became familiar to teens up and down the land who troubled to inspect the labels of the records by their idols Sweet, Mud and Suzi Quatro. In addition, their music came to define an era: their anthemic, pounding records for the aforesaid acts epitomized the Glam Rock sound that then dominated the airwaves in the British Isles. Once that glam boom was over, they proved themselves equally capable of more sophisticated fare with the classy pop-rock they devised for Smokie.

Nicholas Barry Chinn was born on May 16th 1945. "I was brought up in London, then I went off to boarding school at the age of six in Surrey and then I went to public school in Bristol, so one could say I was brought up in London but I always went away to school," he says. Had he wanted, Chinn had an opportunity for a comfortable lifestyle in his family's motor car business. "They wanted me to go in, and for a couple of years I did, but it wasn't for me," he says. "I did it because it was expected and I was still writing. Then I quit."

Chinn had wanted to be a songwriter since his late teens: "I'd always written. I'd written poetry. It started out, I wanted to be a journalist and then I thought, 'Well there's not enough money in it'. I thought a natural extension - I am a writer - 'I'm gonna write songs'. I'd been writing since I was about eight. I'd written a lot of poetry. Well of course the poetry of the day - and still the poetry of the day - are songs."

Chinn was undeterred by the fact that he didn't play an instrument or compose melody, electing to be a lyricist. Chinn secured a break through an acquaintance called Phillip D'Abo, whose brother Mike, as well as being the ex-frontman of Manfred Mann, was also a songwriter. Mike D'Abo had been commissioned to write the songs for a 1970 Peter Sellers comedy called *There's A Girl In My Soup* and invited Chinn to help him. "We did it at his house together," Chinn recalls, adding, "It's always been together. I've never written a lyric to a melody."

A pleasingly good start though this was, Chinn's real turn in songwriting fortunes came when he met one Michael Donald Chapman. Chapman was an Australian, born April 15th 1947 in Queensland. "He was in a band," says Chinn. "A pop band really, Tangerine Peel, and he was the lead singer. We met just months after ...*Girl In My Soup*." Out one night at a club, Chinn had asked the house DJ to do him a favour by playing a song from *There's A Girl In My Soup*. Chapman, working there as a waiter, noticed this and started chatting with him. It transpired that Chapman was disillusioned with the musician's life. Chinn: "The group had had two or three records out and kind of nearly made it and when you've been in a group long enough that's nearly made it... Mike decided, 'I'm getting out of here'."Chapman was now thinking about freelance songwriting. The two decided to see if they could compose together. "We wrote four or five songs," Chinn recalls. "None of them were very good but we did write four or five songs and of course that suggested to us that there was a chemistry. I liked him (that's very important by the way). I just thought he was a really, really good melody writer and I thought he had a lot of talent."

Asked if he himself was handicapped by not playing an instrument, Chinn says no, claiming it made "no material difference at all. Absolutely none... We were pretty much of a duo. Mike would add lyrics and I would say, 'That's the wrong chord, you're going the wrong way or you're going into the chorus the wrong way'. Sometimes I would just say to Mike, 'It's the wrong direction' or whatever, the way you climb from a verse into a chorus or whatever. Or sometimes it may be just the wrong-sounding chord and maybe the person playing it can't tell." Chapman composed on guitar: "Later on he leant some piano but for most of the years we wrote together, it was always on guitar." (Chapman initially expressed interest in being interviewed for this book but ultimately stopped responding to messages.)

When talking of the songs he and Chapman were trying to write, Chinn speaks of an "essential commerciality", saying their orientation was "Very, very pop indeed. Our first hit was 'Funny, Funny'. So we were very pop." Asked who they were influenced by, he replies, "Difficult to say because we were at the beginning of our own era. If you look at the writers of the 'Sixties, no-one was doing what we were doing. I'm talking about independent songwriters. The 'Sixties wasn't particularly an era of rock and roll for independent songwriters. There was plenty of rock and roll from bands and everything. They wrote completely differently to us but I would be tempted to say that if I had to look at songwriters I really admired on a professional basis it would be Roger Cook and Roger Greenaway. They didn't influence us at all but I just admired their professionalism. I remember one night Mike and I were writing. Mike said, 'Well we've had enough now. Let's pack it in'. I said, 'No'. and he said, 'Well, why not?' And I said, ''Cos Roger Cook and Roger Greenaway'll be in bed now. So we'll continue'."

The two had a routine for writing: "First thing is we would meet at ten o'clock in the morning every day, 'cos that's discipline and I think you've got to discipline yourself and we would pretty normally start with the title and then we would develop the song around the title." Despite the regimented style, they would not succumb to frustration if a session failed to produce anything significant: "No, that was fine. We felt that the key was to be together so that if an idea did come up, we could develop it. if ideas weren't coming up, we'd go out to lunch, have a drink. It was pretty loose but it's just that discipline of being together so that if an idea comes up you can develop it, because so often an idea comes up and you're not together and you lose it."

In the pair's early days, they went through the humiliation and distress of rejection. Chinn, though, shrugs off the idea that this was ever going to have a lasting effect, on him at least: "One of the things I always had as a songwriter was total self belief. I think you've gotta have it. If I thought I wasn't gonna have hits, I'd never have sat down with Mike and written songs." Chinn at least had the consolation that he wasn't going to starve: "Fortunately, I come from a reasonably comfortable family and my father had given me some money which I used for that." He was also able to finance the recording of demos.

Two pieces of good fortune occurred at roughly the same time for the would-be hitmakers. The pair played one of their early songs to Phil Wainman, a producer who had taken a four-piece called Sweetshop, later shortened to Sweet, under his wing. The song was the aforementioned 'Funny Funny', an infectious and anthemic pop number which owed something to Barry/Kim's Archies smash 'Sugar Sugar'. "We were aware of 'Sugar Sugar' when we wrote 'Funny Funny'," Chinn acknowledges. "Obviously we didn't nick it because the two songs sound completely different but 'Sugar Sugar', 'Funny Funny' - that was pretty deliberate." 'Funny Funny' - released in early 1971 - was the only Chinn and Chapman song not published by Chinnichap, the publishing company they set up in 1971. This canny decision to publish themselves was something that it usually takes songwriters years to realise the wisdom of.

Before 'Funny Funny' was released, they also played some songs to another producer, one with a somewhat more impressive track record than Wainman: Mickie Most. "As a producer, he was the guy," says Chinn. "No-one was having hits like he'd had in the 'Sixties. Christ, he'd had everything. That's why we went to him. Publishers had been saying no to our songs. It was certainly a few. We took demos in. We'd go and see publishers and they all said no and then one day Mike and I said, 'Well, there's no point still seeing publishers. Let's go and see somebody who makes hits." However, the man who had produced number ones for The Animals, Herman's Hermits, Donovan, the Nashville Teens and sundry others and who had set up his own successful label RAK was hardly likely to allow two unknowns through the door to pitch their wares. Subterfuge was in order. Chinn was friendly with somebody whom he knew was in possession of Most's phone number. He took her out for a drink. Alcohol had the desired effect of loosening her tongue and Chinn left with Most's coveted home telephone number in his hand. Chinn rang Most to tell him that he and his partner wrote songs that would be hits if only they could get a release. Most, intrigued by the effrontery involved in this, invited Chinn and Chapman into his office. Once there, they played him some demos. Most was as honest and abrupt in his critiques as he was on *New Faces*, the talent-spotting TV show on which he was a caustic fixture of the judging panel. "The first day we met him, he turned down four songs that were demos," reveals Chinn. They had written another song they thought might interest him called 'Tom Tom Turnaround' but didn't have a demo of it. Fortunately, Chapman had brought his acoustic guitar and proceeded to play it to their merciless audience. Chinn: "Halfway through the first chorus, Mickie said, 'Stop. That's a smash'. Then we played 'Funny Funny' to him - we played the finished record to Mickie - and he said, 'That's a hit'." Most turned out to be right about both songs: 'Funny Funny' and 'Tom Tom Turnaround' appeared in the British charts at the same time, rising to numbers 13 and 6 respectively. Chinn and Chapman had arrived. They would form long-term professional partnerships with both Sweet and Most.

"He really was a mentor in the early part of our career," says Chinn of Most. Most would often make what Chinn considers to be crucial suggestions to render songs more commercial. This started right at the beginning with 'Tom Tom Turnaround', the original lyric of which had centred around Native Americans: "The Indian tom-toms and all that. He said, 'Love the song but you can't write about Red Indians'. So we went away and it sort of came out as a love song with someone called Tom Tom. Here was Mickie Most who had had God knows how many hits. Very happy to take that kind of advice." Asked if Most had ever been proved wrong about their songs, Chinn says, "Only once or twice. I think he was wrong about 'Dyna-mite'. [Mud's] first big, big hit. Went to number four. I don't think he was potty about 'If You Can't Give Me Love'." The latter was a number 4 for Suzi Quatro in 1978.

Although everybody remembers Sweet - and various other acts for whom Chinn & Chapman would later write hits - New World, the act who took 'Tom Tom Turnaround' into the charts, is no longer a name that springs readily to many lips. New World were a folksy Australian group that had been signed by Most after winning an edition of *Opportunity Knocks* (a show similar to *New Faces*). "I think people forget about them because they were a very soft act," says Chinn. "As personalities, they made no impact and basically I think because of that everyone forgets about them and the hits really don't live on. We were very delighted to have the hits at the time but they're not an act I talk about very often. Nice guys and everything, but maybe too nice. A very soft sort of act that didn't make an impression."

Chinn & Chapman wrote a couple of other hits for New World, 'Sister Jane' and 'Kara Kara': "'Kara Kara' was about an island out in the south seas or whatever and there was this girl and she was called Kara Kara." All the songs were folk-veined: "We wrote all their songs with their style in mind." Mentioning a song that would later be a smash for another Chinn & Chapman act, he points out, "They were the first act to record 'Living Next Door To Alice'."

Though New World's career petered out after a short while (they were of fixing the *Opportunity Knocks* result by getting friends to send in bogus votes), the success of Sweet had greater longevity. Between early 1971 and mid-1974, Sweet notched up 8 top tens (plus some more minor hits), all written by Chinn & Chapman. Amongst early Sweet hits were 'Little Willy', 'Co-Co' and 'Poppa Joe'. The title of 'Little Willy' might seem an obvious attempt to sneak a sexual innuendo into the charts (willy being British slang for penis) but Chinn pleads innocence: "I remember Dick Leahy [MD of Bell Records] coming to my flat to hear it and he said, 'Songs with Willy in it - the name of a person - never make it' and we talked about a few that hadn't made it. It absolutely didn't occur to us." 'Co-Co' and 'Poppa Joe' had an African flavour about them. The latter showed that the pair weren't afraid to write to a formula: "'Poppa Joe' was like 'Son of Co-Co'. We'd done 'Co-Co' and then we had 'Alexander Graham Bell', which stiffed, and really it was 'Hey, we'd better do some of the same if we want to rescue the act'."

Despite this, the Sweet sound did evolve, quite dramatically and rapidly: there is a considerable distance between their early enjoyable but lightweight pop and the crunching sound they purveyed with records like 'Hellraiser' and 'Ballroom Blitz' only months later. "I suppose in some respects it might have been a deliberate switch, kind of almost unconsciously, but we were developing and you don't want to write 'Tom Tom Turnaround' and 'Funny Funny' and 'Co-Co' for the rest of your life," says Chinn. "We thought we'd keep their previous audience and widen their audience. They couldn't stay just doing teenybop. We were developing artistically, no question about that and that whole Glam Rock thing, we were in as much as anybody else. We were part of that thing. No-one was really ahead of us, other than maybe Marc Bolan. We certainly didn't say, 'Ooh, that's happening - let's copy it'."

The Glam Rock sound Chinn mentions was the pre-eminent musical phenomenon in Britain in the early 1970s. Defining it can be tricky, as summed up by Chinn when he points out, "I'm not sure if Glam was the sound or the look." Glam Rock on one level refers to the outlandish and/or sexually ambiguous images adopted by many British pop acts in the wake of the glitter- and boa-festooned Marc Bolan, including Gary Glitter, Slade, Roxy Music, Mott The Hoople and David Bowie. Amongst that list can - quite emphatically - also be included Sweet, who adopted prevailing trends with a vengeance, incrementally adopting frills, skin tight clothing, and garish make-up until they'd arrived at an image akin to distressed transvestites. Yet a glance at that list of artists reveals a variety of sounds so wide as to make a suggestion of a musical kinship absurd. However, there *was* a glam sound insofar as many of the acts of the era practiced a distinct style reliant on punchy riffs, chanted choruses, sly lyrics, a raucous but determinedly melodic ambience, compressed drums and an often vaguely sinister air. (Rock critic Tony Stewart suggested the description Heavy Metal Bubblegum at the time.) After their early pop hits, the records Chinn & Chapman subsequently made with Sweet and other acts like Mud, Suzi Quatro and Arrow certainly met the criteria on that checklist on most, sometimes every, count.

"If you ask me what our first Glam record was, it would have to be 'Blockbuster'," says Chinn. "But I think Glam was a combination of sound and look. I really believe that if the make-up and all that stuff hadn't been around, why would you call it Glam? It wouldn't have been." 'Blockbuster' took Sweet to number one in early 1973 (Chinn & Chapman's first chart topper). It opened dramatically with a police siren and proceeded to melodramatically tell the tale of the titular Buster, a mysterious figure whom none could think of a way to "block out" (such plays on words were commonplace Chinn & Chapman conceits at this time). The song was propelled by a powerful guitar riff which bore a strong similarity to that of David Bowie's 'Jean Genie', a concurrent chart record. In one of those remarkable flukes the charts sometimes throw up, Bowie's record was only kept off the top spot by the Sweet release. Chinn happened to run into Bowie when the records were numbers one and two in the charts. "I met him in a nightclub and I was introduced to him," says Chinn. "He called me a very rude name, and then got up and put his arms around me and said, 'I'm only joking'. He was terrific about it. We didn't nick it from him and he didn't nick it from us. That's a fact. I assume it's just a massive coincidence. I think actually if you listen to 'I'm A Man' by the Yardbirds, that's where the riff was originally. We didn't copy that either. Someone might hear things and unconsciously years later come up with the idea, not realising. It's not plagiarism. It's just unconsciously, it happens."

Staunch populists, Chinn & Chapman decided to continue with the anthemic 'Blockbuster' formula that had been proven to please the public: "We knew what was going on. So therefore, after 'Blockbuster' we weren't going to deviate. We were going to follow with things reflected on 'Blockbuster'. There's no point going in any other direction, so in writing for Sweet and writing for Mud and writing for Suzi, they were all extensions of each other - although they were different."

Other Chinnichap Sweet smashes were 'Hell Raiser', 'Ballroom Blitz', 'Teenage Rampage' and 'The Six-Teens'. These instantly memorable titles did not always originate the same way: "The Osmonds were arriving at London Airport and these teenyboppers [were] up on the roof to welcome them and on the television news the guy covering it said, 'It's like a teenage rampage'. So - bingo. We knew immediately, 'Hey, that's a song'. But generally it wasn't as direct as that. I wish it could have been. They might have been from things we saw, like 'Ballroom Blitz' came from a gig that Sweet were doing and the place was crazy and so it was a ballroom blitz." Like many of the Sweet's tracks, this song featured the band's bassist Steve Priest delivering one of the lines in a hilariously camp voice, isolated to underline its ludicrousness. This became something of a trademark for the group, although the moments of camp drama were not designed at the composing stage: "The line was in there, as a lyric, but it wasn't written for Steve. It came out of the recording session."

Sweet were the first act to garner Chinn & Chapman an American hit: 'Little Willy' went top five there, as indeed did 'Ballroom Blitz', although the latter climbed the American charts a full two years after it made the top ten in Britain. Explains Chinn, "'Little Willy' came out on Bell in America, then that came to an end and we didn't have a recording company so went to

Capitol where we met vice-president of promotion Al Corey and he said, 'That's a smash'. So they signed Sweet. It was a long delay but that's what happened."

Relations between Chinn & Chapman and Sweet ended on a sour note in 1975 when, with the songwriters away in the States, the band decided that they would provide the song for their next single: "We spent four or five weeks in California just lying around, having fun and we came back and found that Sweet had made 'Fox On The Run' in the studio without us. And no-one had told us. That was the key. So we said, 'Right. That's it. Never working with you again'." Was this not an overreaction? "Not at all. It was a dishonest thing to do."

The fact, incidentally, that Chinn & Chapman went on holiday together despite working with each other every day gives an idea of just how close the two were. "Very deep friendship," says Chinn. "We didn't have many cross words. When we did it was a bit of a blow-up but they didn't happen very often at all."

By this time Chinnichap had taken on and made stars of more than one other act. May 1973 saw the first chart appearance of Mud, a quartet with whom they would have ten top 20 hits (including three number ones) over the next few years. "An agent told us about them and we went to see them," recalls Chinn. "They were on at a social club in Nottingham or something. It was quite obvious that if you gave them the right material they were gonna have hits. They were doing covers, 'Fifties rock and stuff like that. They had a lot of personality and a lot of stage presence and Les [Gray] was great as a front man. The band were good." Despite this, the pair insisted that session musicians play on the band's first couple of singles, 'Crazy' and 'Hypnosis'. "In those days a lot of records were made with session musicians and stuff," says Chinn. "Looking back, I think it was silly. It almost says [we] didn't have faith in the band, which was completely wrong. The minute we got onto 'Dyna-mite' onwards, they just showed how absolutely good they were. Just a silly move. I don't think they were too bothered at the time. I think they would have been bothered if it had continued."

Though the pair were acquiring chart action for the band from the get-go, ('Crazy' reached number 12, 'Hypnosis' number 16), Chinn feels it took a while for Chinnichap to get the formula right for Mud. "They're good records," he says. "I don't believe that we made many bad records. They were very well-produced and put together but as one can see from their chart success, if Mud had gone on doing that, they'd have disappeared." The third single, 'Dyna-Mite', reached number 4 in late 1973 but the record that immortalised Mud came in early 1974 in the shape of 'Tiger Feet', a record that, once heard, was impossible to dislodge from the brain. Featuring a title and refrain that meant absolutely nothing, the record boasted a fearsome, cavernous bottom-end upon which sat a lyric of glorious banality and a melody tailor-made for air punching Every chorus was nailed home with succeeding twin guitar runs. The record topped the charts and became the UK's biggest selling single of the year. Even though Mud never wore make-up, it was the very quintessence of Glam Rock. It remains one of Chinnichap's most well-loved creations. "You go to parties and stuff - it is huge," says Chinn. "Absolutely huge. Always 'Tiger Feet''s played. It does define the era."

Chinn reveals that the song had slightly unusual origins for a team that normally insisted on going into the studio with a clear idea of what they wanted: "It was sort of a jam. We demoed a couple of things in a small studio and there was some time left and Mike started strumming a guitar and it just emerged out of there. That was a bit different."

The other number one the pair wrote for Mud (who also hit the top spot with rock and roll standard 'Oh Boy') was 'Lonely This Christmas' (1974). A lovelorn ballad that achieved precisely its intended objective in occupying the UK top slot during the ultra-lucrative Yuletide season, it saw vocalist Gray adopt an Elvis Presley imitation so accurate that many to this day assume it to be one of The King's records.

At around the same time that they started working with Mud, Chinn & Chapman were asked by Mickie Most to supply some material for Mud's RAK label-mate Suzi Quatro. Quatro was a female bassist from Detroit whom Most had failed to turn into the chart sensation he had pictured her as. "Made an album, didn't work," says Chinn of Most's attempt to break Quatro. "And he said, 'Write something for Suzi' and we wrote 'Can The Can' and demoed it and played it to him and he said, 'Why don't you produce it?'" As with just about everything the pair composed at this time, the song was tailor-made: "We never wrote a song and just took it to the act." The exception to this rule was 'Dyna-Mite': "It was tailored for Sweet and they didn't want to do it so we did it with Mud. Other than that, every act we worked with, the songs were tailored: New World, Sweet, Mud, Suzi Quatro, Smokie, all of them." 'Can The Can' was another archetypal Chinnichap anthem about nothing: passionate and urgent in its declamatory chorus and punchy riff but, on closer inspection, bewildering. This same formula had worked wonderfully for Sweet (and would for Mud) but there was a different psychology involved with Quatro, who - very unusually for those days - had a tomboy image. "We knew Suzi pretty well," recalls Chinn. "She spent a lot of time around RAK. I think to us it was pretty obvious who Suzi was and knowing who she was - knowing the sort of gutsy little girl she was - 'Can The Can' was written to suit her personality. That's how we saw Suzi." Chinn & Chapman rewarded Most's obvious faith in them as being a pair who now had the Midas touch: 'Can The Can' went to number one in mid-1973. "People don't realize that when she hit number one she was the first girl to have a number one record for years," points out Chinn. "Funnily enough, then the market was not full of girls. It is now - it's massive with girls."

Chinn is completely upfront when asked if 'Can The Can' actually means anything. "Not really," he says. "Just sounds great". He admits that he and his colleague would do this frequently: "We were very much into how a title rolled. We were very much into metaphors and sound, that would roll off the tongue: 'Can The Can', 'Blockbuster' 'Ballroom Blitz', 'Teenage Rampage'. They sound good. They're easily memorable." Ironically, the follow-up to 'Can the Can' - '48 Crash', a number 3 the same year - also sounds meaningless but is actually about the male menopause, a bizarre subject indeed from the mouth of a woman in her twenties. Chinn explains the lyric's refrain: "The 'silk sash bash' is the sort of smoking jacket tied up with the silk sash. The '48 crash' - you crash [at that age]."

In contrast to the other acts for whom they wrote, their success with Quatro was hit-and-miss. 'Daytona Demon', 'Devil Gate Drive' (another number one), 'Too Big' and 'The Wild One' were all UK top twenties but that run of success was followed by a rough patch before 'If You Can't give Me Love' restored her to the UK top five in 1978.

Mickie Most came to Chinn & Chapman again when he wanted material for another act he felt had potential, the male trio Arrows. In the summer of 1974, Arrows were gifted another of the Chinnichap anthems that were now a fixture on the UK charts: 'A Touch Too Much', which reached number 8. The association with Arrows was short-lived: "We wrote another one for them, 'Toughen Up', and it didn't make it and then it just fell apart," says Chinn. Arrows actually had their own television show in 1976/77 but were unable to release records during this time because of a legal dispute between their management and record company. This potentially tragic tale of one-hit wonders stymied by the rock business was turned into a fairy tale in the 1980s when Joan Jett covered one of their self written A-sides, 'I Love Rock 'N Roll' and not only took it to number one in the States but saw it become one of the 25 most played tracks in the history of American radio. Lately, it has also been covered by the multi-platinum shifting Britney Spears.

Though Arrows were produced by Mickie Most, Chinn & Chapman were by now producing the majority of the records they wrote. Quatro and Mud were produced by the pair from the start of their respective associations with them. Of producing Mud, Chinn explains, "When were signed the band, they didn't have producers. So the reason we thought that was necessary, purely because it was a natural thing to do and felt the ability was there, obviously." The pair took over Sweet's production duties from

Wainman on their summer '74 single 'The Six-Teens'. However, Chinn was soon bored by the long hours in the recording studio that producing necessitated and elected instead to find other ways to make sure Chinnichap product was successful, namely in its marketing and promoting: "It is just as important because you can make the greatest record in the world and if it isn't marketed right and promoted right and you [don't] get the airplay, then you're dead. So I used to spend time at the record companies. I used to drive 'em mad, making sure that no stone was unturned. [Plugging] was all very, very important, as it still is. Airplay is the key. Anything else you do, actually, really is a waste of time if you can't get airplay."

The 1973/74 period was one in which Chinn & Chapman reigned as the undisputed kings of UK pop. This was the juncture where they had reached the point that virtually all the composers in this book did at some stage where their name was so associated with success that musicians were clamouring to receive songs from them. An example of their apparent ubiquity was that when Mud's 'Tiger Feet' was finally dislodged from the top of the single charts after a month in that pole position in '74, it was by another Chinnichap song, Quatro's 'Devil Gate Drive'. However, Chinn & Chapman were probably the first subjects of this book to find that their popularity with the pop audience was in equal parts to their unpopularity with those who commented on pop. By the early Seventies, popular music had grown up sufficiently to have its own critics. These critics - to be found, in the UK at least, writing in the pages of the likes of weekly pop papers *New Musical Express* and *Melody Maker*, etc. - were distinctly unimpressed by Chinnichap, likening them to a sausage production line and sneering at their commerce-first, art-last motivations. (Stock, Aitken and Waterman - subjects of the final chapter here - would face similar disdainful attitudes.) "Now and again, we got a bit angry," admits Chinn. "We're human. But the bottom line was of course we ignored it, because we went and wrote another one that was needed by the act that the critics weren't going to like just as much as the last one. I'm not going to say it didn't hurt

from time it time but, basically, on a professional basis we took no
notice. That's the way you gotta look at it. You just can't let them
win."

The one time the pair decided to retaliate was when *New
Musical Express* scribe Charles Shaar Murray wrote a vitriolic
review of a Suzi Quatro single which reduced the artist to tears.
"He'd been really, really nasty," says Chinn. "Unnecessarily cutting.
There's a point that's okay but when you slaughter a record and
slaughter the artist at the same time, I don't think it is okay."
Chapman dispatched a parcel of pig's brains for Murray's
attention.

Though the critics ridiculed Chinnichap songs as glorified
nursery rhymes, the pair would often sweat over every word. "I
would work on whether it was an 'and', a 'but', an 'if' or a 'when'.
That's how hard we worked on it because it makes a difference
sometimes. The beginning of a line: is it a 'when', is it a 'but'?
We agonised over the whole thing. We strived for perfection.
Whether you get it or not is another matter." This striving for
perfection involved abandoning material that was felt to be going
nowhere: "I've always felt that one of the features of our success
was our quality control. We didn't finish songs that weren't going
to make it. We would get into a song, verse and chorus and
whatever, and suddenly We would be looking at each other saying,
'D'you know what? This isn't a hit - let's bin it'. I think a lot of
time is wasted by writers finishing songs that aren't going to make
it and there is always this danger that every songwriter thinks
that every song he writes is a gem. Well it's not." What about the
music industry practice of using sub-standard material for B-sides?
"We wouldn't do that. Also, bear in mind we had very few B-
sides - we always gave them to the band." The pair worked on
album tracks just as hard as on songs designated for singles: "A
recording is a recording. Therefore quality control is quality control.
It has to be as good as a single." Chinn finds it difficult to cite
exactly how prolific the pair were in terms of finishing songs:
"It's difficult to say per week or whatever. Obviously in that '73,
'74 period when we had 11 or 12 hits each year, we were prolific

but I couldn't possibly pinpoint whether it was one a week or one a month."

The pair would usually present songs as demos to the relevant recording artist: "It was a demo we made at home. We got two-track Revox. We used to make them in the studio originally but we got the Revox and everything. It was cheaper to make them at home." Chinn feels these demos, though by definition relatively sparse, were sufficient to get across the idea of the song: "We used guitar and a drum machine so you certainly got the feel. You had Mike singing and we'd add some harmonies. It was pretty detailed."

Chinn & Chapman experienced disappointment very rarely in their heyday. Chinn cites the complete failure to chart of Suzi Quatro's 'I May Be Too Young' in 1975 as one of those few occasions when what the pair imagined to be a surefire hit failed to click with the public. "I think we thought that 'Alexander Graham Bell' by Sweet was going to be a hit," he says. "But Suzi Quatro, definitely. Although I play it now and I know why it wasn't. It just doesn't sound as good as her others. But then I was convinced it was a smash. We both were."

Chinn recalls fondly the cosy atmosphere of the Glam Rock scene during this period. With Sweet's records appearing on RCA, the other Chinnichap material on RAK and Gary Glitter (one of the glam titans, although not a Chinnichap client) on Bell, it sometimes seemed as though the vast bulk of the glam industry was comprised of a few London record companies all within strolling distance of each other: "Bell happened to be next to RAK in Charles Street," Chinn points out. "There was a lot of activity round there. There was RCA in Curzon Street, a few hundred yards from RAK and Bell. With Bell, we tried to not release records at the same time, 'cos they had Gary Glitter. We tried to organize it so we weren't in competition with each other."

Through Chinn & Chapman had an undoubted magic touch, a factor crucial to having hits was for the relevant act to gain an appearance on *Top Of The Pops*, the BBC chart rundown television programme that had been broadcast weekly since 1964 and which was at the time the only chart programme on the TV airwaves. "It was essential," says Chinn. "Today, *Top Of The Pops* doesn't really sell records. An act goes in to have a hit, enters the charts at whatever, does *Top Of The Pops* and goes *down* the next week. Then, it was absolutely the opposite. You do *Top Of The Pops* and you went up the next week. Sales could double over the weekend. Treble, in fact." In those days of Glam ascendancy, the air in living rooms across the land would be filled with invective on Thursday nights as parents expressed their outrage at yet another appearance of yet another tarted-up glam act, most of which Chinn & Chapman were responsible for the music of. Chinn does add, "But again, *Top Of The Pops* was useless without airplay. You can't show an act to people watching television for the first time if they don't know the record. It'll go out of their minds as quickly as it went in."

Yet it is a testament to *Top Of The Pops*' power in those days (a power now much diluted through the proliferation of music-oriented TV, as well as TV channels) that many cite the beginning of the end for Glam as the point in the summer of 1974 when BBC TV personnel went on strike and caused non-commercial TV screens to go blank for six weeks. "It wouldn't be an exaggeration at all," states Chinn. "I was in the middle of it. The BBC went on strike and I had Sweet out with the Six-Teens and Mud out with 'Rocket'. We got hurt. Sweet went to number nine, Rocket went top ten also but I really, really think we'd have sold more. I'm certain the Six-Teens would have been top three. You've got to live with it." By the time the BBC - and *Top Of The Pops* - was back on air, the interest of the nation's teens had moved beyond Glam Rock.

Chinn & Chapman were far from washed-up without the glam scene. It was around this time that they started working with yet another bunch of unknowns that they planned to turn into stars. The group was called Kindness. "Their manager, Bill Hurley, sent us a tape which we didn't really like," remembers Chinn. "They were singing covers and bits of stuff they'd written and we were saying no. The manager was driving us mad. Well, he was driving me mad 'cos I always answered the bloody phone because it was in my flat that we worked. One day I said to Mike: 'I can't take this fellow any more. I must give him ten out of ten for persistence'. I said, 'They're appearing in Hachette's in Piccadilly - let's go and see them'. And, in fact, for some reason I couldn't make it and Mike went to see them and he came in the next morning, he said, 'They're terrific'. So obviously, they hadn't translated on tape what they were really all about, and they certainly hadn't translated Chris Norman's voice... Chris's voice was just amazing. So from that moment on we knew." In addition to frontman Norman's gravely and emotional delivery, the band had an asset in the form of their intricate, multi-part harmonies. Chinn & Chapman promptly signed them to their production company, re-christening them Smokey in the process.

The band did benefit from the Chinnichap Midas touch - ten top 20 UK hits between '75 and '78 - although experienced a couple of hiccups at the beginning. Their first single 'Pass It Around' was banned by the BBC who were under the impression that it was about marijuana. They also had a problem with their name. Recalls Chinn, "When we released a record in America, Smokey Robinson got very pissed off because quite often at his gigs they would just put 'Smokey', 'cos everybody knew who it was: if it's Smokey, it's Smokey Robinson. He wanted to sue us. Literally - I'm not kidding. And I was staying in the Beverly Hills Hotel and somebody I knew pretty well, Barney Aliff, was checking in at the front desk. So I went up to him, I said, 'Hi Barney, what are you up to these days?' and he said, 'I've just taken over the presidency of Motown'. I said, 'Oh. You're about to sue us'. And he said, 'I don't fuck friends. What's the problem?' So I told him the story. He said, 'Come to my office'. While I was there, he called Smokey Robinson. He said, 'Look, if they change their name to "i-e", will you accept that? I'd be really happy if you would'. And that's what happened."

The soon-to-be re-Christened Smokie still had the 'e-y' ending to their name when they made their belated first appearance in the British charts. 'If You Think You Know How To Love Me'

was a top three in the summer of '75. It heralded a new direction
for Chinn & Chapman. Smokie's music was soft rock, featuring
acoustic guitars and sensitive lyrics (and furthermore lyrics which
actually meant something). Chinn calls it an "enormous shift.
You've got to bear in mind, that era was coming to an end. That
was also part of why we went with Smokie. We knew that
something different was needed and of course when you hear
Smokie, those are the sort of songs they ought to sing. Smokie
were never going to do a 'Ballroom Blitz'. I think it was our
progression but also a progression made necessary. We were
moving on." The new songs sounded much more sophisticated in
subject matter and structure. "We probably got a bit more
sophisticated ourselves," says Chinn. "[The titles] got much longer
and much less important was the alliteration. The alliteration
actually stopped." Smokie records were lent an additional gravitas
by Norman's extraordinary voice, which would crack with emotion
at all the right junctures, and the en masse back-up singing.
"Fantastic," enthuses Chinn. "You heard that voice.. Sent shivers
down my spine. And then the whole harmonies. Just amazing.
You hand it over to them and it's just fantastic."

Though they never hit the top spot, Smokie consistently graced
the charts with their always pleasing singles over the next four
years, among them 'Don't Play Your Rock 'N Roll To Me',
'Something's Been Making Me Blue', 'I'll Meet You At Midnight',
'Lay Back In The Arms Of Someone' and 'Oh Carol'. The latter
is nothing to do with any song by Neil Sedaka (or Chuck Berry)
but is a Chinnichap original, one in fact whose jaunty gait and
flirtatious lyric was unusual for the mellow, adult love songs the
pair usually provided for the band. Two Smokie songs that certainly
were resurrections were 'Needles and Pins' (they took the old
Jackie DeShannon/Searchers number into the top ten in late 1977)
and 'Living Next Door To Alice'. The latter of course was first
done by New World when Chinn & Chapman were young hopefuls
but had not bothered the chart compilers. Perhaps it was the way
Norman's voice ratcheted up the emotionality in this ballad about
a man who has loved the girl next door all his life but has never

declared that love that made it 'take' this time round: Smokie's version went to number five and became arguably their signature song.

The Smokie rendition was a (then) rare American Chinnichap success, reaching the top thirty Stateside in early 1977. Chinn & Chapman had a more significant American chart success in 1979 by teaming Chris Norman's voice with Suzi Quatro's. Chapman was in Germany and called his writing partner: "He said, 'I've seen Suzi and Chris singing together and they're great. Let's make a duet with them'." The result was 'Stumblin' In', which went to number four in the States (though curiously peaked outside the top 40 in the UK).

Though their chart success was mainly British, Smokie's hits were usually written in America. In 1975, Chapman had decamped across the Atlantic to spend more time with a woman with whom he was involved. Chinn remained in the UK but would fly over for several weeks at a time to compose with him. "I enjoyed it," recalls Chinn. "I enjoyed the travelling to and fro. Actually it was a great life. Maybe a bit tiring." He says the two never wrote over the phone.

Though Chinn & Chapman had made a deliberate shift when Glam was going through its death throes, there was no attempt made on their part to accommodate punk: "Some people say actually that Sweet were the first punk band and in some respects I suppose they were. Punk changed a lot of things. We went on writing but punk, they always wrote for themselves and punk was angry. We weren't angry and the songs we wrote weren't angry. We carried on our own sweet way and we carried on having hits."

In contrast to the sophisticated material they were turning out for Smokie, Chinn & Chapman proved they were still capable of concise and simple pop gems with the songs they wrote for the group Racey in 1978/79. Mickie Most (probably by then the only producer to whom they would have given songs without insisting on producing them too) asked them for material and they delivered him 'Lay Your Love On Me' and 'Some Girls', bouncy tracks which reached UK peaks of 3 and 2 respectively. 'Some Girls' was actually originally offered to Blondie, whom Chapman - keen to expand his production career - was in discussion with about producing their third album, *Parallel Lines*. "She didn't need it," explains Chinn. "Time has proved that. It was like in reserve but once she started writing her own songs with Chris Stein then it was quite obvious she didn't need it, so Racey got it." Fate smiled on Racey on that occasion but worked the other way with another song with which the pair came up for the group, 'Kitty'. "Mickie recorded it a couple of times and just said to us, 'I can't get it right'," recalls Chinn. 'Kitty' sat on the shelf for a while, an almost unknown occurrence for a Chinnichap song, due to their made-to-order practices. "I was in my office in America and somebody came in with Toni Basil as an artist, looking for a hit," recalls Chinn. Basil had had a career as a choreographer but was looking to become a singer. "I said to him, 'Funnily enough, I never, ever have a song in stock, as it were, but have a listen to this...'" The name of the titular love interest was changed to Mickey to suit Basil's gender and a UK number two and US number one resulted. "Completely unchanged, other than the 'he' and 'she''s had to be changed," notes Chinn. One critic, it should be noted, assumed that the song's line "I'll take it like a man" - unchanged in the Basil version - referred to anal sex.

Though the UK success for the song was no doubt pleasing, American success was a more treasured affair for the pair. Chinn admits that incredible as their achievements in the "Rest Of The World" - music business parlance for the territories outside the USA - had been, the stuttering nature of their success Stateside had rankled with them slightly: "I think it's important to any songwriters. Very important. Because you can't feel you've been successful on a worldwide basis until you've got America. Let's fact it, it's half the world market. It was nice to have everywhere else, but it was very important."

By the time Basil hit with the song, Chinn had taken the plunge and relocated to America. In 1980, the pair set up the Dreamland record company. The omens seemed reasonably good for it.

Though they were not the cultural presence they were in the UK - where they not infrequently were interviewed by the press - they were well-known in industry circles in the States: "Clive Davis desperately wanted to do something with us. We had so many hits over here and round the world. And of course we'd had 'Little Willy', we'd had 'Ballroom Blitz'. 'Ballroom Blitz' was a big record in America. It wasn't just that it was number five. It was like: 'Wow - "Ballroom Blitz".' It seemed to make a big impact. People just remembered the record."

Yet the stuttering nature of Chinn & Chapman's American success didn't seem to change despite the relocation and despite them in 1978 scoring, through the group Exile, their first US number one. Exile had been in existence since 1973 and had acquired a sufficiently good reputation for the pair to go and see them live. The song they gave the group was 'Kiss You All Over'. This sensual number occurred to Chapman when Chinn was in their home country and it prompted Chapman to demand his partner's presence in the States to help him finish it: "Mike called me and said, 'I've had a great idea, come over'. I said 'It's a long way to come to write a song'. I did go over the next day and we did write it." The song's lyrical hook was memorable but potentially hazardous: "It was risqué and we knew it was risqué. In fact, it was risqué to the point where I insisted that 'Over and over again' went into the lyric, because that had a different suggestion. 'Over and over again' means on and on and: I'm gonna kiss you and I love kissing you." Despite the self-censorship, the record still met resistance in places: "ABC in New York refused to play it, in their words, 'Until it gets to number one'. And it did. Then they had to play it." Not that this meant that they had necessarily cracked America: "We had a lot of disappointments with Exile, 'cos that was number one and we never, ever did it again. We thought we made good records and good songs but it's so had to get played in America." There was also nothing like the instant, massive and free advertising that an appearance on *Top Of The Pops* constituted. Chinn: "Television in America meant bugger-all. It was all about airplay. And you got to spread it. There are a lot of stations to get. You could even have a smash in one area, like the mid-west, and you can't break out of that. It's not a hit anywhere else so obviously it's in the chart but it's not flying up it. To break the whole of America, you got to have a lot of radio stations. It's not easy."

In fact, Chinn & Chapman's success in America often seemed as accidental as their chart placings in Britain had so frequently appeared to be the result of sheer will. In a story similar to the Toni Basil scenario, Huey Lewis, early in his career, hit number 8 in the US in 1983 with their 'Heart And Soul'. "'Heart And Soul' was written for Exile and didn't make it," says Chinn. "Huey Lewis's mob heard it via a publisher and he'd made the album and they wanted a surefire poppy kind of single to launch it with and that was the one." A similar story lies behind Tina Turner's top five US success with their 'Better Be Good To Me' the following year. It was picked up by Turner when she was recording her album *Private Dancer*. "We'd recorded it with a band called Spider that we were working with," Chinn recalls. "They didn't have it out as a single but they had it on an album. (We didn't have any hits with them.) It was with our publisher and he sent it to Tina Turner's manager, Roger David, and he gave it to Tina. He liked the song very much. Apparently she said, 'I don't want to do it' and he said, 'But Tina, this is the story of your life - better be good to me'. And of course it is - all that stuff with Ike and everything. And she said, 'You're absolutely right' and she recorded it. It was a big hit and a very influential song for Tina. It's always, always done on stage and she announces, 'This is one of my favourite songs'."

Although Chinn & Chapman had irregular success in the States, it should be pointed out that by this time Chapman had established himself as a top producer: Blondie's *Parallel Lines* album spawned the US number one 'Heart Of Glass' and made the band superstars. His work for The Knack had led to comparable success. As acts like this were self-sufficient song-wise, this was an area in which Chinn's services were not required and it's possibly this that caused the curtain to come down on the partnership of he and Chapman: by the time both 'Heart And Soul' and 'Better Be Good To Me' were hits, they had ceased working together. For his part, Chinn isn't willing to discuss the details of the reasons behind their break-up in 1982. "It was, I think, personalities and all kinds of things," he says vaguely. "In many ways, it is something I don't want to talk about but it's not something I don't want to talk about because it's too hard to talk about it. I just think it's probably a private matter, as it often is when songwriters split up. It was eleven great years and we split up because we split up - like a lot of songwriters - and that's really it."

Mike Chapman continued both as a successful producer and songwriter (the latter often in collaboration with Holly Knight). Chinn also tried to hook up with other collaborators, working with Paul Gurvitz and (separately) Steve Glen. However, his enthusiasm waned quite quickly: "Mainly I wrote lyrics and would have ideas, just like I did with Mike. With Paul we got a cover with Kim Wilde but it didn't really do much. With Steve we got a cut on a Roger Daltrey album, 'Is There Anybody Out There?'. But in reality I just didn't find the chemistry anywhere near what I had with Mike. I was never particularly happy. Which is why I stopped. Very prestigious. I was happy at the time. But this is a business where you want hits, not prestige." Would he not have been content to move over to writing album tracks? "Not really for me. I always wanted hit singles." He says he no longer feels any hunger to write: "[I did] a TV interview quite recently. They said to me, 'Why did you stop writing?' and I said, 'Because I think pop songwriters have a shelf-life'. And I think we do. I listen to the radio now and I hear Robbie Williams and Craig David and I say to myself, 'I couldn't write lyrics like that now'. Craig David is 20 or 21. I'm 56. I don't think that way anymore. It's as simple as that. I'm sure that all those years ago, songwriters who were older said, 'God, I couldn't think the way "Ballroom Blitz" has been written'. I just don't think that way anymore. That was our generation. We were tuned in with the young people."

Chinn won't be drawn on the worst Chinn & Chapman songs

("There's nothing that makes me cringe") but is certainly happy to go on the record about his favourite creations. The track he retains most fondness for is Sweet's 'Ballroom Blitz': "I think the performance is great. Love the song." He also cites 'If You Think You Know How To Love Me', 'Living Next Door To Alice', and 'Lonely This Christmas', adding, "Look, there aren't any we wrote that I don't like. The hits."

He feels that the state of songwriting today is pretty healthy. "When I listen to Travis or The Stereophonics or Craig David, Robbie Williams, I think the state of songwriting is just fine. When I listen to a lot of the boy bands I'm not so sure. I'm not into the dance music but then I hear something like Eminem, I think he's great. So I think the state of songwriting is pretty fine. If I go back to the early Seventies, it was pretty fine but there was still some dross around." He adds that he is surprised that rap has broken through to the UK marketplace: "I'm not surprised it's happening in America. It's quite an urban thing in America, although mind you it's certainly not black anymore. It's absolutely crossed over to white. It's a music phenomenon. I perhaps would have thought it would be more American but it's not."

The glam generation whose songs Chinn & Chapman so enraptured has now grown up and has been instrumental in rehabilitating the Chinnichap songs that were once held - in some quarters - in contempt. While the continued healthy sales of compilations of acts for whom the pair wrote belie their onetime reputation as disposable trash, the media (for the most part now in the hands of those who grew up on Chinnichap product) have come round to the idea of Chinn & Chapman's production line being no more reprehensible than Motown's - i.e., not at all.

Chinn: "About ten years ago, Sweet started selling a lot of the old stuff around the world and the whole concept of Chinn & Chapman and Sweet - and the other acts for that matter, but particularly Sweet - absolutely changed. Now it seems total respect, which is great. The whole thing changed completely."

11
STOCK/AITKEN/WATERMAN

"I'd like to make this point," says Mike Stock. "It's not very often made: in reality, Matt and I throughout all our success were the band, we performed on all our records. We were writers, we were a band, we were musicians - we were the artists, really and they were the guest singers. Nobody's really given us credit for that."

In Britain during the 1980s, Stock, Aitken and Waterman were names that were synonymous with pop success. A teaming of songwriters Mike Stock and Matt Aitken with Pete Waterman - who wrote no music or lyrics but acted as a publicist, industry insider and talent-spotter - their names appeared on around six dozen top 20 UK singles, either as producers or songwriters, usually both. In one particularly remarkable three-year period - 1989 to 1990 - they achieved the almost unbelievable feat of having at least one record in the top 75 every single week. Rick Astley, Kylie Minogue, Jason Donovan, Mel And Kim and Bananarama are just some of the artists for whom they composed a string of hits. They also basked in a cachet status that saw long-established acts like Donna Summer, Cliff Richard and Georgie Fame beat a path to their door in order to benefit from their Midas touch. Stock's comments indicate a dimension to this success which makes it even more remarkable. Stock and Aitken used every modern device at their disposal in crafting their records, taking advantage of the rapidly advancing technology of that decade to ultimately dispense with musicians. Some have claimed that this led to a displeasing sonic uniformity: "All their records sound the same!" was the commonly heard cry of their detractors, many of whom could be found in the industry. For Stock/Aitken/ Waterman - as the trio were billed on their records, or S/A/W as they were commonly known - their seal of approval always came from the general public, who dwarfed their detractors in number by literally millions. Yet the public could not save the success of a partnership Stock and Aitken consider to have been ultimately doomed by industry jealousy: the two remain convinced that resentment at the success they achieved on budgets which called into question the wisdom of traditional record company profligacy ultimately led to them being virtually frozen out of record making.

Mike Stock was born on December 3rd 1951 in the coastal town of Margate. He was raised in Swanley, just on the border of South London. His household boasted a piano, reflecting the fact that his family was a musical one, ".. although my father and mother weren't trained musically at all. [My father] was a travelling salesman for most of his life but he tinkled on the piano and played the ukulele and stuff. My mum had a good singing voice. My brother is a trained classical violist. My sister has been classically trained. My other brothers and sisters are all interested in music to a degree." However, he adds, "I'm the only one who's ever gone into the pop field professionally." Stock was precocious to say the least: "I wrote my first songs when I was seven. I kept a compendium of my first songs that I'd written. I wrote the lyrics and I illustrated the lyrics. About thirty or forty songs. They're all very naïve. One of 'em's called 'The Thunder and the Lightning'. I suppose they were plagiaristic. I can't even remember now. I suppose they were all based on something [that] had influenced me." He adds, "I still believe that you can't be totally original, because you'd probably create a tune that was unrecognisable as a melody if you were going to be that original."

Stock has a wider grounding in popular music than most: "I knew lots of things like Rogers and Hammerstein and the great musicals. I loved the popular song. Popular music for me doesn't just date from Elvis. To me it goes probably back into the Victorian age." Nonetheless, Stock was, like just about any aspiring young musician in the 'Sixties, smitten by The Beatles: "They were a major influence but I was already writing songs at the time. They were the ones who [made me want] to be a pop star or something, stand up on stage, without a doubt." Stock is fluent on both piano and guitar but has had lessons on neither. "Obviously I can't read music," he says. "I play my attempts at little classical pieces as well on piano by listening to it and learning it and repeating it. On guitar, I got a chord book. It had like a thousand chords in it so I learned very quickly. I invented when I was that age a chord wheel. You look at sheet music, it gives you the chord shapes. If it was in 'E'-flat and you're trying to play it on a guitar, you just set your chord wheel round to 'E'. If the key's too difficult to play, just turn it round and all the chords then become transposed. I thought I was quite clever in doing that because some of the songs were written in difficult keys [for] the guitar."

After completing his schooling, Stock hit the hippie trail in his gap year. "Then I went to university," he recalls. "That didn't agree with me very much, so I left that without completing my course and then worked selling double glazing. I always wanted to be involved somewhere in music. I just didn't know for certain that there was a way of earning a living at it. in the end I got on my bike. I bought myself a little electric piano and a rhythm box and a microphone - I went into pubs. That was in 1975 or something. First of all you find out which pubs do live music and then you ring 'em up. They'll try you for a night and if they like you they let you back." These modest beginnings to Stock's life as a professional gradually grew into bigger things, with him acquiring the occasional bit of work as a session singer (including on the infamous Seventies *Top Of The Pops* albums, which featured sometimes unintentionally funny re-recordings of contemporary hits. "I did a couple of television shows as well - talent contests," he recalls. "I don't want to say [which] in case someone digs out the video." By the time Stock met Matt Aitken in the early 1980s, he was playing in two bands. One was an ensemble who performed original songs, written and sung by Stock. The other were purely covers merchants.

Ironically for a pair destined to create so many new songs, it was the latter group which led to them hooking up. "Because Mike's guitarist got drunk and fell offstage and didn't turn up to the gig one night and somebody knew us both and recommended me," recollects Aitken. "We spoke on the phone and I turned up with me guitar. He said, 'Have you got a suit?' I turned up with a blue suit on but Mike's band were immaculately kitted out in designer stuff and he had diamante on his lapels." Initially, their working relationship was somewhat prosaic. "It was hire-and-fire at the time," says Aitken. "Because I was doing other work elsewhere and he was quite happy just to have somebody that was reliable that turned up. So that went on for probably nearly a year. And then in conversation it turned out that Mike had another band that was involved in playing stuff that he'd co-written. He didn't know at the time that I was into doing original material as well. We said, 'We'll give it a go', so we ended up doing Mike's original band and the cover thing as well."

Matt Aitken was born in Coventry on August 25th 1956 and was raised in Astley. "Which is between Manchester and Liverpool," he explains. "So I've always considered myself to be a Lancashire lad even though I was born in Warwickshire." Aitken's father died when he was very young. When his grandfather also passed away, he and his mother ended up living with his grandmother, who happened to possess a piano, one with which Aitken had previously toyed on visits to his grandparents' home. "When that happened, I'd be eight," he says. "It was the first musical instrument I had any access to. When I was a small boy I used to go in and sort of make tunes up with one hand. Then I sort of invented my own boogie woogie. That was, again, untutored. And then I decided I wanted to play guitar, which my mother wouldn't allow because we had a piano and she insisted that I do proper piano lessons and if I did then maybe I'd get the guitar. So I went off and took classical piano lessons for two or three years. I'm so glad that I did that. Because I got the theory side of it together reasonably well, when I did come to take up guitar, all the stuff that most people avoid when they pick up a guitar, I already had and I could work a lot of things out for myself just by understanding the relationships between the notes and things like that. But again I started with a chord book and some blues records. I'd be about eighteen."

Aitken was not quite as precocious as his future partner in the writing stakes: "My creative aspirations were down to really extemporisation on melodies really, variations on themes. I didn't really sit down and write a song although I would [write] little piece-ettes on guitar." Aitken left school at the age of eighteen or nineteen and took a delivery job which lasted for nearly a year. "I had an eight-track cartridge in the van so I could listen to the music. I'd do that, then I'd go home and practice guitar in the evenings." Aitken worked as an accountant for three years, a job which enabled him to buy an electric guitar. "Then I started to find my way into semi-professional groups. Initially just amateur groups and then I found that you could do semi-professional work as well as working in accountancy and it was ten quid cash at the end of the night, which was very handy at that time." Though these were all exclusively cover bands, the lure of musical work proved stronger than that of accountancy: "When I was about 22 or 23, I got offered a professional job, which entailed me leaving work, obviously, and it was a big move but I thought that if I didn't do it then I probably never would, so I just did it."

Aitken started venturing properly into composition after moving to London: "I joined some original material groups and became a co-composer. There was a group which was a studio band and we started writing stuff together, all very much around the same time I started playing in Mike's cover band. But I wouldn't ever have described myself as an experienced songwriter."

The pair's first professional contact with Pete Waterman was in 1980 and came about as a consequence of a song called 'One

Nine For A Lady Breaker', a Stock composition celebrating the then-ultra trendy CB radio. "My brother was a member of this group and they wanted to write a song for their club members so they could sell it as a record to them," explains Stock. "So I made the record, wrote the song for them. Did it in an eight-track studio. And we sold about seven or eight thousand copies of it. Privately pressed. Someone said, 'Why don't you send it off to somebody?'" The obvious recipient seemed to be Peter Collins on the grounds that he had been the producer of a novelty hit with a car radio theme called 'Car 67'. Collins' career was looked after by Waterman, who was at that point a manager of record producers. "And they liked it and made a proper version," says Stock. "Got released on Logo. I sang under an assumed name. It was like a major release but it majorly didn't get anywhere" Stock's association with Waterman at this juncture was fleeting: "I met him just about. He wanted me to do the B-side myself in the studio." Aitken, with whom Stock had very recently started playing, can be heard playing on that B-side.

In the early 1980s, Mike Stock built a studio underneath his house, a venture made possible by the tidy sums he was earning on the live circuit: "Before Matt joined me, I had gigs for months on end, every single night and twice on Sundays. When we did functions at the hotels, we were getting a couple of hundred quid a night each and that turned out to provide us with enough of an income to do other things. It was professionally done and we were getting a professional wage for it so we could afford to spend more of our time in the studio developing any ideas that we had. 'Cos we always knew that doing what we were doing in a covers band or the pubs and clubs was just a short-term thing. My view is if you're on that circuit for more than two or three years, you'll be on it for all your life." The home studio was a rudimentary affair with a very cheap 24-track two-inch recording machine. "Sometimes we had to stand there and wind it round ourselves because the motors wouldn't work," Stock recalls. "The desk was originally a road desk. We just put it together. We actually knocked holes in the walls to put the doors in." Nonetheless, this rudimentary studio marked the beginnings of the studio-as-instrument S/A/W technique, the result of which would define their sound. "You're always writing songs and making them," recalls Stock. "You're not just with a sheet of paper, dots. You're creating records as well as songs, so good songs for us are kind of indivisible from the record. We rely on the studio." Aitken adds, "We only ever once sat down to write songs when we weren't actually making a record, and that was much later on. There's only one occasion where we actually wrote songs in a void where it wasn't recorded as we did it."

Of the studio work, Stock says, "Originally, Matt joined to be just the guitarist in the band. Then we expanded our relationship to include both the bands." Aitken: "I became the sort of second engineer at the studio as well at that point because I found that side of things quite interesting and nobody else would do it." Aitken's perspective now started to change: "I think my ambition would have been to be a performer [but] I realised that the studio aspect of it was much more important - and much more interesting actually." Stock: "We were being quite enterprising. We had our own studio, we were trying to do our own little label, and write some songs, make some records, sell the studio time to outside people, do some productions for them. Did some adverts for people, corporate stuff." Aitken: "The idea was to be able to support yourself at the same time as hopefully landing a major deal."

Stock recalls that the compositions on which he and Aitken began collaborating were "..guitar-based pop-rock", mentioning The Police as a big influence. At this point, Aitken acknowledges that he was something of a junior partner: "Mike was always the one that would be more likely to sit at a piano and start writing a tune. And at a point when we did start writing together, I'd just chip in and interfere or be a sounding board. It developed from that later on into a joint venture." However, Aitken brought a distinctive contribution to the table. Stock: "Matt, was the guy with the skills, as a guitarist. He was a lead guitarist, so he could transfer that to keyboard or sometimes some guitar solos."

Their musical ventures during these early days were many and various, something partly attributable to their lack of concern about being stars. Stock: "Success for me was always something to do with the charts. Having a record that you were involved with in some respect in the hit parade. Now if we were making it, writing it or performing it, it wouldn't have mattered which had come first. As long as we were getting that hit record, somehow." However, in the early days, significant success eluded them. Much of their work was done for the tiny independent label Monarch and they would write and play music for anyone who asked. "We got the recording costs, which kept us going, and we delivered the record," recalls Aitken. "Keeping occupied, keeping amused, keeping the wolf from the door, hoping that one of them might become a major success and then we're launched." Typical in a way of their ventures of this period was 'The Upstroke', a 1984 record - credited to Agents Aren't Aeroplanes and featuring two outrageous female singers - revolving around an invented dance that the pair claimed was the favoured style of a species of yuppie. "Everything was all about these Sloane Rangers at the time," says Aitken, "and we [affected] knowledge of these secret clubs where these Sloane Rangers were going. It had everything: it had a unique marketing ploy. The basis we sold it on was that it wasn't just a record. There was more to it than that. It was all lies, of course."

The man who had vision enough to see the record's potential was Pete Waterman. "We thought, 'Well who can we take this record to?' and the third person we thought of was Pete Waterman," recalls Stock. "He was a manager of producers, so that's what we thought would happen. He'd managed a producer who was being successful. Pete himself isn't a producer in the sense that I'd call a producer. He's a bit more like a film producer. He puts people together. So Peter Collins had had these hits and I thought, 'Well I'll sent our stuff to Pete [Waterman] and maybe Pete'll either get Pete Collins to do it or manage us to do it...' Matt and I really didn't have a lot of money so we walked around London. We had three appointments: RAK, Red Bus and Pete

Waterman. We turned up at RAK and he was off with 'flu. Nobody broke the appointment. We turned up and he wasn't there. Went down to Red Bus. He heard the track, understood what we were doing, said he'd like to think about it. Walked over to Pete Waterman, Pete Waterman got it immediately. Understood what we were trying to say. Didn't want to see the band, knew that it was created in the studio. We shook hands with Pete [to] make the record properly in the studio. He wanted to re-make the record so he could own the recording or whoever would buy it. (I realise that now, I didn't realise it at the time). In the evening, guy from Red Bus rang me at home and said, 'I wanna do the deal with you'. I said, 'I've just shaken hands with Pete Waterman'. Pete organised the studio time in a top studio for us to make the record. It was number one in the dance charts - the Hi-NRG Boystown or whatever they called it at the time - and it got to 60 in the national chart." Aitken: "60 was great. And it got played on John Peel's show. We knew we'd arrived at that point. We'd just got into the car to go and get some chips or something, turned it on and we both thought it was the cassette. It wasn't, it was the radio."

Meanwhile, Stock and Aitken had managed to get the gig to write the Eurovision Song Contest entry - for Cyprus. "One of the guys had came down to the studio under my house and he was managed by a Greek female who was backing him," explains Stock. "She loved him, thought he was great. So she asked us to write him a couple of songs and write a song for Cyprus's entry. They'd take it over to Cyprus and get it played. Like they do over here: have a song contest, find out which one the public voted for. Of course, we had to pretend that he'd written it, because you had to be a Greek Cypriot to write the Greek Cypriot entry. At PRS we registered it in our own names. To our surprise, the Greek people voted for it. This all coincided with 'The Upstroke' deal with Pete. All of a sudden, Pete is saying, 'Hang on, these guys are bringing in all sorts of interesting things'." Stock, Aitken and Waterman as a full-time partnership was beginning.

It was Waterman who secured the pair a gig producing the

transvestite film star Divine. 'You Think You're A Man', though not written by them, became the first S/A/W single to hit the British top twenty. When 'Whatever I Do (Wherever I Go)' by Hazell Dean hit number four in the summer of 1984, Stock and Aitken had their first major self-composed hit. The first number one with which they were associated - Dead Or Alive's 'You Spin Me Round (Like A Record)' followed just a few months later. It was another hit they didn't write. Though of course happy to top the hit parade, Aitken says of production jobs, "It's not the same thing at all. Somehow you feel more that you're actually being used in a way. You're merely being employed to do a job." Stock: "And neither we nor Waterman had much vested interest after the record was made." The pair do add that Dead Or Alive frontman Pete Burns approached them because he liked the sound for which they were becoming known. Aitken: "Pete had written the song having heard Hazell Dean. A little light had come on for him because before that they'd done a dodgy version of 'That's The Way I Like It'. He'd heard our techno-based sound - which it was: there were no real instruments on it, it was just sound, it was totally synthetic... Pete Burns wrote those first four songs or whatever off the back of hearing what we'd done with Divine, with Hazell Dean because he'd realised that you could marry pop songs that you were writing to these beats and then bought it back home, as it were, and we developed it to its logical extent. In truth, if we'd bickered about it, we could have probably wheedled ourselves a songwriting credit." Despite the foregoing, Aitken feels that the Divine record was more the first 'proper' S/A/W record than 'Whatever I Do': "If you were musicological about it you can trace the ancestry down from the first record and you'll find common bits in both and how things evolved." In any case, the early Stock and Aitken style was shortly to change due to the limitations of hi-NRG, a speeded-up and somewhat depersonalised form of disco. Aitken: "What we tried to do is marry pop with Hi-NRG. Dress the song up in a contemporary way that had a market. I think we found it very restrictive to write in that format all the time [Hi-NRG]. The more times you're restricted to a tempo and a certain rhythm it becomes harder and harder to think of new ideas."

They found a way out of that impasse with 'Say I'm Your Number One', a piece of modern soul which young chanteuse Princess took to number 7 in the summer of '85. Such switching between genres is something they do not find difficult. "It's easy for us to do it creatively," says Stock. "We love to. It's just difficult to persuade Pete and other people to take anything else from us than the stuff that you're very highly successful with. 'Cos Pete just wanted to do more of the same." Aitken: "There'd been a sort of rebirth of R&B from America generally - Jam & Lewis and those sort of techno-drummey, breakbeatey sort of records were starting - and we perceived we had this Hi-NRG area sewn up really. We knew how it worked and who marketed it well and what labels to go with but there was this other emerging dance area that we could look to move into if we could write songs that were good enough."

Stock and Aitken weren't actually to achieve a self-written number one for a further three years. However, their compositions began to appear with increasing regularity in the UK singles chart, with Princess doing particularly well. Stock and Aitken were a name act and the pair claim they could have continued to be so on their own. However, they recognised that Pete Waterman was an individual who could sustain their success and for that reason were happy to do something that many songwriters would find astonishing: grant him equal status - and equal financial rewards - in a three-way partnership. The familiar S/A/W credit had not yet quite been settled on when 'The Upstroke' appeared. "The credit on that record would have been 'A Pete Waterman production, directed by Mike Stock and Matt Aitken'," says Aitken. Stock adds, "We were having an argument about how we should be credited. He wanted to be credited *a la* a film producer. He called us the directors, like we were the creative artistic ones behind the camera. Of course the music industry didn't really go along with this on that and we only suffered it for as little time as we thought it would get us somewhere. A few months later it all changed and we called ourselves 'Stock, Aitken and Waterman'. That was six months after." Of the negotiations which led to that eventual credit line - one which would become familiar to so many during the next decade - Aitken says, "There were several meetings and several slagging matches. It was clear that if there was a way forward, it would have to be through that route. Pete was only concerned to protect his own position because in truth he was more than a manager but because there isn't a niche called 'Bloke That Goes Out And Does The Business'..." Asked what Waterman could give them that they couldn't get on their own, Aitken says, "Contacts, initially. At that point, he'd got a team of producers working in the studio and he knew that in order to keep that relationship going that he would have to go out and secure work and he, like us had done previously, went out and secured work or, if that wasn't available, invented something and sold it on the basis that it would be successful." Stock: "The point about this is that obviously Pete Waterman would have liked to have maybe just been the producer and us been the musicians. It was his own ego."

Of the decision to grant Waterman a third of the publishing money, Stock reasons, "What I really wanted was our songs pushed forward. We thought it was better to harness Pete in to a team than have us all go off at different directions. If we could go off and do what we want, then he could go off and do what he wanted. I just wanted to keep things going, keep things together. That's a trait of my life. All we had to do was iron out the little difficulties. The little difficulty was, 'Pete, we want to be known as producers'. 'Okay, how we gonna do this?' The best way was to share everything. The best way was to say 'Stock, Aitken & Waterman'. Share the proceeds of our work equally." Stock says that this gave Waterman the incentive to "..keep him on the ball and to push our songs.. He had to get a publisher. What he got was, for himself, 9%. The publishing company, of which he was the owner, got its 20%, which you'd have had to pay anyway. So he paid for the administration out of his third."

"At the time, it was very equitable," says Aitken. "We didn't agree to split the songwriting 'til '85, when it was clear to us that we needed to either get a publishing deal or not and we had had hits that we'd written, the two of us, at that point. It just seemed sensible to do that - to make sure that we were all committed to each other's cause. At the time, EMI would have given us half a million quid to sign to them. We were looking like a couple of likely lads to have some more hits. So you could have signed your publishing away but you would have had to have sold the control away to EMI." He adds, "Looking for your next hit, they're only interested in collecting the dosh you've earnt from your last one. [Waterman] had a vested interested in pushing them forward and making them successful."

Waterman has contended that he played an active but limited role in the studio, famously stating that he would grant his two colleagues the use of his ears (i.e., he knew which songs would sell). Stock and Aitken dispute this. (Waterman declined to be interviewed for this book.) Stock: "When we were flying - we're talking about '88, '89, '90 - Pete was not there. Pete was absent. Pete was doing a radio show and a TV show and he was the voice of the industry. He was in every magazine and every article. He had no time to be at the studio. For about three years he turned up on about Thursday afternoon I think for an hour." Aitken does accept that Waterman would sometimes be a useful sounding board: "He would walk in as a fresh pair of ears and go, 'Fuck me - that's great!' or, 'I don't understand this'." He adds, "Which sometimes was very good, especially if you felt you were struggling and somebody else thought it was really good, but ultimately it could be very frustrating particularly if you were still in the very formative point of trying to dig to make a song work by trying various different chord sequences around the vocal or whatever. If somebody comes in and pours cold water on what you're doing, without realising where you are, that can be equally discouraging. So it was a mixed blessing."

Waterman did come up with the odd title, such as 'Never Gonna Give You Up', a hit for Rick Astley. Stock: "Sometimes he would come up with a title which was too verbose but the idea was good: 'There Are Too Many People Walking Around With Broken Hearts', but there I begin to falter as for any more." Stock asserts that Waterman even managed to soil the contributions he did make: "I didn't want him telling the people that he wrote 'Too Many Broken Hearts' sitting on the toilet, which was what he said! He didn't. He came up with a title that was unusable that we turned round. We made that song and wrote that song and made the record."

In 1986, S/A/W released their first collaboration with Bananarama. This three-girl vocal group had already achieved a string of UK chart hits but with voices that were perceived to lack any character, they had little credibility. The team didn't hesitate to accept the approach to produce them, however. "They'd been having hits" reasons Aitken. "They had an awful lot of credibility as far as I was concerned because they were very successful. We were too old at the time to think about credibility. It didn't matter to us at all." Stock reasons, "We'd done the Eurovision Song Contest entry for Cyprus!" Stock adds, "We thought they were great. There was nothing wrong with that: three ordinary girls who dressed up and looked glamorous and they were lively, energetic and compelling. They had a track record when they came to us." The first S/A/W-produced Bananarama single was a resurrection of 'Venus', originally a hit for Shocking Blue in 1970. This new version - which included elements of the Hi-NRG sound - was a hit on both sides of the Atlantic, actually reaching the top spot in the US. Stock points out, "In the Japanese keyboards that you buy, Casio things, you get a version that's built in of several songs one of which is 'Venus', and it's always our arrangement. It's not the original, it's the things that we invented. The things that we put in are now associated with that song."

Stock and Aitken subsequently started writing Bananarama's singles. 'I Heard A Rumour', 'Love In The First Degree', 'I Can't Help It' and 'I Want You Back' all achieved top twenty UK placings. Though the pair don't begrudge Waterman the third of publishing he received from their songs, they now acknowledge the lack of wisdom in giving the Bananarama girls part of what became a six-way writing split on their records, and not simply because of the unfairness of it. Stock: "To a degree, the reason we had to accommodate them in the writing: they had a publishing deal they needed to fulfil. The only way we could get our songs in was if we let them take a bit of the publishing. It was the same deal we'd done with Pete, effectively. It was out of hand and it was wrong. What they did is helped you with the lyric. I'm not gonna take it away from them. They sat there and it wasn't an entirely pleasurable experience because it was mining for gold in a very barren landscape." Aitken remembers one particularly distressing writing session: "'I can't sing the word "rich".' 'Why not?' 'I don't know. I just can't'. 'But it's called 'Strike It Rich' - what shall we call it? "Strike It Milk"?' That was like being a schoolmaster. That was quite horrible really."

Towards the end of 1986, S/A/W launched the career of Mel and Kim, two chirpy black cockney sisters whose records would bear the influence of the nascent house genre, another depersonalised, de-commercialised disco variant. Aitken: "The first thing we did with them was actually an R&B record. They wanted to do R&B - that was the idea that was presented to us - and we did a song, which was on the album, called 'Everybody's Got A System'. It was a good record and it still sounds quite good now but nobody got excited about it. Then we got these tapes over from Chicago, the house thing that was happening, and we thought, 'Well nobody's doing this - and more specifically, nobody's actually writing songs'. There was Daryl Handy but it was very 'unsingy' song. Nobody's doing singy songs with these kind of things so we thought, 'Let's try this with them' and that's why we wanted a groovy title for the first one that we attempted."

Said groovy title was 'Showing Out' (subtitled 'Get Fresh At The Weekend'). "We were searching for a trendy phrase," recalls Aitken, "and one of the tape ops happened to be in the room at the time, called Jamie. We said, 'Jamie, any trendy phrases you've heard down at the clubs this weekend?' And he sat and he thought and he scratched his head and he said, 'Yeah - "showing out".' And as it happens, since then we've learnt that 'showing out' was actually used on a Peter Sellers record in 1963." Stock: "It just means 'showing off'. We weren't [looking for] any old phrase. We were looking for something that summed up what Mel and Kim did. They were quite flash girls out on the town." Stock also points out that thinking of a title is often a creative spur for them: "If Matt and I are going to sit down with a blank sheet of paper, the first thing we're going to do is, 'Can we have a title, please'. Then that's the bullseye to aim at." The cherry on the cake for the launch of this record into the public eye was the incalculable sales-push given the record by the loveable personalities of Mel and Kim Appleby. "All we ever looked for is a vehicle for a song," says Stock. "Mel and Kim were a great vehicle. They were brilliant for that. I think we've lost quite a few really good songs for the want of a decent performer."

'Showing Out' climbed to number 3 in Britain. The following year, 'Respectable' took the sisters to the top spot - the first self-written S/A/W number one. This bad girl anthem featured an artificial vocal repetition in the choruses ("Tay-tay-tay-tay" - the first part of the word "Take") that was the epitome of the S/A/W studio-as-instrument writing style. Aitken: "There was a thing on 'Showing Out' that went "Show-show-show-show, show-show-show-show' and when we were flying the vocals in, he [Stock] did the 'Tay-tay-tay-tay'." Stock: "The technology to do that was new and we were just probably one of the first to put it into a pop scenario. On another Mel and Kim one, ('FLM') it was a vocal sampler triggered by the hi-hats. You could hear a strange, almost rhythmic use of vocals. We were experimenting as we go." Aitken: "We nicked all our ideas at that time from what was coming out of Chicago. [Dub] was DJs playing with records and sounds and that was the same thing that was happening in Chicago, really. What it did is, it just blew away fucking ten years of bullshit because after the death of disco you couldn't ever put a hi-hat record on a record. Because it was disco and disco died and disco sucks and der-der-der-der-der. We went through all this New Romantic stuff, we had all these Hi-NRG records that we made, and we were not allowed the one most single effective thing to make the record really work. Then suddenly these gay guys in Chicago said, 'Fuck all that, we want this, because we wanna dance to it' and suddenly it was acceptable again. Also, they started using pianos on records, or sampled pianos. What sounded like a real piano, and again that was something you couldn't really do on a dance record for ten years." Stock adds, "Mind you, all these things are never the public. It's only the industry who gets these bees in its bonnet. Trendy buggers who wouldn't know an 'A'-flat from an elephant's bum."

SAW had two further UK top tenners with the sisters before Mel and Kim's career was brought to an end by the illness and subsequent tragic death from brain cancer of Mel Appleby. (The pair, incidentally, dismiss the rumour that a S/A/W-produced single called 'I'd Rather Jack' credited to the Reynolds Girls was really Mel and Kim under a pseudonym.)

That S/A/W were not proud about which artists they chose to produce and write for is illustrated by the example of Samantha Fox. Fox was a national icon in the UK in the Eighties but - initially - only through being a very well-endowed topless model. After achieving a couple of hits she turned to S/A/W in order to sustain her pop career. They gifted her the top ten 'Nothing's Gonna Stop Me Now'. Though they tried to not give Fox anything too demanding for her limited vocal range, they insist that they didn't give her a lesser song than they would have presented anyone else. "They came off the pen as they came off the pen," says Stock. "We had them queuing up to record the songs. By her own admission she's not the world's best singer. We're not going to try and give her something that she couldn't cope with but we wouldn't ever have written an inferior song for anybody". Aitken adds, "I think she murders it though. Didn't quite ever get to the note."

It's perhaps partly because of this undiscriminating provision of songs that S/A/W achieved their strange status of being loved by the public but despised by critics and certain sections of the industry. It was to some extent weariness with this dichotomy of public adoration and critical brickbats that led them to record

'Roadblock'. This brawny, horn-augmented pastiche of Seventies-style funk was released in the summer of 1987. It was a project designed, almost literally, to fool people into liking a S/A/W product. It was released with a blank label and infiltrated into clubs. The trendies who disparaged S/A/W were soon enthusing over this mysterious record, which they assumed was a rediscovery of an act from the previous decade. Aitken points out that they were able to maintain the secrecy of the record's origins because of a remarkable turnaround time: "It happened so quickly. From mixing it to us scratching all this stuff on the white label, that was probably ten days. Two weeks maximum. And then it was in the clubs the following week. So probably a month before it was getting some kind of recognition." When that recognition came, the pair unmasked themselves and an official release - credited to Stock/Aitken/Waterman - reached number 13 in Britain. "It wasn't the public we were trying to fool," avers Stock. "As soon as it became a *bona fide* release, we put our name on the single. It was only the trendy club DJs and the radio DJs who hated us that we were trying to fool. We succeeded in that, so when that job was done it didn't matter. Game's up. Once you've told them, 'Ah-hah - it's us'." This utterly untypical S/A/W record enjoys a status as the sole piece of S/A/W product their detractors are prepared to admit a liking for. Some still find it difficult to believe that the creators of supposedly characterless pop could author something so soulful. "I played it to Siobhan out of Bananarama," Stock recalls. "She was always nagging about us doing other than this pop stuff we were doing: 'Oh can't you give us something trendy to do?' I said, 'Hey what do you think of that?' She said, 'Yeah, well, you could never do something like that'. I said, 'What do you mean?' She said, 'This. Seventies groove record.' I said, 'It's us - we made it last week'. She said, 'No you didn't'. She didn't believe me. So we had to do 'Mister Sleaze' [for Bananarama], a similar record, just to prove [it]."

Ironically, 'Roadblock' was made with virtually the same mechanical process as generated al the other S/A/W hits. Although the vocals are sung and the percussion is in free time, Aitken points out,: "The whole bass and drum track is four bars long, and that just repeats endlessly. Things change over that. The saxophone is played by a sax player [but] we sampled it and got the one that was right and then fiddled around with the rest of it. , all the percussion overdubs are done in free time, they're not sequenced. It didn't sound genuine to us: anybody with any knowledge at all would listen to that instantly and know it couldn't possibly have been an old record. It could have been a re-mix of an old record, and I suppose that's what people - the cognoscenti - thought. That we'd taken the master and the max track and put modern beats on it." Stock: "In reality, ordinary record buyers didn't rate it. Still don't. Don't even know who did it. It's only the trendy guys who want to point out, 'Oh, they're alright really 'cos they did it'."

Perhaps part of the reason for the hatred felt by some for them was S/A/W's growing belief that musicians - other than themselves - were more trouble than they were worth, especially in an age where almost everything was beginning to be possible on synthesiser. Aitken: "We used a guy called Andy Stennet when we were doing the R&B stuff, 'cos he had very good knowledge. He was a good soul boy. We used various occasional programmers on things that we did from then. But it would be 90% [Stock] or me. Always. On many, many examples, it would be *just* him or me. It was very often more problematic to use somebody else but at our busiest phase, when we had two studios going more or less constantly, we had a guy called George who helped us out for a year or so and worked under direction and worked very well. He would either work for me or Mike or both of us at the same time. We used to burn them out. They'd burn out after six months. They'd be gibbering wrecks. They couldn't keep up." Stock: "We were better than all of them. That's the truth. By that time, we were quicker, harder-working, more directional. Our ideas were crisper and cleaner than all of theirs. Matt and I developed, playing on stage, sets of other people's hits. We were playing thirty or forty songs in an hour-and-a-half. You've got to keep people dancing. You can't stop and take a breath. So you're segueing things. Some of the songs we were writing are complex musically. Trying to explain that to session musicians from the pop world was sometimes actually not easy. They were funny. Difficult. Nothing for them to read. 'You've got to learn this like a band. You've got to be like in the band with us, jam along'. What Matt and I often did was jam along for hours with the track: 'That's a great bassline - I love that bit. Keep that'. 'Ooh that's a good change there'. You do grow the music. Getting people to do that with you... Session musicians, say, 'Okay - what do you want me to do?'"

The arrival of the Emulator into the market in 1985 sounded the death knell for any significant involvement by musicians in S/A/W records. For Aitken, this sophisticated sampling keyboard was a revelation: "Much more user-friendly than stuff we'd been using before: you just put a disk in and it loaded a piano up. We could put a string section on.. That single instrument when it arrived suddenly reduced everything. And these boxes would keep arriving from America with new sounds. It increased your possibilities endlessly, but it made it much more easy to do things that you'd always wanted to be able to do, so in a way it was a catalyst." Yet Aitken is anxious to make the point that they were in no way in thrall to technology: "There is this conception that everything was done in a computer. That we had this Boolean logic formula, that we'd just turn out hits by typing three words in and away you'd go and that everything was played by screen-based computers, which couldn't be further from the truth really. In fact we eschewed that in favour of being able to physically get on a keyboard and make mistakes in order to find the one bit that works." Stock points out, "We were always quite quick about getting new technology but there was a point when it was really working for us, we didn't change. We could have gone software-based much quicker than we ever ended up doing." Aitken: "We were still using a relatively archaic system when everybody else was using Atari-based systems and we spent so long trying to get a system that was reliable that having [ironed] the bugs out of that system over two or three, four years, there was little point going to something that was going to keep crashing on you." Stock: "And which would take you several weeks to reinstall properly. We didn't have that luxury. So that was a problem by 1991. We did swap around a little bit. It caused us a few problems."

As musicians themselves, did they not in their heart of hearts think that if they had five human beings playing the parts, they could make the record better by getting them to play off each other and think up little licks and progressions? Stock: "I imagine, I can't be sure, that only the very best in the world would have been able to keep up with us at the time." Aitken: "It wasn't really necessary most of the time. In fact, sometimes it was positively counter-productive if you were in a hurry. If you were under a cosh and under a deadline, it was generally speaking quicker and more efficient to do it yourself." Stock: "When we were on the run - when we were doing things at our most productive - we would be writing the song, getting the artist in, finishing the recordings and mixing it all in a day. So that what happens overnight, the engineer would come in and in the mornings, at 11 o' clock, when we arrived, we would check his mix, approve it, strip it down, write the next song, get the artist in at lunchtime, finish off the recordings in the evening, go home, wait for the mixer to come in and start again."

The next individual who S/A/W's common touch turned into a superstar was Rick Astley, a diffident, fresh-faced young man with a voice like a modern Paul Robeson. Astley was legendarily the tea-boy in the S/A/W studio plucked and groomed for stardom. Though the reality is slightly more complex, Stock and Aitken confirm it is partly true. "Rick doesn't want us or anybody to really say that 'cos he thinks it's insulting," says Stock. "We mean it in the opposite. We mean it as a great tribute. What he was, he came down and mucked in while he waited for us to get our shit together so we could work with him and make a record with him. We heard him sing and we liked his voice and we discussed what we could do. We just didn't have the time to do it immediately. So he came in and mucked in, made some tea, got us the food. I say that as a great tribute to him because it wasn't beneath his dignity.

In truth he did do that - for about a year. Matt and I weren't entirely convinced of his voice because it was either on or off. It was very big and powerful. It was very difficult to get him to sing quietly. It was a very powerful voice - coming out of his frame it was quite unnerving. The first thing we recorded with him was an old Motown song Pete wanted us to do for him - 'Ain't Too Proud To Beg'. That was the first time we'd worked with him. 'Bloody hell - what have we got here? We've got a voice that sounds like that and we're doing this. It's not quite right'. So then your brain starts ticking over and eventually you come to write him a song. We did 'Together Forever' and 'Never Gonna Give You Up', songs like that which are kind of to be projected. And they are projected by him and he did it brilliantly." Stock points out that writing specifically for people was very much their norm: "Very rarely Matt and I sat and wrote a song without an artist in mind, without the capability of that artist. We knew who we were gonna work with the next day."

'Never Gonna Give You Up' was an important S/A/W record for more than one reason: it was the first record they'd written to get to number one in America. "It's nice," says Aitken, "but we didn't ever - except later on - specially try to tailor anything for America. It certainly wasn't in our thoughts when we were working with Rick. It took off there for a variety of reasons. There was a whole chain of events that led up to it being an American number one. It was number one here for seven weeks, so that's usually an indication you've got a record... In fact, Rick had two number ones in the States and one here."

Stock and Aitken have mixed feelings about making it in the world's biggest record market where, despite eventually securing seven top 10 hits as writers and/or producers, they never enjoyed the same cultural presence as they did in Britain and, to some extent, Australia. "We obviously were creating in the UK our own wheels that could just turn and get the hits going, and we were jumping off into Europe," says Stock. "America was always a mystery. You've always been told that you've got to do records specially for the Americans. We never believed that." They say they were never tempted to concentrate on breaking America. Aitken: "We were massive here, massive in Germany, massive in Japan. Why throw the baby out with the bath water?" Stock: "It's not that we don't like Americans but we don't hold having a hit in America in such great esteem as everyone else seems to." For his part, Aitken reserves a degree of bitterness over one aspect of their failure to be as prominent in the US market as in their home country: "The thing that really floored me with all of that is that Kylie - all the fucking world-wide success that we had with her - couldn't get arrested in the States and then they started importing Tiffany and Debbie Gibson, who were crap. Because somebody somewhere didn't turn the right key in the right door. She could have been absolutely fucking massive out there. But because she wasn't, they looked at what was happening over here and they said, 'Ooh, this pop thing's happening so we're gonna do our version and export it to them'. We just basically got trampled on by the American machine."

Though Astley had four further top 10 hits under the aegis of S/A/W - 'Whenever You Need Somebody', 'When I Fall In Love'/ 'My Arms Keep Missing You', 'Together Forever' and 'Take Me To Your Heart' - he very soon expressed a disinclination to continue making records with the people who had given him his star status, citing lack of artistic fulfilment. Luckily for S/A/W, they had another superstar-in-waiting in the form of Kylie Minogue, for whom they'd written a number one hit, 'I Should Be So Lucky', at the beginning of 1998. Minogue at the time was an actress in *Neighbours*, a clean-cut Australian soap opera that was just about to become massively popular in Britain. Before long, she was the biggest-selling female singer in the UK.

The pair's relationship with Minogue got off to a rather inauspicious start when they responded with blank looks when she turned up at their studio ready to lay down a track. "We had never met or heard of her," recalls Stock. "It had been arranged with our business affairs guy at PWL, David Howells, that she would come in to record a song with us but somebody forgot to tell us. And of course we're working with artists every single day and we've got them queuing up. So this girl arrives and says, 'I'm going back to Australia this afternoon'. And I don't like necessarily saying, 'It only took us 20 minutes to write the song', but it did. We were under pressure. We had to get it together. We got it together, we got her in, we got her on her way. We then put the effort into finishing off after she'd left. But in fact, it underplays it to say it was a 20-minute song. It obviously has all our experience and at the time we were on fire. We could sit down and write it. We wouldn't be able to do that now. We're sort of out of training for that." Stock, incidentally, dismisses a story told many times by Waterman that he came up with the title: "Fuckin' nonsense. Pete was in Manchester, nowhere near the bloody building." Aitken takes up the story: "We were thinking of doing a song that we'd already written 'cos she was in a rush. I wanted to do one of the songs that perhaps hadn't made it onto a Bananarama album 'cos we were under the cosh and Mike didn't want to do that. And I said, 'If we do something that we haven't spent time on, it might not be as good as it could be'. And either he [or I] said, 'She should be so lucky to have one of our second-best songs'. Stock: "As you're sitting down to write the song, you think actually this would be better if it was 'I Should Be So Lucky'."

Before the record was finished, there was a slight technical problem to overcome. Stock: "I came up with this tune for her to sing in the verse. The chords are, in the verse, 'A' major to 'F' sharp minor to 'G' to 'E'. I'd written the tune on the third, on the 'C' sharp, and when she came in to sing it, I realised her voice was actually pitched a lot higher. So I just got her to sing that same tune at exactly parallels on the fifth instead of the third. It's lucky that worked out, otherwise it would have been a nightmare. She couldn't sing that well. She wasn't projecting well. She hates the fact that she sometimes sounds like a little tweety bird but I loved her for that. It was engaging and I thought it was fragile and she was vulnerable."

The public certainly responded to Minogue's engaging, girl-next-door image and, after a slow start, 'I Should Be So Lucky' - released on the new label PWL (Pete Waterman Ltd.) - became one of the biggest hits of the year. Not bad for a song whose basics were knocked together in less than half-an-hour. However Stock does acknowledge that that achievement is not so impressive as it sounds. "At a time when we were working under a great deal of pressure, because you're [recording] records as you're writing them, you couldn't actually have turned up in the studio with no idea what you were going to do," he explains. "I always had a library of tunes in my head that I've had over the years because as a kid, writing them, they never got exploited. So at some point I'd say to Matt, 'Hey what do you think about this?' as a start-off for this act or whatever we're doing today. You couldn't do it otherwise. You couldn't just turn up with your guitar plugged in and your keyboard switched on and go, 'Right...'"

This period in the S/A/W story - the state produced by the combination of their services being so in-demand and their craft being so honed that Stock describes it as being "on fire" - is probably the appropriate place to explore Stock and Aitken's technical approach and general philosophy about songwriting. They have firm ideas about what a good chorus should feature. Stock: "It contains the melodic hook and it contains the synopsis of the story really and the focal point of the story, which is the focal point of the song." That focal point was always something the pair kept to something easily assimilable to the audience. Aitken: "If you're working backwards from the title which you think is a good title, it may suggest four or five different story lines and then through a process of debate we argued our own corner for the one we think is the most likely scenario." With the subject and story decided, the basics of the song would be settled on. Aitken again: "We'd get the melody as well as the title and how does that work melodically, rhythmically and what is the story we're trying to tell. You've got one across and one down and now you've got to do all the nitty bits in the middle and that generally can be the easy bit but sometimes it's fucking hard. You never know."

Stock says there are two main types of song: cyclical and linear. Of the former he explains, "Standard or classic would be an introduction which was the chorus but the tune version, just the melody, instrumentally, and quite often in a different key from the ultimate chorus or from the verse so that then you've got a change into the verse and then the verse would set up the story line and then the bridge would take over that and the bridge would lead you into the chorus - and we'd hope that we'd at that point been raising the melody up through the scales so that at the point it comes to hit the chorus is the highest point of the song, because there is no point in making the chorus drop. It has got to lift to the climax. So those sorts of songs with the intro, the verse, the bridge, the chorus, then the verse - we took them as cyclical, a cycle that's repeated and therefore if you're starting from the chorus and working back that's how those songs grow. The other sort of song we've done quite a number of are more organic and more linear: you start here and you're moving here and moving here and moving here and moving here. You don't actually go round in circles. Things like 'Especially For You' were more linear than cyclical. But you don't over-analyse what you're doing. You just do it and get on with it, put it in the pan and come back to it later and see if you've got it right."

The pair had favourite chords, which they half-joking refer to as "The universal chord sequence". Stock: "Don't take this too literally, but 'Never Gonna Give You Up', 'I Should Be So Lucky', 'This Time I Know It's For Real', some of our biggest multi-million selling singles had a similar chorus chord sequence. There were variants in that - it wasn't quite as simple as that - but they have tension in-built into the sequence. They'd feel emotional, normally because your roots aren't necessarily the same as your chords and you'd build in this sort of... I don't know how you would describe it. The same chord sequence as 'Land of Hope and Glory'. It feels stirring. When we've got those chord sequences going it's really great. You can feel it - it really does take off."

"We used to debate between major and minor," adds Aitken, "because we always felt that being in a major key was better for an up-lifting chorus than a minor key and we tended, in the early days particularly, to write the verses in a minor key, which is a bit more 'down', and then hopefully lifted up. But on a particular song that we wrote, I can't remember which one it was, we decided to use a particular set of chords which had been used a million times, which happened to suit us very well because it is major, but it's rooted on the fourth of the chord rather than on the actual key, top tonic, and, in that it creates its tension. You're actually in a major key but it's not that major, it's less major, because you keep descending into the relative minors, the minors surrounding it. It never actually settles until the very end of the chorus and you give the game away then and everybody's happy by then. We used that and developed that and endless variants over the time and then we got hits with the 'More I See You The More I Want You' chords which again are a slightly different variation on that which keeps modulating between two keys and we used that for many songs. And then we went into the descending bassline period, where we rediscovered an old thing and we used that one three or four times and then there was the sequence with the ninth on the top that you imported and we used that several times and did as many variants as we could. But we as writers are old fashioned in the sense that we always like to start from a chordal, harmonic sequence of pre-determined chords, rather than starting from somebody just singing something and then fitting it around, which I think a lot of DJ-types today would tend to do: give you the beat and a focal note and hope that the singer actually develops something which you can pin stuff around. That's not really songwriting."

A favourite trick of the pair was to have such a smooth transition between verse to chorus to bridge that the audience would almost not register it. Stock: "Sometimes we'd shock with an impossible key-shift to lift it but very often we'd put key changes into the chorus or something. The smoothness was how we managed to get the melody to go through those key changes imperceptibly, so that people didn't realise they were being lifted up, otherwise it sounded awkward: 'Oh, we've gone up a key'. As a device, that would be too obvious." Aitken adds, "Very often the hardest problem that we ended up with was we got from the first bridge chorus, chorus - fine, and then suddenly we'd have this bomb that's the verse and sometimes that would be the real hard point, would be disguising it back down somehow and some are better than others. But then sometimes we'd say 'Fuck it, it sounds great to suddenly go brrrrr like that'."

This belief in classic pop values and methods combined with an occasional impatience with those same forms borne out of creative restlessness informs much of their music of this period. Stock: "We did restrict ourselves with a scaffolding. First of all we knew it was a three-minute pop song. We knew we had to get everything in and out in those times: three choruses at least so everyone's heard it and so that general restrictiveness meant you had to be more creative within the framework. We've never sat down and gone. 'Lets write a symphony'. All those restrictions that you place on yourself force you to be a bit creative." Stock: "It's how you break those rules that make [the song]. But you've got to know them and stick to them and then it's the breaking out of that which gives you your unusual twist sometimes: 'Oh hang on, this bridge could be two bars. That's going to throw a few people. It means the chorus is going to come in quicker, people are going to be taken aback by it'. That's a device that has worked. Or sometimes come out of the chorus into a section where nothing's happening as a sort of release." There was also a more practical reason for some of the incidents of dismantling the 'scaffolding', as Stock explains: "When we sat down to write for artists under the sort of constraints that we were forced to work - which is like, 'Get it done today the artist is coming in at two o' clock' - you know you do have to plan your work and work your plan otherwise you get lost. So sometimes we would deliberately break our mould and say, 'This gap here, we'll hope we can invent something'."

A drawback of the fact that the pair had created a pop empire that relied almost solely on them for its every note was a back-breaking workload that probably no songwriting or production team had ever experienced hitherto. Without the direct involvement of the pair, S/A/W records simply could not be made. "We started

regularly at around 11 in the morning and finished regularly at
around 10 at night and we did that five nights a week, every
single day," Aitken recollects. "If we went beyond 10, we'd go
down the pub then for an hour. If we came back to the studio it
would only be to listen to a mix or have an argument, it wouldn't
really be to do with much more work because if we then had
gone on for a couple more hours and you end up going until two,
three o'clock in the morning, then you don't come in the next day
until two o' clock in the afternoon. By that time we were supposed
to have finished and be writing the song for the next. You've got
to pace yourself."

The pair found it helpful rather than a burden that they were
almost always working on two or three songs at a time. "We'd
very often jump tapes in the middle of a session and get onto
something else," says Aitken, "particularly if we'd hit a flop or
we'd finished a particular part: 'Do we fancy finishing this off or
shall we move onto the one that's nearly finished?' So it was
tape off, tape on, faders up, you would remember where you
were and in some ways it was easier to be objective because
sometimes its difficult to see when something's working because
you've just been through the pushing-the-rock-up thing and you
don't realise you're actually at the top - you don't need to push it
any higher."

Both Stock and Aitken (the latter especially so) bristle at the
suggestion - repeated many times - that their songs all sounded
the same. "I don't reject it out of hand but the actuality is that it
isn't," contests Aitken, "and if you chronologically go through it,
you'll find after four records, if you skip back six records
previously... Well I can certainly point to things and go 'Well that
isn't the same because this is this and this is this'. Now as a
punter if it all sounds the same to you then I can't really comment
on that, because I'm not a punter." As an example, he posits
'Got To Be Certain', Kylie's Minogue's follow-up to the chirpy,
uptempo 'I Should Be So Lucky': "Harmonically they're
completely different, rhythmically they're completely different.
Rhythmically, harmonically, melodically different. The common

factor uniting those is a) we played them and b) she sings them with the same 'band'. Its going to sound a bit the same isn't it?" Stock says, "Well I don't think there is much wrong with somebody [who] hears it going, 'Its instantly recognisable as Stock, Aitken and Waterman'." However, he adds, "Princess is English R&B, and people came to us thinking that came from New York. What we were doing with Mel and Kim was Chicago house - earlier than anybody else had gotten onto it. What we did with Venus was amalgamate a rock song, rock guitars and a boogie bass and Hi-NRG. Dead Or Alive was its own type of record. And Hazell Dean was a breakthrough in its own way." Aitken: "If you laid them all out chronologically, things changed as they went on. What the problem was, when we got to our most prolific phase, which was when we started to do Kylie as well as all the others, there was such an outpouring of stuff that inevitably ideas overlapped. Inevitably. There's only so many notes and so many ideas. So you'd get three or four records that had three similar things on. But then you'd move on. So there was never any constant theme. That's in your mind." Stock: "But we were the writers and the musicians on everything, and we are the backing band." Stock also says, "You could recognise a record of ours probably partly because it came at you as obviously a hit: it obviously had brightness and freshness. That's the similarity, really."

Stock and Aitken would only very rarely produce an entire album. "We only ever thought we were doing singles," says Stock. "Kylie was the only one where we really took a bit more care. The first two or three albums, because we realised she was special. Don't get artists like that. Only once in a generation. If someone said to me, 'I've got the new Kylie down the road', I would crawl 200 yards on broken glass to sign her"

The pair admit that they found it difficult to cope with opinions other than their own about the music they were making. "From '86, not deliberately, we were so oiled and so on the ball about what we were doing that most artists would come in and be swept along and swept out of the door before they even knew what had hit them," reveals Stock. "We wouldn't have given them any opportunity for any input. We didn't want their input. We struggled when we dealt with opinionated, self-contained groups like Dead Or Alive or Brilliant. Being a lone girl or three kids straight out of school who wanted to have a go at it, then we could, as long as we could be dictatorial in a sense - 'You're here to work with us'. It's when you get people with opinions that we do have problems. So it depends what people want from us. If people want us to give them a record, turn round and earn loads of money, that's what we do best. It becomes more and more complicated when we've got to accommodate their opinion." During the in-demand period in question, when musical figures both minor and major requested their services, iron rules were laid down, with Waterman or David Howells making it clear to the recipients of S/A/W productions that Stock and Aitken would be 100% in charge in the studio. This applied even to the British musical legend Cliff Richard who - with 96(!) top 40 UK hits and 31 recording years under his belt, availed himself of the S/A/W magic with his 1989 single 'I Just Don't Have The Heart'.

"Cliff insisted on hearing a demo first," says Stock. "We said, 'We've never done demos. He wanted to hear the song and learn it. We said no. We had to persuade him to trust us. It wasn't easy." As with all their other artists, Stock and Aitken laid down the backing track before Richard arrived, although they found they had to re-lay it when it transpired they'd made a miscalculation about the artist's vocal range based on a record he'd made a decade or so previously. Thankfully, the technology about which the pair were so enthusiastic helped make this an elementary process. Stock: "The programmed keyboards edit were in sequences that we'd lay down on the tape and the sequences were already in the sequence machine and we just kept them. So we re-laid it and then he came in and sang it." Richard went outside and had a coffee while they executed this process. At the end of that session Richard requested a copy of the song to take home. Stock: "He said, 'I always take demos home'. 'Well I don't want you to take it Cliff 'cos you'll only play it to people and get an opinion of it'. 'No, no, I want to take a copy. I promise I won't play it to anybody. I've been doing this for 30, 40 years'. In the end I relented and run him off one. When he came back after we'd finished it, he said 'Oh, I played it to my mum.' 'Cliff...' 'It's alright - it's only my mum. She loves it'. 'Okay, fine, terrific'. 'And I played it to the milkman'. 'You played it to the *milkman*? What did you play-' He said, 'I play every single one of my records that I have ever made to my milkman, and if my milkman likes it I go with it'. I thought he was joking. And I said, 'What did the milkman say?' 'He loved it'. So we were able to finish it off, but, you know..."

Despite this, Stock says he wishes they had done some more work with Richard, although Aitken is slightly scathing about Richard's motives. "It would have been number one, that record, but he decided to go and play tennis and sun himself on a yacht and he wouldn't come back to do *Top Of The Pops* on the right week," he alleges. "Reading between the lines, I think he got like two-thirds of an album done and realised he didn't have a hit and, 'Who should we go to? Who's hot at the moment?' I think it was probably one of those situations."

It was a situation the pair claim happened fairly frequently, them citing Brother Beyond (for whom they wrote two top tenners in 1988) and Samantha Fox as examples of artists who used them as a form of salvage operation. Not that this bothered them unduly: few acts were turned away by PWL. The pair do admit that Take That and Boyzone - both destined to be massive successes - were turned down on their behalf. "Most of the decisions as to who would get past the door were made by David Howells," says Stock, "and basically he would be checking the business affairs out more: 'What's your deal?'"

The pair had a string of further successes with Minogue: 'Got To Be Certain', 'Je Ne Sais Pas Pourquoi', 'Hand On Your Heart', 'Tears On My Pillow' (the latter two both UK chart-toppers) and 'Never Too Late'. *Neighbours* provided S/A/W with another readymade teen idol in the shape of Jason Donovan, who played Minogue's fiancée in the soap and happened to be her real-life lover. Donovan was as wholesomely attractive as Minogue, although initially his vocal power was less impressive. At first, the pair were sceptical about the wisdom of taking on yet another TV-actor-turned-singer but decided to give him a song called 'Nothing Can Divide Us' and in so doing passed the baton from one S/A/W male idol to another: the track had been laid down for but rejected by Rick Astley. "We knew it was a number one with him singing it," says Aitken. "It was brilliant and he didn't want to know. Bosh. So that was the end of our relationship with Rick - not because he'd fallen out with us particularly but for various other reasons. Jason had been recording in the Work House with Pete Hammond and presumably Pete thought it would be a good idea to try and get Jason to sing on it, so we got Jason in to sing on it. That was a nightmare session. We didn't actually unpick this until about two years into it: he has got a very good tone but he had some blockage between his ear and his sinuses and it made if very difficult for him to actually pitch. It was about a year and a half later when they actually got to the bottom on that, and he had some operation and from that time his singing went up to the point where he could go on stage and do *Joseph* [*and the Amazing Technicolour Dreamcoat*]. But in the early days it was very hard. He hated the headphones."

'Nothing Can Divide Us' reached number five in Britain in the Autumn of 1988 and Donovan proceeded to have as phenomenal a chart career as Minogue, effectively becoming her male counterpart as he racked up successes that included the number one 'Too Many Broken Hearts'. It was immediately after his first single that his and Minogue's status as the nation's joint sweethearts was cemented with their duet 'Especially For You'. It sailed to number one. Bizarrely, Stock and Aitken only wrote the song because of an erroneous rumour in the music retail industry. "We were told that Woolworths had come in for an advance order of 400,000," explains Stock. "'cos everyone told them there was a duet coming out." Though the pair were by now used to intense pressure and expectation, this was the hardest task with which they had ever been presented. Stock: "You're not just told, 'You've got to write a song', you're told all of a sudden that they are going to take 400,000 of it and it's to be a duet with one bloke who can barely sing and one of them who can sing okay, they're in Australia and you've got to get it out within two weeks otherwise you miss the deadline, and we've got nothing. What do you do? So you sit down and off you go and you hope that God smiles on you." God did just that in the unlikely shape of Timmy Rotherford, a PWL promotions man who gave them a title that kicked off the writing process. "I said, 'Gawd we're stuck for this title, we've got to come up with something for Kylie and Jason'" says Stock. Rotherford, knowing the record was intended to tie-in with the Christmas spirit, pointed out a greetings card bearing the inscription Especially For You. Stock: "It was simple, straightforward. Went off and worked with that."

Though many found the artists staring into each other's eyes as they mimed it on Top Of The Pops and the like touching, Minogue and Donovan never actually sang the song together. Stock: "They are both in Australia so May McKeno, who is a session singer, and I sing the song we had written. She sings Kylie's part. Matt and Pete go to Australia and get Kylie and Jason on it and come back. It took them four hours." Aitken adds, "And the B-side, which was also a duet."

1988 had been a year when the objective both Stock and Aitken had effectively long ago discarded - being famous in their own right - became a reality. The public were beginning to become as familiar with their names as those of their artists, partly due to them taking rare breaks from the studio to grant interviews. The bulk of the publicity, however, was handled by Waterman. In retrospect, the pair feel that Waterman's brashness in his dealings with journalists helped kill the goose that laid the golden egg. Stock: "What we actually did was a marvellous story in itself. He gilded the lily so much sometimes that people just had enough of him. And the results in flack for us was quite hurtful. We weren't like Pete. We weren't bragging about it, we were just getting on with it. We thought what we were doing was making our records quickly and cheaply - and cheap because we're not spending overlong on them - and they're hits, so record companies are putting their money in and getting their money's worth. The artists are earning a living. We're all doing fine. It's a fabulous world. What we didn't like were the indications that we were somehow evil. We were voted the second most hated people of the '80s, behind Margaret Thatcher. It wasn't *Smash Hits*, it was some other magazine, similarly trashy." While the pair could laugh at the puerility of that sort of criticism, they both admit that they found the hatred they engendered bewildering and deeply upsetting. The lowest ebb for them in this respect was an evening when they attended the Albert Hall to pick up a prize for a record they'd made with Bananarama. "We got pelted," Stock recalls with horror. "We got pelted by the trendy DJs. We got cans of piss thrown at us. We had to run off that stage and shelter. They were evil to us and as we came back here we were all shocked at the end of it - 'What have we done? We made some fucking pop records'." That wasn't the end of their trials that day: "Went to the pub and some bloke picked a fight with Pete. We had to get the bouncer to get them apart. Started throwing punches." Stock points out that the vitriol they were subjected to was "always from the industry, not public. Never from the public. From the record executives who were embarrassed that we were doing it with four people. The American bosses of the major labels saying, 'Why have PWL got 28% of the market place?'"

Of all S/A/W's successful chart years, 1989 was the most incredible. It started with the Kylie Minogue and Jason Donovan duet climbing to number one and was followed by S/A/W securing 25 UK top tens, seven UK number ones and both the Christmas UK number one (albeit as producers only) and number two singles. Asked if they contemplated at the time that they would look back on this juncture as their peak, Aitken says simply, "No, we were too busy." However, he does admit that he tried to savour success by structuring his Sundays so that he would be driving in his car as the top 40 radio chart countdown was played.

It would have been difficult to foresee from the bright start that S/A/W made to 1990 with a number one for Kylie Minogue in the shape of 'Tears On My Pillow' that this year would mark the beginning of the end of their phenomenal run. Though it would have been an exhilarating year for anyone else, their tally of six top tenners (of which only the Minogue record reached the top spot) was, for Stock, Aitken and Waterman, mediocre. When Minogue departed the S/A/W stable, things deteriorated rapidly as, for the first time, there was no new teen idol to replace either her or the declining Donovan. "Pete was off the pace," says Stock. "Pete was out being Pete Waterman, a big industry man. He wasn't taking care of business so we weren't getting a throughput of artists anymore. We were getting the dregs and anything would do and people started going, 'You could make anyone a hit' so [would] just give us crap." Aitken adds, "At the time they changed the chart as well and they changed it from Gallup to Miller Brown, different company." Chart success was therefore, he claims, not so easy to come by: "Suddenly the slew changed away from pop... The BPI got together and said, 'Look, they're kicking our pants and we're not making any money and they're making us look like idiots' and the first thing they did was change the basis on which the chart was assembled."

Of the artists with whom they were now working, Aitken says, "What came along after Kylie and Jason was Sonia who not only did she have the audacity to be ordinary but she wasn't particularly good-looking either and on top of that that she had the audacity to have a number one with her first record ['You'll Never Stop Me Loving You']. The guy that was in charge of [her label] Chrysalis at the time went in *Music Week* the week after saying how deeply embarrassed he was about it. He got the sack. Then we got Big Fun, who couldn't shout coke from a break van and I think that was the final straw. I think people couldn't take it anymore."

Both Stock and Aitken evince a remarkable lack of bitterness at what some might consider to be sheer ungratefulness by Astley and Minogue in flying the nest of the men who'd made them. "Rick only stayed with us for six months," says Stock. "Don't forget, Rick made and produced half of his first album - we only did the singles. He had a real deal, a great deal but it wasn't enough for him." On the subject of Minogue, Aitken says, "We couldn't move fast enough for Kylie, that was the problem." There was no rancour at the time? Aitken: "I didn't feel that with anybody." Stock: "I've not actually fallen out with the artists." Waterman, however, was another issue. The relations between the three became more strained in this period. Stock: "In 1989 he bought the building next door and started to move and break up the team. We had an office with half a dozen girls and they were fending for Matt and me. We were able to concentrate on our job because we had people helping us administrate and run the office. Pete, who had outstayed his welcome in the media field because of the things he'd said and his television show had been cancelled and his radio show had been knocked on the head, one day walked back in. It was a Monday morning and Pete Waterman was there all of a sudden. 'What the fuck's he doing here?' That was a bit strange. Then there was a break-up. We were slowly deconstructed. Stock, Aitken and Waterman and the PWL integrated group of people who were all there for the one reason, to make our records successful, started to become broken up and then he did a deal with Warners, had a separate label to do this trendy dance music." Asked why Waterman would want to break things up, Aitken offers: "Because he'd spent all the money on PWL. He'd got himself into massive financial difficulties, nothing to do with us, and he wanted to bail out... Now whether he felt that if that would be easier to do if he didn't have the burden of taking us on..." Stock: "By the time we had started to take off there's no role for him so he goes off and finds by the end of 1989 he's feeling isolated and he comes back in and he would rather derail the whole thing than see it going on without him. That's a failing he has."

Aitken: "He sought to convince the record companies that he was the fountainhead and regardless of whether we were involved or not it wouldn't matter and it was all him." He adds, "I think actually Pete consciously or sub-consciously decided to deconstruct what he'd constructed and he'll go in the media and say that we weren't able to write the songs that he wanted." Stock: "The thing is, I do not believe that our songwriting would ever have dropped below a standard. That just doesn't make any sense. I don't believe that. We were being marginalized. Matt and me were being edged out of the scenario by Pete for his own reasons."

Though there might be disagreements about the reasons why, there was now indisputably a problem in getting S/A/W records into the market, unthinkable even a few months previously. "In the last year that we worked together there," says Stock, "we made as many records as we always did, but we just didn't get any releases and Matt left and I stayed with Pete for a further year or so and the last year, which was '93, I recorded and wrote as many songs as I did in 1989 but I only had 3 releases and none of them was on PWL." The S/A/W imprimatur was now one that people wanted to positively not be associated with.

Aitken became particularly demoralised by the situation. "We weren't getting the releases," he says. "We weren't getting the commitment. We were strong when we had our own label. We could put Kylie out and if you put a record out on EMI you could always bounce off the two. If you just put all your eggs in one basket and EMI don't get a hit - they are just as likely to fuck up the record as they are to be successful with it - what have you got if you haven't got your own label? Plus, our records were starting to sound the same to me, which is always a bad sign." Aitken claims that Waterman was also allowing other producers to tamper with their recordings: "So we'd make it, I'd leave a record in a state that I thought was mixable and it would turn up a month later with completely different drums and bass on it and not work and sound horrible. Plus he was selling the company to Warners. Nothing made sense anymore."

Aitken called a meeting with his partners. "I said, 'You know, maybe we should all take a break' and they didn't want to." Aitken's frustration manifested itself in a blazing row - which he now admits was about nothing of any importance - followed immediately by his departure from the stable in 1991. Stock and Waterman soldiered on. "It didn't bother me," says Stock of his new creative isolation. "Matt and I used to work in a way - we'd all go off and do separate parts and when we were really busy we might have two studios going. So if I'm working on a chord up here, he was working on a bass down there, or if he was doing a guitar over there, I'm doing a vocal over here. We often worked separately. We didn't always sit and hold each other's hand."

There were still occasional hits but the fact that the most successful Stock/Waterman artists of this period were either gimmick-led (WWF Allstars) or are now forgotten (Sybil) illustrated how far they'd fallen. However, it was not that lack of success which eventually ruptured the relationship between Stock and Waterman but rather a publishing agreement to which Stock was unable to agree. "He wanted me to work with Pete Burns again from Dead Or Alive," Stock recollects. However, Pete Burns came with a nominal writing partner in Steve Coyne. Stock: "So in fact I was going to have a song shared four ways, do all of the work and only get 25%. So I said to Pete [Waterman], 'Pete look, if you want me to work with Pete Burns and Steve Coyne, incorporate them into the publishing, then all I want is 50%. You and I have a deal: 50/50. But if you want me to work with them, you pay it out of your fifty'. He flew off the wall. He said, 'I'm not going to be your junior partner'. So he just basically said, 'Well if you don't like it, we can't work together'."

Stock and Aitken subsequently launched a high court action against Waterman over something that made that dispute pale into insignificance when they found out that Waterman was selling the recordings made by PWL to BMG. "That was appalling," says Stock. "What he was trying to do was bail himself out. I don't know how he got into such financial trouble other than the obvious. He had about 20 Ferraris, helicopters and farms and cows and trains and God knows what else." Their court case was ultimately unsuccessful and Stock remains extremely bitter about it: "We thought we had a claim in the recording copyrights. He did it all secretly. That was the point. He didn't tell us what was going on. It was all being de-constructed. We were in the studio giving our whole life - our whole working life - 12 hours a day, every day of the week to the cause of making Stock, Aitken and Waterman and all the people that were employed, successful. That's what we did. We were the engine house. We drove it all along and I felt we got kicked in the bollocks by Pete. He had no respect for us at the end of the day. We were sitting there doing it. He was out swanning around being a superstar. I didn't want the limelight, but we didn't want the opposite. Didn't want to be kept in the dark and then shit on."

Stock and Aitken hooked up again creatively not long after Stock's split with Waterman. They have had the odd burst of massive success since - three singles they produced for TV stars Robson and Jerome in the 1990s were UK number ones - but both admit that they badly need a talent- spotting figure like Waterman or Howells. "I'm waiting for an act with a good deal and a good manager," says Stock. "We need a bridge between us and the industry because you can't work outside of the industry. It's no good getting some young girl singer. I could do it myself, round the pubs, look in *The Stage*. What you need is a girl/boy group in a deal with a major who wants to make pop records. If all that's in place, it's a vehicle for us to put songs on. The vehicle will then sell millions of records and everyone make lots of money. I'm waiting for that act."

Waterman has subsequently achieved success with the pop vocal group Steps but Stock asserts that his role in that is a titular, not a real, one: "Pete's put out a lot of very, very poor-to-average records in the last six, seven years. His only success has been Steps and I can say that he knows it was nothing to do with him at all. The band wasn't recruited by him. They were signed up with Tim Burn."

Asked what are the best and worst songs for which they have been responsible, Stock offers, "The worst song we ever wrote never got released, so you wouldn't have heard of it. That was terrible, 'Beat the Clock'." Aitken explains, "We did a song with a Japanese girl who couldn't say her R's but it had to be called 'Beat The Clock': 'Beat The Crock'." However, Aitken says that even worse than that was 'Terry', written for Bill Wyman's ex-wife Mandy Smith.

As for the opposite end of the scale, Stock says, "Best song I've ever written is one I'm writing next week. I'm hoping to write the best pop song ever and I'm ever hopeful that next time I start that will be it. Obviously I like the ones that have been most successful. There are a couple of songs buried away on albums which I'm proud of as songs, despite their success or lack of it: a couple of Donna Summer ones are really good on the album that she did [*Another Place And Time*, 1989]. It was quite a mature album, because at the time we were coming out with Kylie and Samantha Fox or something we also did some slightly older ones. I like 'Another Place And Time' as a song. I certainly don't like the verse of Samantha Fox but I like the chorus. The worst verse we ever did was that one." Aitken, meanwhile, is belligerent in his belief in the wisdom of the buying public: "Best songs are 'Never Gonna Give You Up' and 'I Should Be So Lucky'. By definition we are writers of popular songs and they are the most popular songs, so therefore they must be the best."

The two are poles part when discussing the state of songwriting today. Stock feels that technology has reduced the talent pool, a particularly apposite subject - and ironic point of view - considering that many blame S/A/W for starting the freezing-out of the musician - and latterly, in the shape of dance records, the song - in the music industry. "I would compare it [with the fact that] kids today take calculators to school to do simple arithmetic," says Stock. "Kids are taught how to use a calculator, they are not actually taught how to work out. If you don't know how to de-construct something, you can't really pull it together again in another form very easily and I think what is being lost is the ability to construct from zero, from nothing, a song, because most of what I hear these days starts from a sample of a drum loop, or a bass-line or something like that. There is still the great songs in the ballad tradition of the Americans, like Whitney Houston or Celine Dion might sing, there's still those people out there, but they're basically using the old-fashioned method. They're still the old guys doing it."

"We live in this wonderful nostalgic world," demurs Aitken,

"and if you look at the charts from 1966, you will find two good ones that you remember and you'll find eight crap ones that you've no recollection of at all." Aitken feels that the quality of songs is still high but that the market is open for criticism: "I think the last couple of Westlife songs have been good songs. I think the Martin guys who do the Backstreet Boys write good songs. Because I am that much older, I can generally spot where most of it's come from, even if they don't. The problem is that records don't get long enough to entrench themselves in the public psyche. I thought the Westlife one before last was an absolute fucking monster, I thought it was a brilliant song, but it was number one for two weeks and then it's gone and they're already releasing the next one. Maybe the songs are better than we're giving them credit for, because there's so much."

Asked what they feel was S/A/W's contribution to music, Aitken says, "I think we were the first people - need to be careful about this now - to put ostensibly white melodies on top of black rhythms, if that makes any sense." Stock - while citing their innovation in using fragments of vocals as a form of instrumental break - feels they were craftsmen rather than pioneers: "I don't hold any elevated opinion of our corpus of songs. I really don't. If someone said to me, 'We liked Stock, Aitken and Waterman because they are in a traditional mould of popular songwriters', that was about all you can say. I don't think we broke any moulds or we did anything different." However, he certainly feels there was a huge achievement in the manner in which they achieved and sustained success: "I don't want to be big-headed or anything but I think what we did, which differs from any other successful songwriters, including Lennon and McCartney, which was bigger than them, was we worked and wrote for many different acts and coped with many different levels of talent. In the main, The Beatles wrote for themselves. We've actually sat down and written for I don't know how many different artists.

"Has anybody had as many different successful hit records - or number ones, even - with as many different artists? I don't think anybody has achieved that."

APPENDiX
RE(OMMENDED LiSTENiNG

Notes on the recommended listening entries in this book:

By the nature of what they do, collecting the work of the freelance songwriter is not always easy. On many an occasion, they will have written a solitary hit for an artist. If that hit has not been gathered on a Various Artists compilation featuring other material by the writer(s), the reader will need to buy the relevant artist's greatest hits in order to obtain it. For practical reasons, such instances of single hits are not covered by these recommendations, but see the special mention at the end.

The recommendations are not always for aesthetic reasons. On some occasions, they are included because they cover interesting junctures in the career of the writer(s) or give a rare insight into their craft.

The reader should take care to ensure that the discs they are buying contain original recordings. Re-recordings never match the magic of the original.

CD catalogue numbers are given for compilations so as to avoid confusion with other, similarly-titled collections.

LEIBER AND STOLLER

Elvis Presley: *Elvis The King Of Rock 'N' Roll: The Complete 50's Masters* (RCA, 1992; cat. no. 67966-2 07863)
A five-CD box-set that contains all the L&S tracks recorded by Presley in the 1950s. The single disc compilation *Elvis Sings Leiber & Stoller* (also RCA) is easier on the pocket but, at the time of writing, quite rare.

Peggy Lee: *Mirrors* (1976)

Elkie Brooks: *Two Days Away* (1977)

Various Artists: *Leiber & Stoller Present the Spark Records Story* (Ace, 2001; cat. no. CDCHD801)
Interesting collection of tracks that were issued by the pair's Spark label, including material by The Robins.

Various Artists: *The Leiber & Stoller Story 1* (Ace, 2004; cat. no. CDCHD1010)
First of an intended series of three compilations gathering records of the pair's songs. This one focuses on their early, Los Angeles years.

Also: Any comprehensive **Coasters, Drifters** and **Ben E. King** compilation containing original recordings from the 1950s and 1960s.

MANN & WEIL

Barry Mann: *Inside the Brill Building* (Brill Tone, 1995; cat. no. BMW 111)
A rather rare three-CD collection of Aldon Music demos of songs written by Mann with a variety of collaborators, including Weil, as well as songs by other writers.

Various Artists: Soundtrack: *An American Tail* (1986)

Various Artists: Soundtrack: *Muppet Treasure Island* (1996)

Barry Mann: *Soul And Inspiration* (2000)
Mann's versions of songs he and Weil provided to others.

Also: Any comprehensive **Righteous Brothers** and **Paul Revere and the Raiders** compilation containing original recordings from the 1960s.

GREENWICH & BARRY

Various Artists: *The Red Bird Story* (Charly, 1991, cat. no. CD CHARLY 296-4)
A massive four-CD collection of Red Bird releases containing many of the hits the pair wrote for that label.

Also: Any comprehensive **Archies** compilation containing original recordings from the 1960s.

HOLLAND-DOZIER-HOLLAND

Various Artists: *Hitsville USA: The Motown Singles Collection 1959-1971* (1992, Motown/Pgd; cat. no. 6312)
One could complain that this misses out as many H-D-H classics as it includes, despite it being a four-CD set, but this collection serves as a splendid taster to both Motown and their most celebrated writing team.

Various Artists *Invictus Chartbusters* (Sequel, 1999; cat. no. NEMCD986).
An adroitly judged collection of tracks from the trio's post-Motown labels.

GRAHAM GOULDMAN

Graham Gouldman: *The Graham Gouldman Thing*
Gouldman's 'Sixties solo album, featuring his versions of some of
the hits he provided for others, as well as newer songs.

Also: Any comprehensive **Herman's Hermits, Hollies** and
Yardbirds compilation containing original recordings from the
1960s.

BOBBY HART

Boyce & Hart: *The Songs Of Tommy Boyce & Bobby Hart*
(Varese Sarabande, 1995; cat. no. VSD-5670)
A very useful collection of hit songs written by Boyce and Hart,
separately and together, plus their own greatest hits as joint
recording artists. Some might quibble over the omission of '(Theme
From) The Monkees' - surely their most well-known piece of
work - but the compilers acquire kudos for the inclusion of the
original Monkees TV show version of 'Valleri'.

JOEY LEVINE

Ohio Express: *The Best of the Ohio Express: Yummy Yummy
Yummy* (2001. Buddah/BMG; cat. no. 99800)

Various Artists: *25 All-Time Greatest Bubblegum Hits* (Varese
Sarabande, 2000; cat. no. 302 066 132 2)
As well as being a supremely listenable introduction to bubblegum,
this compilation is highly useful for those wanting to check out
Joey Levine's various ventures in that genre: not only does it include
(of course) 'Yummy, Yummy, Yummy' but it also collects 'Gimme
Gimme Good Lovin'' and 'Quick Joey Small (Run, Joey, Run)',
as well as the two bubblegum anthems that would not have existed
without him helping invent the medium, 'Captain Groovy and his
Bubblegum Army' and 'Bubble Gum Music'.

The Third Rail: *ID Music* (Rev-Ola, 2003; cat. no. CR REV 48)
A collection of material Levine recorded with Artie and Kris Resnick.

CHIP TAYLOR

Chip Taylor: *The Hit Man* (1996)
Taylor's own takes on some of his most famous compositions.

Also: Any comprehensive **PP Arnold, Hollies, Janis Joplin, Troggs,** and **Billy Vera and Judy Clay** compilation containing original recordings from the 1960s.

TONY MACAULAY

Various Artists: *Buttercups And Rainbows - The Songs Of Macaulay And Macleod* (Castle/Sanctuary, 2001; cat. no. CMDDD 347)
Excellent and beautifully packaged two-CD, 50-track compilation of the titular pair's work for the Pye label.

David Soul: *The Best of David Soul* (Music Club, 1994; cat. no. MCCD152)

CHINN & CHAPMAN

Any comprehensive **Arrows, Mud, Smokie, Sweet** and **Suzi Quatro** compilation containing original recordings from the 1970s.

Mike Chapman *Michael Donald Chapman* - Rare Australian compilation of Chapman's work both with and without Chinn. So rare, in fact, that label details are unknown at the time of writing.

STOCK/AITKEN/WATERMAN

Various Artists: *The Hit Factory: Pete Waterman's Greatest Hits* (Universal Music TV, 2000; cat. no. 5606692)
A selection of the most successful S/A/W compositions and productions, along with some later Waterman work.

SPECIAL MENTION

Various Artists: *Bubblegum Classics...* (All Varese Sarabande)
   Volume 1 (1995; cat. no. VSD-5535)
   Volume 2 (1995; cat. no. VSD-5575)
   Volume 3 (1996; cat. no. VSD-5719)
   Volume 4 (1996; cat. no. VSD-5890)
   Volume 5 (1996; cat. no. VSD-5896)
These compilations of bubblegum and light pop from Varsese Sarabande are highly useful for those who wish to collect songs by writers featured in this book. On these discs you can find songs by Jeff Barry, Bobby Hart, Joey Levine and Tony Macaulay that are otherwise difficult to acquire for the reason mentioned in the first paragraph of this appendix.

ISBN: 0-9545750-0-8

SICK OF BEING ME
A ROCK 'N' ROLL NOVEL
By Sean Egan

This is the alternately exhilarating and harrowing story of guitarist Paul Hazelwood, from his childhood on a London council estate where he nurtures his dreams of stardom to his agonising realisation on the cusp of his thirties that talent doesn't necessarily bring success. Respected music journalist Sean Egan portrays the reality of being a struggling musician and of achieving low-level success in that profession with an authenticity that spurns the sensationalism and cartoon nature of previous literary depictions of this milieu. Similar compelling verisimilitude informs the drug scenes, which reveal the touching pain that can be hidden beneath an unpleasant junkie exterior.

Vulnerable, truthful, moving and beautiful, Sick Of Being Me is one of the great coming-of-age tales of our times.

> *"Few rock 'n' roll novels are as dead-on in their realism and few writers are able to describe both drugs and rock with such vivid and compelling language. Where 'High Fidelity' and 'About A Boy' were light and fluffy, Egan's 'Sick Of Being Me' is dark but honest, though it never loses sight of its pure rock 'n' roll heart."*
> ~ Charles R. Cross, author of 'Heavier Than Heaven: A Biography Of Kurt Cobain'

Acclaim for Sick Of Being Me

"Something of Roddy Doyle's gritty realism in the dialogue... Harrowing descriptions of junkiedom rival Irving Welsh... A snorting good read." ~ *Uncut*

"Sick of Being Me is about the world that haunted Jim Carroll. It's about the world that plagued William Burroughs and Herbert Huncke circa Tangiers in the early 1950s: a shockingly real ride through the dirtiness of addiction and denial and egotism told with the sure-eyed realism of a practicing journalist." ~ *The Electric Review*

"Compelling but painful reading... told with an at times shocking candour." ~ *ITV Teletext*

"Sean Egan has taken a clichéd formula and turned it into something of a quiet masterpiece." ~ *Venue*

"This is pop fiction with a difference and one of the best books of its genre out there." ~ *What's On UK*

"I found myself gripped by the life, experiences and feelings of Hazelwood.... Egan writes his ass off in a fine effort." ~ *Discoveries*

"He tells of the rock scene in such a realistic way that it's hard to believe it's fiction... Readers will enjoy their backstage pass." ~ *Fife Free Press*

"Finally gives rock 'n' roll the work of fiction it has always deserved." ~ *alive.co.uk*

"Grippingly told... Descriptions of the junkie's lot are graphic, while the struggling muso backdrop is, by and large, spot-on." ~ *Ink*

"A positively uncomfortable, but totally essential and ultimately satisfying read, it will challenge your perceptions on many levels. Recommended without reservation." ~ *Powerplay*

"In a novel that is heavy on realism and light on glamour, Egan has given life to a character whose grimly humorous and ultimately affecting story lingers unforgettably." ~ *Goldmine*

Printed in the United Kingdom
by Lightning Source UK Ltd.
101519UKS00003B/46-102